INTRODUCTION TO MICROSOFT EXCEL FOR THE PERSONAL COMPUTER

ALAN L. ELIASON
with Gary June

PRENTICE HALL, *Englewood Cliffs, New Jersey 07632*

Editorial/production supervision: bookworks
Interior design: Alan L. Eliason

If your diskette is defective or damaged in transit, return it directly to Prentice Hall at the address below for a no-charge replacement within 90 days of purchase. Mail the defective diskette together with your name and address to:

Prentice Hall
Attention: Ryan Colby
College Operations
Englewood Cliffs, NJ 07632

Printed in the United States of America

10 9 8 7 6 5 4 3 2

ISBN-0-13-500307-5
ISBN 0-13-500315-6 {INSTRUCTOR'S EDITION}

Prentice-Hall International (UK) Limited, *London*
Prentice-Hall of Australia Pty. Limited, *Sydney*
Prentice-Hall Canada Inc., *Toronto*
Prentice-Hall Hispanoamericana, S.A., *Mexico*
Prentice-Hall of India Private Limited, *New Delhi*
Prentice-Hall of Japan, Inc., *Tokyo*
Prentice-Hall of Southeast Asia Pte. Ltd., *Singapore*
Prentice-Hall do Brasil, Ltda., *Rio de Janeiro*

CONTENTS

TO THE INSTRUCTOR

Welcome to the powerful and innovative educational spreadsheet---the *Microsoft Excel Promotional Edition*. We offer this book/software package with a site license. This means that you can teach the fundamental concepts of Microsoft Excel at a fraction of the full-version cost. We want you to know that although this promotional version is limited, it can be used with either the student or the full version of Microsoft Excel.

We've developed this book and software package to help you deliver quality instruction in introducing Microsoft Excel as an automated business tool. You will be able to use this tool for making worksheets (or, if you prefer, spreadsheets), applying built in mathematical functions, designing charts, creating databases, and building macros (programmed routines to simplify the use of the software). You and your students will discover that this promotional edition is very powerful. For example, it can be used to create 64 row by 16 column worksheets. Second, it contains a run-time version of Microsoft Windows. This allows you to introduce your students to such things as pull-down windows and pop-up dialogue boxes. Third, it contains a full-range of built in functions. These mathematical instructions can be used directly on a worksheet. Fourth, it permits your students to build a complete set of charts, a substantial database, and personalized macros. This should convince you that the promotional edition is a powerful educational software product.

There are some limitations associated with this edition, however. These include:

* There is no online tutorial. (The standard version of Microsoft Excel contains an 18 lesson tutorial.)

* There is no online help available.

* There are no descriptions of each built-in function and the book does not contain a separate reference guide. If these two items are important, we suggest you use the larger Microsoft Excel text, the *Microsoft Excel Student Edition*.

* There are only three print fonts to choose from.

* The software only supports two types of computer printers:
  1) the HP LaserJet printer series and
  2) the Epson FX series.
  The software also assumes that the printer is connected to LPT1:

* There are no descriptions of the built-in macros. These too are supplied by Microsoft with the full edition of the software.

* Worksheets are limited to 64 rows and 16 columns.

Besides these limitations, there are a few others

* No support for international keyboards.

* The heading, "Microsoft Excel Promotional Edition" appears on all display screens, and on all printed output.

* The control panel is not operational.

* Footers cannot be added to a page.

Even so, these differences and limitations are not major factors when building smaller worksheets. Moreover, you can use this Promotional Edition of the software to perform all the functions of the full version. The major limitation is one of scale.

Required Equipment

The minimum equipment to use for this promotional version does not differ from the full or the student version of Microsoft Excel. This equipment includes:

* An IBM (R) Personal System/2 (TM) model 30, 50 or higher, with a 80286 or 80386 processor, an IBM PC/AT (TM) computer, a COMPAQ DESKPRO 386 (R), and 100 percent 80286 and 80386 compatible computers.

* VGA display, or one that is 100 percent compatible.

* A full 640 Kb of conventional memory.

* A hard disk.

* A Microsoft or IBM PS/2 Mouse.

* DOS 3.0 or higher and a minimum of 640K of memory.

* 3 1/2 inch 720K, or 1.4m disk drive, or 5 1/4 inch 1.2m disk drive.

* Either a Epson or an HP LaserJet printer, if printed output is desired.

Note that a mouse is included in this list of equipment. While the keyboard is sufficient to perform all the exercises in the text, a mouse greatly simplifies the use of Microsoft Excel.

Technical Support

Technical support for the *Microsoft Excel Promotional Edition* is provided by the College Software division of Prentice-Hall and NOT THE MICROSOFT CORPORATION. For support, you can call anytime from 9:00 to 5:00 EST, (201) 461-4049 for answers to your technical questions.

The Site-licence Agreement

The *Microsoft Excel Promotional Edition* requires a hard disk to be used successfully. While we do not expect you or your students to re-install Microsoft Excel upon each visit to the computing laboratory, the Microsoft Corporation and Prentice-Hall do expect each of your students to purchase the *Microsoft Excel Promotional Edition*.

About the Text

The organization of the text follows the pattern of providing basic concepts and skills in each of four areas: worksheets, charts, databases, and macros. Sample worksheets are included with this promotional version. Students will be working with these samples in Chapter 1. They will be building and printing simple worksheets by the time they finish Chapter 2. When students complete the text, they will know how to perform a number of complex processing tasks. These include:

* Designing several types of worksheets.

* Using a variety of build-in Microsoft functions.

* Designing several types of charts.

* Constructing and using a database.

* Creating and using macros.

We developed this text by writing a series of student walk-through exercises. Over 60 were written for the six chapters of the book. In most cases, the solution to each exercise is given. We took this approach to reduce the frustration normally associated with a new software product. What we are asking students to do is to replicate a design shown to them in advance.

As you will observe, we also took a highly visual approach in the writing of text material and student exercises. We wanted students to be able to look at a picture in the text and find the same picture on their computer display screen.

For those of you who want your students to solve problems without any answers given, you can do this as well. The end-of-chapter projects contain over 20 problems for students to solve. Many of these projects extend or modify student walk-through exercises.

In preparing this text, we attempted to select problems that would appeal to your students as well as to demonstrate the functionality of Microsoft Excel. The text contains exercises and problems that deal with accounting, finance, operations management, marketing, and personnel. We hope that you and your students will like this approach.

Setup Information

Setup information for the Microsoft Excel Promotion Edition is found in the README file. This file indicates that setup is done via a batch file called SETUP.BAT. SETUP.BAT will copy the required Microsoft Excel files to a directory called XLDEMO on your hard disk. By default, SETUP assumes that your hard disk is drive C: and your floppy disk is drive A:. The Getting Started Section explains how you copy all files to your hard drive.

TO THE STUDENT

For those of you who are new to the use of an automated business tool, get ready for an adventure. You will soon discover that Microsoft Excel is a marvelous software product, capable of doing much more than helping you to solve trivial business problems. For example, you can use Microsoft Excel to help you prepare and balance your budget, prepare your taxes, bill your customers, prepare a chart of your expenditures, keep a database of all the people you know, and analyze how you are spending your money.

What do we mean when we refer to Microsoft Excel as an *automated business tool*? In simple terms, it is a tool that helps you to manage and analyze data. It does this by making calculations for you, charting results, finding data with specific features and properties, and reporting information in a way that is understandable. As an automated tool, all calculations are made by the computer. You command Microsoft Excel to take specific actions; Microsoft Excel translates your instructions into a set of computer processing activities.

As you work your way through this book, you will learn the skills needed to command Microsoft Excel to perform a wide number of tasks. How will you learn these skills? Our approach is called "learn by doing." We believe this is the best way to understand how Microsoft Excel can help you solve business problems. Beginning in Chapter 1, you will find material to read and exercises to complete. These exercises require you to load and use Microsoft Excel. By the end of Chapter 2, you will be preparing worksheets and printing materials to document your mastery in using Microsoft Excel.

Best wishes on working with this powerful and innovative software product. When you complete the chapters and exercises contained in the book, we expect you to be quite skilled in using Microsoft Excel. We fully expect that you will be able to design your very own set of Microsoft Excel worksheets.

GETTING STARTED

Before beginning to explore the use of Microsoft Excel, let's review what you can do with this software product.

1. *You can build worksheets.*

A worksheet (also called a spreadsheet) is the primary document you will use to store and manipulate data. A *worksheet* is a ruled ledger pad consisting of rows and columns. Without the computer, adding the amounts in rows and columns requires an adding machine and a skilled operator. With the computer, Microsoft Excel can be instructed to add row and column totals---as well as do much more.

2. *You can create charts.*

Microsoft Excel comes equipped with a complete charting package. A *chart* is a graphic presentation of data. Microsoft Excel has seven types of charts to choose from: area, bar, column, line, pie, scatter, and combination. These seven chart types are available in 44 predesigned formats. As a consequence, you can use this charting package to visualize your worksheet data.

3. *You can build and analyze databases.*

A *database* is a collection of data organized in a special way. With Microsoft Excel, the data in a database are placed on a worksheet. For example, you might decide to create a database of coins you have collected, noting the characteristics of each coin (type, date, condition). With Microsoft Excel, you can conveniently manage this database and be able to ask questions about data stored on the database.

4. *You can create and use your own macros.*

A *macro* is a custom program made up of a set of instructions that you create for Microsoft Excel. These instructions tell Microsoft Excel how to perform a specific task that you need to perform frequently. For example, with Microsoft Excel you can create a macro to do a common function, such as to underline text placed on a worksheet.

The organization of this book follows the order of building worksheets, creating charts, creating and using a database, and recording and running macros. Before we start with worksheets, you should be familiar with the notational conventions used throughout the book and know how to install the *Microsoft Excel Promotional Edition*. The next sections tell you how this is done.

Notational Conventions

The following terms and notational conventions are used throughout this book and are critical to understanding the meaning of the student exercises:

* *Keynames* are the names of keys on your computer keyboard. The names ESCAPE, ENTER, CONTROL, and so forth appear in capital letters. On your computer keyboard, these names might be abbreviated or represented differently. The ESCAPE key, for example, might be labeled Esc.

* *DIRECTION keys* are the four arrow keys on your computer keyboard. We use UP, DOWN, RIGHT, and LEFT to indicate the direction the arrow points.

* *Key combinations and sequences* are shown is two ways: First, with a plus (+) sign between two keynames (for example, CONTROL+END), or a keyname and a character (for example, ALT+e). Second, with a comma (,) between two characters (for example, f,s). The plus (+) sign indicates those keys that must be pressed at the same time. For example, ALT+e means that you should press the ALT key and hold it while you press the letter e and release it. Then release the ALT key. The sequence *f,s* means press the f key and release it. Then press the s key and release it.

* *Italics* are used in two ways: to highlight key terms in the text and to indicate words and characters you type in the exercises.

* *One bold letter* is a special notation. It is used to indicate the name of the Microsoft Excel command to select with the mouse as well as the keystroke letter to press with the ALT key to activate the command if you do not use the mouse. The term **E**dit (ALT+e), for example, means click on the command "Edit" using the mouse or press the ALT+e keys to choose the same command from the keyboard.

* *Shortcut keys and function keys* offer a quick way to perform an activity directly from the keyboard. A complete list is provided at the end of the text. As examples, the F11 function key will create a new chart, while the F12 function key will save a new file.

Installing the Microsoft Excel Promotional Edition

Microsoft Excel requires Microsoft Windows to run. You will soon discover that Microsoft Windows is a flexible, powerful user interface that helps you to manage the building of computer applications.

For users who do not have a full version of Microsoft Windows, version 2.0 or higher, the *Microsoft Excel Promotional Edition* contains a pre-configured version of Microsoft Windows. While this version is not the full Microsoft Windows program, it is more than adequate in building and executing all the exercises contained in this book. This version loads automatically when Microsoft Excel is run.

The *Microsoft Excel Promotional Edition* is easy to install. If you have a full version of Microsoft Windows version 2.0 or higher installed on your computer, skip to Part II. Otherwise, do the following:

Part I. Loading Microsoft Excel and Windows

1. At the prompt, type *A:* to switch to drive A.

2. Insert the 3 1/2 inch diskette in drive A.

3. Type *setup*.

4. Read the message which explains the default drives, and either change the default, as instructed, or press ENTER.

5. Type *h* if your printer is a HP LaserJet, or type *e*, if your printer is an Epson FX printer. These are the only types of printers supported by this software. After typing the letter, all files will be copied to the hard disk and placed in the directory XLDEMO.

6. Use the C: prompt to run Microsoft Excel from this directory. At the prompt, type *excel*. This typed command loads Microsoft Excel into memory. After loading, you are ready to begin Chapter 1.

Part II. Microsoft Excel for Full Windows Users

If you use a full version of Microsoft Windows (version 2.03 or later), you do not have to use setup at all. Instead, do the following:

1. At the prompt, move to the Windows directory on your hard disk.

2. Copy the following files to this directory: EXCEL.EXE, PREV.FON, ANNUAL.XLS,EAST.XLS, WEST.XLS, SALES.XLS, REPORT.XLS, DEMO.XLW. For example, to copy excel.exe, type: *copy a:excel.exe*

c:\windows (and press ENTER). To copy all .XLS files, type: *copy a:*.xls c:\windows* (and press ENTER)

3. Once this is done you can start Microsoft Excel as you would start any Windows application. For example, from Windows using the mouse, double click on EXCEL.EXE. Begin Chapter 1 when you are ready to begin using Microsoft Excel.

CHAPTER 1 - EXPLORING THE MICROSOFT EXCEL WORKSHEET

When you first start Microsoft Excel, you will see on your display screen a blank worksheet named Sheet1 (see **Figure 1-1**). You can use this blank sheet to build a new worksheet, or you can write over it by using a worksheet built earlier and saved on disk. In this chapter, you will not be asked to build a worksheet. Rather, you are asked to investigate worksheets built for you. By working with existing worksheets, it is easier to explain the terminology needed to explore the Microsoft Excel worksheet.

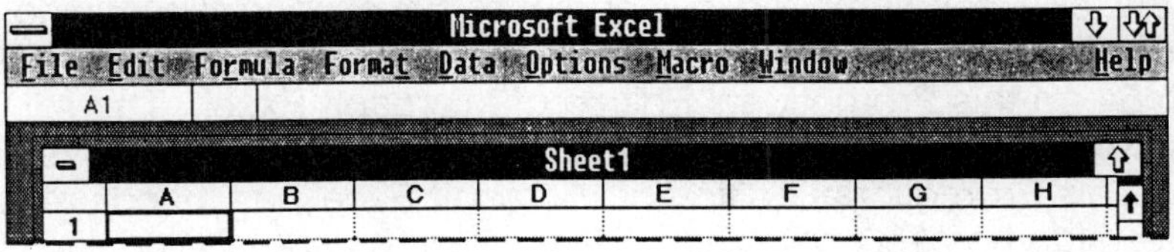

Figure 1-1 Worksheet menu bar

In working through each chapter, there are a set of tasks you should be able to do upon careful reading and study. When you complete this chapter, you should be able to:

* Explain the terminology used in selecting a command using a mouse or the keyboard.
* Move around a worksheet using a mouse and the keyboard.
* Understand the difference between a drop-down window and a dialog box.
* Define the eight categories of Excel worksheet commands.
* Open and close a worksheet window.
* Move and size a worksheet window.
* Exit from Excel.

1-1 What is a Worksheet Window?

Microsoft Excel is based on the concept of displaying or opening a window for you to use on the computer screen. The *worksheet window* is the rectangular grid of rows and columns that fills most of the screen when you first start Microsoft Excel. Another type of window will be available when you work with charts. Consider the top of the worksheet window shown on Figure 1-1. Whenever you start Excel, the words **F**ile, **E**dit, Fo**r**mula, Forma**t**, **D**ata, **O**ptions, **M**acro, and **W**indow will appear on a bar called the *menu bar.* This list of eight words represents the different types of worksheet menus.

Figure 1-2 tells you more about the worksheet window. Besides Sheet1, the worksheet name, the *active cell* and the *cell reference* are indicated. The active cell is the boxed cell. The name of this cell, A1, is the cell reference, where A is the name of the column and 1 is the name of the row. The *cell* is the basic unit of a worksheet. It is used to store text, numbers, and formulas.

A row and a column on a worksheet have special meaning. With Microsoft Excel, a *row* is a complete horizontal line of cells, numbered 1 through 64 on this Promotional Edition of Microsoft Excel. The full version of Microsoft Excel contains 16384 rows. A *column* is a complete vertical line of cells. This Promotional Edition of Microsoft Excel has 16 columns; while the full version has 256 columns. These columns are labeled (A,B,C,...Z; AA,AB,AC,...IV).

Information on the worksheet is entered and modified (meaning edited) through the *active cell*. Only one cell on a worksheet can be active at a

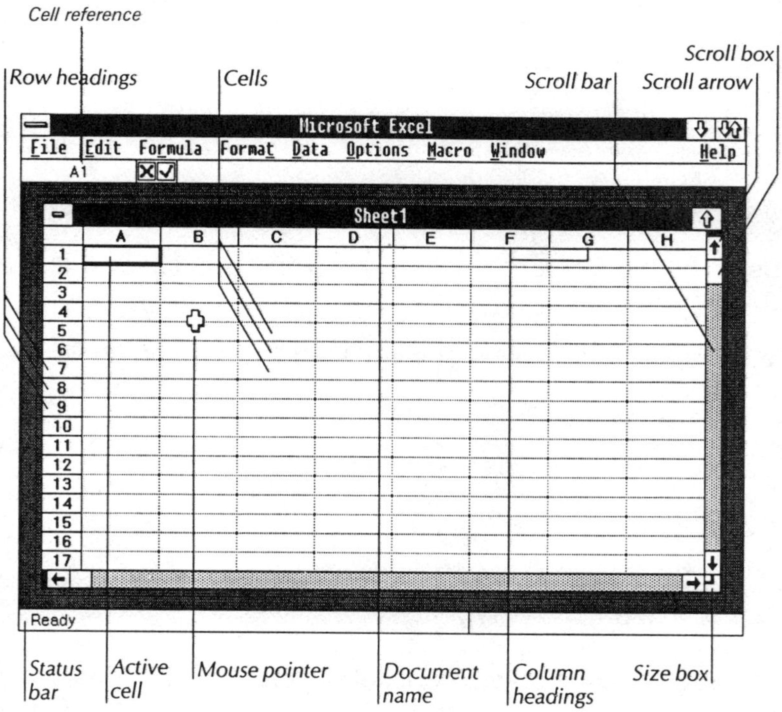

Figure 1-2 Expanded worksheet window

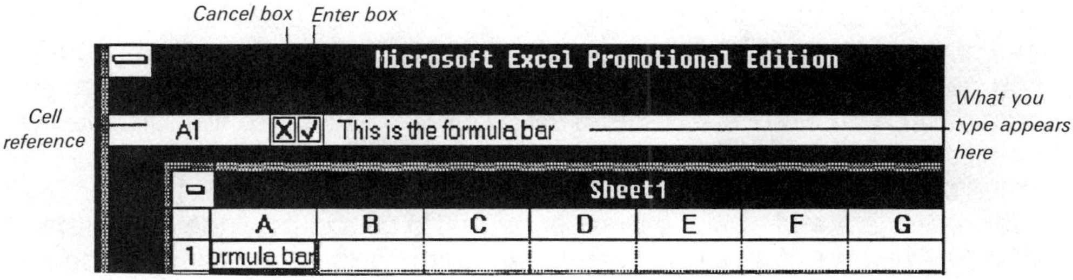

Figure 1-3 The formula bar

time. This is why the active cell is highlighted on the terminal screen and why the cell reference is displayed. Both pieces of information tell you where you are on the worksheet.

As information is entered into the active cell, it is also displayed on a second bar the *formula bar* (see **Figure 1-3**). As indicated, this bar contains a reference area, two check boxes--an enter box and a cancel box---and an area to display typed information. An *insertion point* is placed at the end of the typed information to indicate where the next information is to be placed if keyed. This point is indicated by a vertical line (|).

At the bottom of the worksheet is a third bar called the *status bar* (see **Figure 1-4**). This bar displays information about the currently selected command and the current mode of operation. When you first examine the

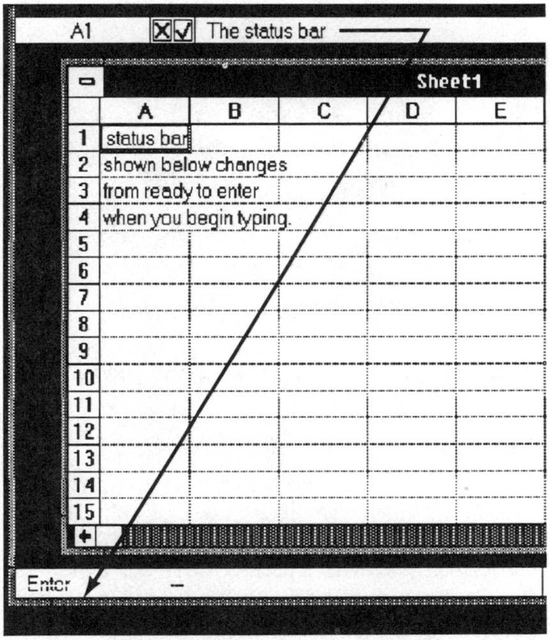

Figure 1-4 The status bar

Microsoft Excel worksheet, the command mode will be set to READY. This means that Microsoft Excel is ready for you to perform some activity. When you begin typing a letter or number into the active cell, the mode changes from READY to ENTER. The ENTER mode also activates the formula bar, by displaying the two check boxes, the *enter box* and the *cancel box*. The enter box (the box with the check mark) is used when you want to edit information appearing in the formula bar. The cancel box (the box with the x) is used when you want to cancel an edit or entry. Besides the cancel box, you can press the ESCAPE key (marked Esc) to cancel an entry.

1-2 Moving and Selecting With the Mouse

Both a mouse and the keyboard can be used to command Microsoft Excel to take action. A *command* is a special term. It is an order issued to Microsoft Excel to carry out a specific type of action. For ease of use, Microsoft Excel uses categories or sets of commands, organized by *drop-down* (or pull-down) menus.

After you choose a command, Microsoft Excel may pull down a menu or display a *dialog box* (or pop-up window). Each menu or dialog box features a prompt for further action on your part. Before asking you to use a drop-down window and a dialog box, let's consider how to use a mouse. If your computer does not come equipped with a mouse, read this section and skip the exercises. The next section, section 1.3, deals with the use of the keyboard.

1-2-1 Moving the mouse

A *mouse* is a small pointing and input device designed to fit under your hand. It is used to control a pointer on the terminal screen and to take a variety of mouse actions. These actions include:

* Selecting menus and choosing commands.

* Moving and selecting cells on worksheets, charts, and databases.

* Scrolling through worksheets and windows using the scroll bars.

* Moving and changing the size of windows.

* Choosing an action from several alternatives.

With Microsoft Excel, a single- or multiple-button mouse can be used to enter user input instructions. If a two-button mouse is to be used, only the left-most button is active. The right-most button is always inactive. The mouse button is clicked once or twice. If clicked twice, it is called a double-click. A double-click is an important technique. Instead of clicking on a selection and moving the mouse to enter the selection, a double click tells Microsoft Excel to both select and enter.

The mouse controls a pointer on the terminal screen. By moving the mouse in an up-down or left-right direction, the pointer can be moved from one side of the terminal screen to the other. If you run out of room for the mouse---the edge of the desk is reached before the pointer is moved to where it should be---lift the mouse and put it down where you have more room. Lifting the mouse does not move the pointer on the terminal screen.

As shown by **Figure 1-5**, the mouse pointer can take several shapes, depending on where it is placed on the terminal screen. These shapes are called icons. An *icon* is a graphic symbol designed to represent a function to be performed. As an example, the first icon represented as an arrow means to point and select.

1-2-2 Mouse terminology

Besides understanding the meaning of several different types of icons, you must understand mouse terminology. **Figure 1-6** describes nine terms important to using a mouse. Of these, the words Click and Drag are of most importance. *Click* means to press and release the left-most mouse button; *Drag* means to hold down the left-most mouse button as the mouse is moved.

EXERCISE 1-1
Using the mouse as a pointer

1. Load Microsoft Excel. For example, if you have placed Microsoft Excel in the XLDEMO directory, type *cd xldemo* and press ENTER. Then, type *excel* to load Microsoft Excel into memory.

2. With an empty worksheet facing you, move the mouse to the body of the worksheet (for example, cell C8).

3. Move the mouse pointer to the formula bar.

4. Move the mouse pointer to the menu bar.

5. Move the mouse pointer to the status bar.

Pointer shape	Screen location	Mouse action
	Found in a menu bar, scroll bars, and in chart window	Used to point and select
	Inside worksheet	Click to select cell or cell range
	In formula bar and in text box within a dialog box	Click to place insertion point where you want to start editing text or numbers
	Along row headings	Drag to adjust row height
	Along column headings	Drag to adjust column width
	Along window border corners	Drag to size window vertically and horizontally at the same time
	At vertical split bar	Drag to move split bar and divide worksheet window into vertical panes
	At horizontal split bar	Drag to move split bar and divide worksheet window into horizontal panes
	In upper-left corner of screen (displayed when Control Split command is chosen)	Drag to move both the vertical and screen horizontal split bars and divide worksheet into vertical and horizontal panes
	On sample pages when previewing before printing	Click to select and magnify a part of the page for closer printing
?	Near center of screen when you press SHIFT+1 for help	Click the command or area of screen you want help on (inactive with this edition)
	In Help window on a word underlined by a dotted or solid line	Point to the word or phrase with dotted underline and hold down mouse button to see definition (inactive with this edition)
	Any area of screen	Means "wait for command or action to be carried out"

Figure 1-5 Mouse pointer shapes and actions

Technique	Description
Point	Move the mouse until the tip of the pointer rest on the object you wish to point to.
Press	Hold down the mouse button.
Click	Press and release the mouse button (one click).
Drag	Press and hold down the mouse button, then move the mouse.
Double-click	Press the mouse button twice (two clicks) in rapid succession.
Choose click.	Select a command by pointing at the menu name. Then Next, point to the command you want and click.
Scroll	Click on a scroll arrow or drag the scroll box. This moves a document in its window to make a hidden part visible.
Select	Point and click or drag to identify the area of the worksheet you want the next command to change, or to change a setting in a dialog box.
Turn on/off	Click on a check box to toggle---turn on or off---a setting.

Figure 1-6 Basic mouse techniques

6. Move the mouse pointer to the very edge of the window (the thin gray border).

7. If you want to exit from Microsoft Excel at this time, jump ahead to the last section of this chapter. However, we recommend that you complete the first six exercises before exiting.

Questions:

1. How does the mouse pointer change shape as you move from one area of the worksheet to another?

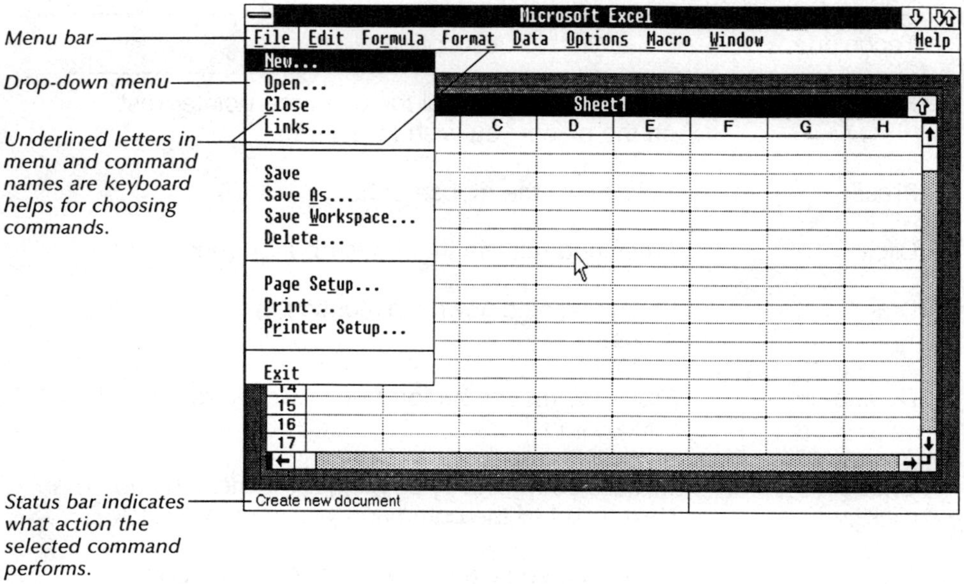

Figure 1-7 The File drop-down menu

1-2-3 Choosing commands with a mouse

A mouse can be used to open a drop-down menu and to choose a processing activity. **Figure 1-7** shows what happens when the worksheet menu named File is clicked. The drop-down menu shows that the File menu contains a set of file commands. These commands permit a new file to be opened, or an existing file---one previously saved---to be opened. They permit an old file to be saved or a new file to be named and saved. They allow a workspace to be saved. Finally, they allow a file to be deleted, set up as a page, and printed. The printer setup command is used to ready your printer. The exit command, the last command on this menu, shows how you exit Microsoft Excel.

EXERCISE 1-2
Opening menus with a mouse

With a blank worksheet facing you, do the following using the mouse:

1. Click on **F**ile and examine the drop-down menu.

2. Click on **F**ile again.

3. Follow the same procedure for all other names on the menu bar. Click on **E**dit, Fo**r**mula, Forma**t**, **D**ata, **O**ptions, **M**acro, and **W**indow.

Questions:
1. With Microsoft Excel, how many Edit commands are available?
2. What is the advantage in using a mouse to open and close a window?

1-2-4 Scrolling with a mouse

Besides using a mouse to point and click, a mouse can be used to scroll through a list or through worksheet rows and columns. **Figure 1-8** illustrates two scroll bars---one to the far right side of the worksheet and one at the bottom. Inside each scroll bar is a scroll box. To scroll with a mouse, drag the box up or down in a vertical scroll bar or side to side in a horizontal scroll bar. At the top and bottom of each scroll bar are scroll arrows. To move to the next item in a list, the next row, or the next column, click on the down or right-most arrow. To move back to the previous item

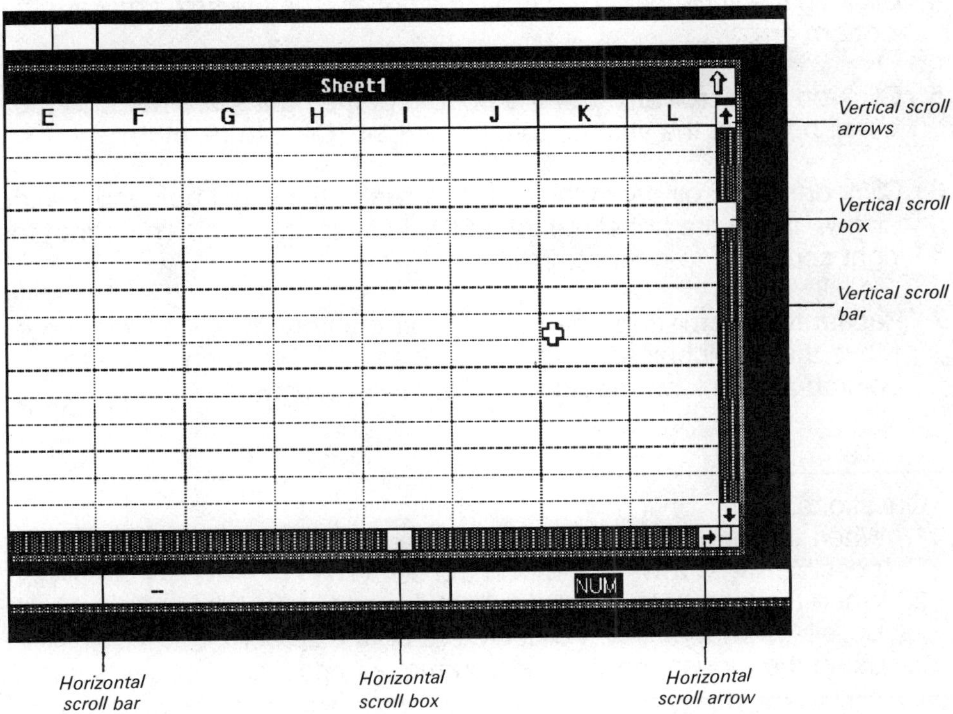

Figure 1-8 Scroll bars, boxes, and arrows

in a list, the previous column, or the previous row, click on the top or left-most arrow.

EXERCISE 1-3
Scrolling with a mouse

With a blank worksheet in front of you, do the following:

1. Drag the scroll bar on the far right-hand side from the top (row 1) to the bottom of the worksheet.

2. Drag the scroll bar on the right-hand side from the bottom to return it to row 1.

3. Click on the scroll arrow at the bottom of the right scroll bar.

4. Click on the scroll bar in the gray space between the scroll box and the bottom arrow.

5. Click on the scroll arrow at the bottom of the right scroll bar until the scroll box is at the very bottom of the bar. Click twice more.

6. Click on the scroll bar in the space between the scroll box and the top arrow. If you are not at the top of the worksheet by this time, drag the right scroll bar to return to row 1.

7. Repeat the exercise for the scroll bar at the bottom of the worksheet. Move the scroll box as far to the right as possible; then return to column A. Click on the right- and left-most arrows.

Questions:

1. When the vertical scroll box is dragged down as far as possible, what rows appear on the screen?
2. When the horizontal scroll box is dragged to the right as far as possible, what column numbers are on the screen?
3. Using the mouse, how would you move to column Z on the screen?

1-2-5 Selecting from dialog box options

Microsoft Excel features a number of dialog boxes. These are boxes that are displayed on the screen when a command is selected. The important rules to remember when working with dialog boxes are three:

* If a command name ends in an ellipsis (...) on a menu, Microsoft Excel will display a dialog box, asking you to provide further information.

* While inside the dialog box, you specify processing requirements by selecting from the choices given.

* When you finish with dialog specifications, choose the appropriate command button to carry out the command. In most cases, pressing ENTER chooses the OK button.

The terms important to using a dialog box are shown on **Figure 1-9** (the dialog box shows you what print fonts are initially set for you). These terms mean the following:

List box---a boxed area that displays a list of choices for a command.

Text box---a box in which you can type information needed to carry out a command.

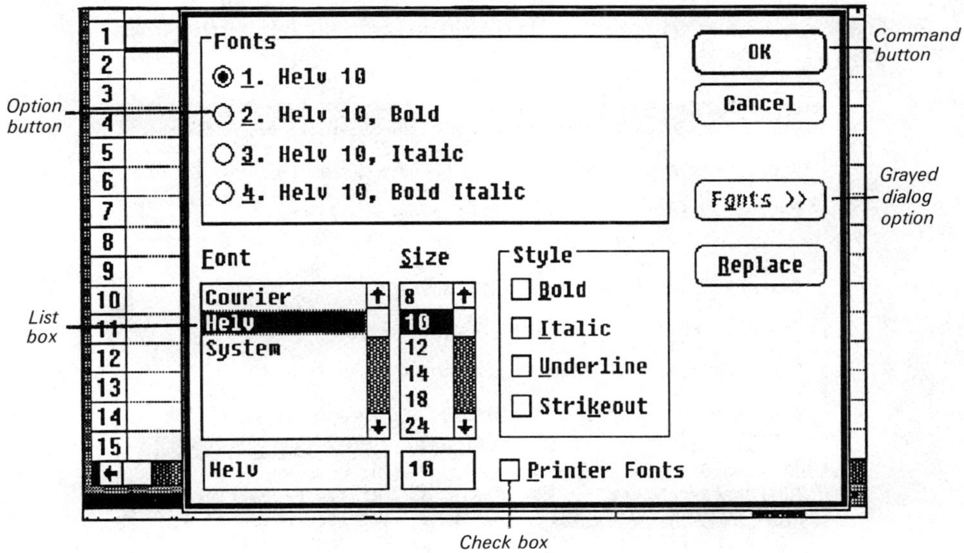

Figure 1-9 Terms important in using a dialog box

Option button---a round button used to select an option.

Check box---a small square used to turn on and off an option.

Command button---a large button, labeled to indicate what action it carries out. The OK button closes the dialog box and carries out the command. The cancel button closes the dialog box and cancels the command.

Grayed dialog option---a grayed or dimmed box that indicates that the option is not available at this time or that you may need to complete an action before the option becomes active.

EXERCISE 1-4
Working with a dialog box

For this exercise we ask you to use the dialog box to check the setup of your printer. Do the following:

1. Click on **F**ile, to open the File menu.

2. Click on P**r**inter Setup, to open the printer setup dialog box.

3. Click on **S**etup to examine the printer setup dialog box (see **Figure 1-10**).

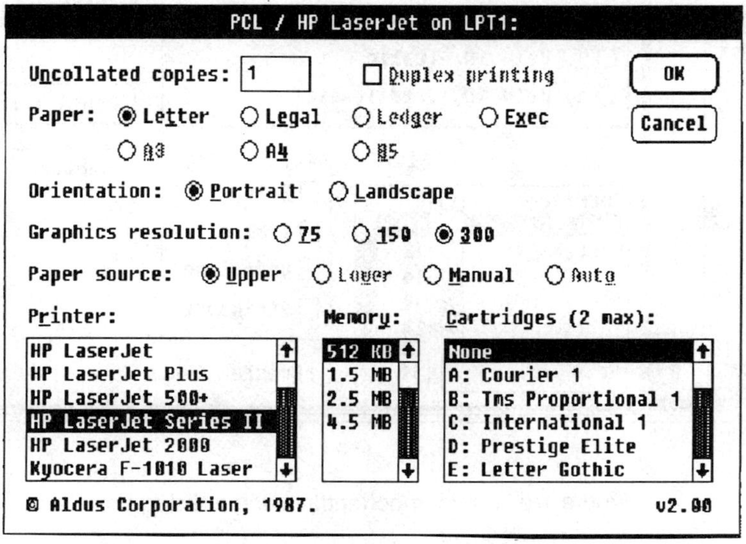

Figure 1-10 The Printer Setup dialog box

4. Click on Legal to transfer to legal-size paper.

5. Click on Letter to transfer back to letter-size paper.

6. Drag the Printer scroll bar from top to bottom. This allows you to identify the printers supported, as directed by your setup instructions.

7. Drag the Cartridges scroll box. This allows you to identify the types of fonts supported by your printer (provided the cartridge is available on your printer).

8. Scroll the Cartridges box back to the initial setting.

9. Click on Cancel to return to the printer setup box.

10. Click on Cancel to remove the pop-up window from the display screen.

Questions:
1. What are the advantages of pop-up windows?
2. What are the advantages of using a mouse in selecting dialog box options?

1-3 Moving and Selecting With the Keyboard

If your computer does not include a mouse, the keyboard can be used instead. Even if your computer does have a mouse, you can do with the keyboard whatever you can do with a mouse. More importantly, the keyboard is required to enter values into an active cell. This is the only way of telling Microsoft Excel what data you need to process.

1-3-1 Moving around the worksheet

The keyboard can be used to move around the worksheet using the direction keys (LEFT, RIGHT, UP, and DOWN), the PAGE UP and PAGE DOWN keys, the HOME and END keys, and other key combinations. **Figure 1-11** describes the keys you should become familiar with for now. For example, to move to the lower-right hand corner of a worksheet, press the CONTROL+END keys.

Besides keys for moving and selecting, Microsoft Excel uses a large number of ALT+(control-key combinations) to perform a variety of tasks, such as opening a drop-down menu and working within a dialog box. The control key is identified by the letter underlined in a word. For example, to

KEYS FOR MOVING AROUND THE WORKSHEET

To	Press
Move to the beginning of a row	HOME
Move to the end of a row	END
Move left, right, up, down	DIRECTION keys
Move up one window	PAGE UP
Move down one window	PAGE DOWN
Move to upper-left corner	CONTROL+HOME
Move to lower-right corner	CONTROL+END
Move to edge of data block	CONTROL+DIRECTION key
Select row	SHIFT+SPACEBAR
Select column	CONTROL+SPACEBAR

Figure 1-11 Keys for moving around the worksheet

open the **F**ile menu, press the ALT+f (or F) keys on the keyboard. To close the menu, press Esc (Escape).

The alternative way to move from one menu to another is to press the function key F10 to activate the menu bar. Following this, press the DOWN key to drop down a menu, press the RIGHT key to move to the next drop-down menu. Once again, press Esc to escape.

As suggested above, each of the function keys are reserved for highly performed tasks. **Figure 1-12** lists the main task for each key. As examples, to activate the formula bar in Edit mode, press the F2 key; to create a new file, press the F11 key. The appendix contains a complete listing of the commands or actions provided by each function key. Each key can be used to perform several types of actions.

Finally, the INSERT, DELETE, and BACKSPACE keys are used for changing information in an active cell. (You will use these keys in the next chapter.)

EXERCISE 1-5
Opening menus using the keyboard

This exercise is the same as Exercise 1-2. You are asked to open all worksheet menus using the keyboard instead of the mouse. In writing this exercise, the notation followed is to indicate the item to be selected using the mouse, where the single keystroke letter is shown. Following this, the complete keystroke requirements are shown.

Key	Command or Action
F1	(Inactive on this edition)
F2	Activate formula bar, in Edit mode
F3	Formula Paste Name command
F4	Formula Reference command
F5	Formula Goto command
F6	Next pane
F7	Formula Find command (find next cell)
F8	Toggles Extend on and off
F9	Options Calculate Now command
F10	Activate menu bar
F11	File New command
F12	File Save As command

Figure 1-12 Main uses of function keys

1. Select **F**ile (ALT+f) to open the file menu.

2. Press ESCAPE.

3. Follow the same procedure for all other names on the menu bar. Press the ALT key plus the letter underlined to open and close all other

menus. Select **E**dit (ALT+e), Fo**r**mula (ALT+r), Forma**t** (ALT+t), **D**ata (ALT+d), **O**ptions (ALT+o), **M**acro (ALT+m), and **W**indow (ALT+w).

4. If you have a drag-down menu open, press ESCAPE.

5. Press F10 to activate the menu bar.

6. Press the RIGHT key to open the worksheet menus.

7. Press the LEFT, UP, and DOWN keys.

8. Press Esc.

Questions:

1. What is the advantage in using the keyboard to open and close a worksheet menu?
2. What happens when you press the LEFT, UP, and DOWN keys?

Next, we want you to work with a worksheet stored on the diskette you used to get started with Microsoft Excel. The name of this file is EAST.XLS. The name of this worksheet is EAST. The XLS extension is added to all saved Microsoft Excel worksheets. In contrast, a XLC extension will be added to all saved charts, a XLM extension will be added to all saved macros, and a XLW extension will be added to all saved workspaces.

EXERCISE 1-6
Moving around a worksheet

With a blank worksheet facing you, do the following:

1. Select **F**ile (ALT+f).

2. Select **O**pen (press o, or DOWN plus ENTER). This will open the dialog box shown on **Figure 1-13**.

3. If the EAST.XLS is on a different disk drive, such such as drive a, click on **D**irectory A (ALT+d) and click on OK (press ENTER). The alternative way is to type *a:* and press ENTER to change to drive a.

4. Select EAST.XLS (type *EAST.XLS*). This selection loads into computer memory the saved worksheet stored on disk.

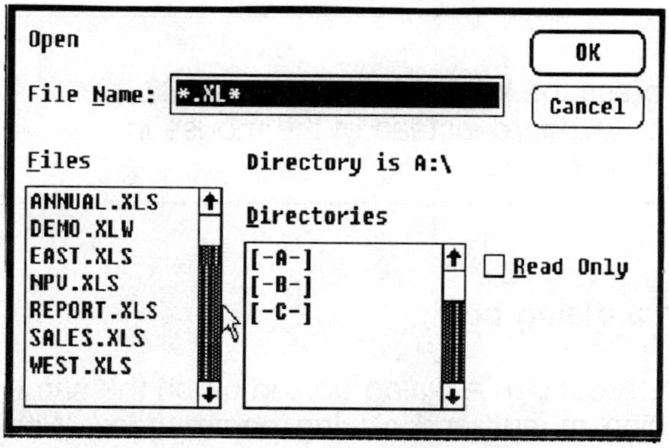

Figure 1-13 The File Open dialog box

5. Choose OK (press ENTER). **Figure 1-14** shows the stored worksheet.

6. Using the keyboard, press the following keys:
   a. Press HOME.
   b. Press END.
   c. Press CONTROL+END.
   d. Press CONTROL+HOME.

7. Leave this worksheet open if you want to begin work on the next exercise. Otherwise, to close this worksheet, do the following:
   a. Select **F**ile (ALT+f).
   b. Select **C**lose (press c).
   c. You will be asked: Save changes in 'EAST.XLS'? Select **N**o (press n). This will return you to a blank worksheet, named Sheet1.

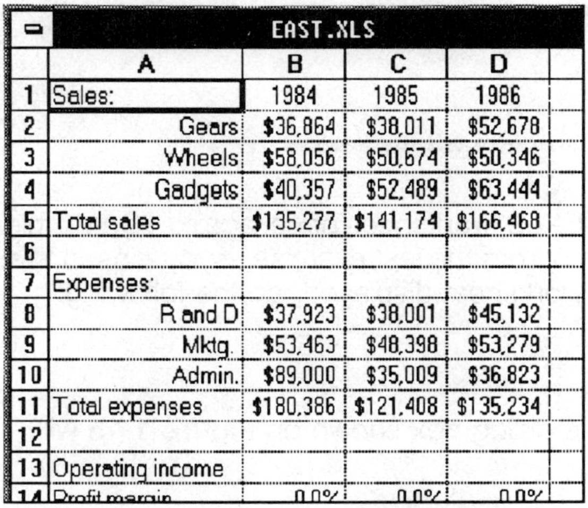

EAST.XLS

	A	B	C	D
1	Sales:	1984	1985	1986
2	Gears	$36,864	$38,011	$52,678
3	Wheels	$58,056	$50,674	$50,346
4	Gadgets	$40,357	$52,489	$63,444
5	Total sales	$135,277	$141,174	$166,468
6				
7	Expenses:			
8	R and D	$37,923	$38,001	$45,132
9	Mktg.	$53,463	$48,398	$53,279
10	Admin.	$89,000	$35,009	$36,823
11	Total expenses	$180,386	$121,408	$135,234
12				
13	Operating income			
14	Profit margin	0.0%	0.0%	0.0%

Figure 1-14 The EAST.XLS worksheet

Questions:
1. What happens when you press the key sequence in step 6?
2. When is it better to use the keyboard instead of the mouse in moving around in a worksheet?

1-3-2 Using the keyboard in a dialog box

You can also use keys to move around in a dialog box, in much the same way as keys are used in opening menus and closing commands. With keys you can select as follows:

* Press TAB to move to the next list box, text box, check box, command button, or group of option buttons.

* Press ALT+key for underlined letter or number to move directly to a list box, text box, check box, command button, or group of option buttons.

* Press the DIRECTION keys to move and select within an active group of option buttons.

* Press the SPACEBAR to turn on or turn off an active checkbox or choose the active command button.

* In a list box, press the key for the first letter of an item to move directly to the item and select it. This method is faster than using the TAB key or the DIRECTION keys.

EXERCISE 1-7
Moving within a dialog box

For this exercise, use the EAST.XLS worksheet once again. Open this worksheet using steps 1 through 5 from the last exercise, if you closed this worksheet. With the EAST.XLS worksheet displayed, do the following:

1. Select **O**ptions (ALT+o).

2. Select **D**isplay (press d). The dialog box shown on **Figure 1-15** will open.

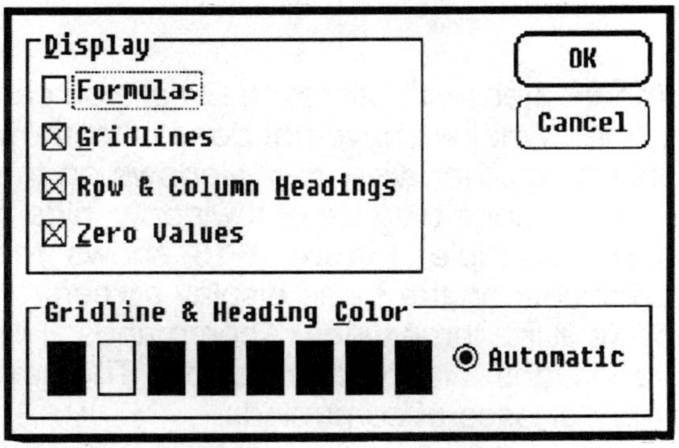

Figure 1-15 The Options Display dialog box

3. Click on **G**ridlines (ALT+g).

4. Click on Row and Column **H**eadings (ALT+h).

5. Click on **A**utomatic (ALT+a) to turn the default color off.

6. If you have a color monitor do this and the next step. Otherwise, do step 8. Select the color RED (continue to press LEFT until you reach the color RED).

7. Select OK (press TAB and ENTER).

8. Select OK to continue.

9. Repeat steps 1 through 8 except turn gridlines back on, the row and column headings back on, and set color to automatic.

10. Select **F**ile (ALT+f).

11. Select **C**lose (press c).

12. Select **N**o (press n) when asked: Save changes in 'East.XLS'? This will close the EAST.XLS worksheet, not saving the changes you made.

Questions:
1. What happens to the display screen when you select the color RED?
2. What does this exercise teach you about the Options, Display command?

1-4 Using Windows

As the last two exercises have demonstrated, with Microsoft Excel, you can open more than one window at a time. What we have not done is to show you how to move from one window to another, view two windows on the same display screen, move a window, change the size of a window, hide a window, and close a window. For example, **Figure 1-16** shows the WEST.XLS and the EAST.XLS worksheets on the same display screen.

The procedures for using windows utilize three types of commands: File commands, Window commands, and Control menu commands. The next three sections review these important classes of commands.

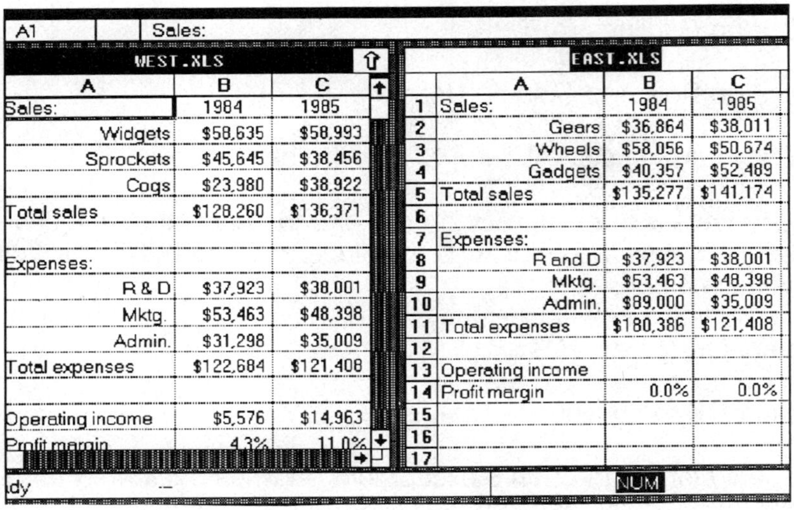

Figure 1-16 The WEST.XLS and EAST.XLS worksheets

1-4-1 File commands

File commands are used to create, save, and print Microsoft Excel worksheets. The File commands of most importance in using windows are File Open, File New, and File Close. These commands differ as follows:

* *File Open* opens an existing worksheet stored on disk and displays it on the screen.

* *File New* opens an untitled, empty worksheet, such as Sheet1. This name is the default. When you save a sheet, you must provide a new title.

```
Window
-----------------
New Window
Show Info
Arrange All
-----------------
Hide
Unhide
-----------------
1 WEST.XLS
2 SHEET1.XLS
3 EAST.XLS
```

Figure 1-17 Window commands showing active windows

* *File Close* closes the active window. A variation of the File Close command is *File Close All*. This command appears on the menu bar when you hold down the SHIFT key when selecting the File menu. It replaces the File Close command.

1-4-2 Window commands

Window commands are used to open and close windows, when multiple windows are open, to split windows into horizontal and vertical panes, and to arrange several windows on a single display screen. The window commands we ask you to become familiar with at this time are Window Activate Window and Window Arrange All. These commands work as follows:

* *Window Activate Window* activates the window you choose. As an example, consider window menu shown on **Figure 1-17**. These windows are shown as open: **1** WEST.XLS, **2** EAST.XLS, and **3** SHEET1. You can activate one of these windows by clicking on the number 1, 2, or 3 with the mouse or by typing the appropriate number.

* *Window Arrange All* rearranges all open windows to use the available display screen space efficiently. This command is very helpful in allowing you to determine what types of information are stored in a particular window.

1-4-3 Control menu commands

Control menu commands allow you to manipulate windows in other ways. The way to open the control menu is to click the control icon hyphen (-), located to the left of the name of the worksheet (see Figure 1-14). Clicking on this icon with the mouse (or typing ALT+-) opens the Document Control menu shown on **Figure 1-18a**. On each worksheet, there are two types of control menus: the *Document control menu* and the *Application control menu*. Both are indicated by the same icon [the hyphen (-)]. The Application control menu (see **Figure 1-18b**) is located in the far upper left-hand corner of the display screen. It is used to change the workspace for any document on the display screen. For now, do not use this application control menu.

The Document control menu, the menu we want you to use, is located to the left of the title bar of a worksheet. This menu contains six commands: Maximize, Restore, Close, Move, Size, and Split.

* *Control Restore* restores the active window to its previous size.

* *Control Move* allows you to move a window from one location on a display screen to another, without changing the size of the window.

```
Restore   Ctrl+F5
Move      Ctrl+F7
Size      Ctrl+F8
Maximize  Ctrl+F10
-------------------
Close     Ctrl+F4
-------------------
Split
```

Document Control Menu

```
Restore    Alt+F5
Move       Alt+F7
Size       Alt+F8
Minimize   Alt+F9
Maximize   Alt+F10
------------------
Close      Alt+F4
------------------
Run...
```

Application Control Menu

Figure 1-18 Document and application control menus

* *Control Size* allows you to change the size of a window by making it larger or smaller.

* *Control Maximize* enlarges a window to allow you to see as much of the worksheet as possible. In so doing, it hides other worksheets from view.

* *Control Close* closes the active document window.

* *Control Split* allows you to divide a window into panes.

The next four exercises help you to understand the use of these document control commands.

EXERCISE 1-8
Arranging two worksheets on a screen

For this exercise, use the EAST.XLS worksheet and the WEST.XLS worksheet. Both worksheets are stored on file. Do the following:

1. Select **F**ile (ALT+f)

2. Select **O**pen (press o). This will open the dialog box shown on Figure 1-13. If the EAST.XLS and WEST.XLS worksheets are stored on a different drive, such as drive a, click on **D**irectory A (ALT+d) and click on OK (press ENTER). The alternative way is to type *a:* and press ENTER to change to drive a.

3. Select EAST.XLS (type *EAST.XLS*).

4. Choose OK (press ENTER).

5. Select the document control menu icon (ALT+-) and drag to Ma**x**imize (press x).

6. Select the document control menu icon (ALT+-) and drag to **R**estore (press r).

7. Repeat steps 1 through 4, but open WEST.XLS next. This will leave three worksheets on the screen: WEST.XLS, part of EAST.XLS, and part of SHEET1.

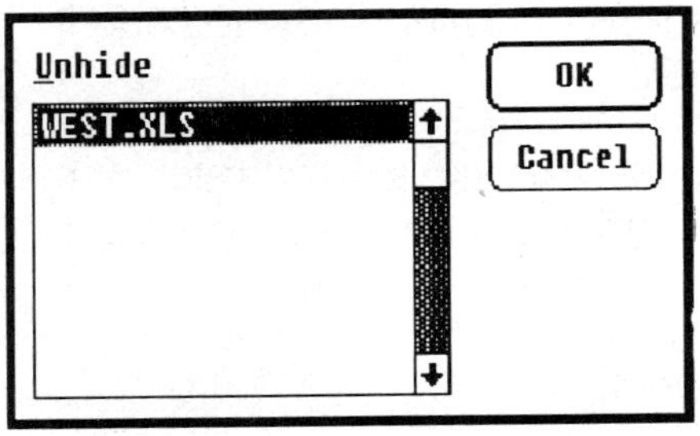

Figure 1-19 The Window Unhide dialog box

8. Select **W**indow and drag to EAST1.XLS (ALT+w and press 1).
9. Select **W**indow and drag to WEST1.XLS (ALT+w and press 3).
10. Select **W**indow and drag to **A**rrange All (ALT+w and press a).
11. Move the mouse to Sheet1 and click (ALT+w and press 2).
12. Select the Sheet1 Control Menu icon (ALT+-) and drag to **C**lose (press c).
13. Select **W**indow and drag to **A**rrange All (ALT+w and press a).
14. WEST.XLS should be the active window. If it is not, move the mouse to WEST.XLS and click (ALT+w and press 2).
15. Select **W**indow and drag to **H**ide (ALT+w and press h).
16. Select **W**indow and drag to **U**nhide (ALT+w and press u). This will open a dialog box (see **Figure 1-19**).
17. Click on OK (press ENTER).
18. Press SHIFT, select **F**ile, and drag to **C**lose All (SHIFT+ALT+f and press c).
19. If asked whether or not you want to save changes, click on **N**o (press n).

Questions:
1. What happens to EAST.XLS when you select the document control command Maximize? What happens when you select Restore?
2. What happens to the display screen when you activate the Arrange All command?

3. What happens to WEST.XLS when you activate the Hide command? When you activate the Unhide command and select WEST.XLS?
4. What happens when you select the Close All command?
5. What does this exercise teach you about using windows?

1-4-4 Moving and sizing windows

Besides opening, closing, hiding, and unhiding windows, Microsoft Excel allows you to maximize and restore a window and to move a window to a different location on a worksheet. Moving and sizing a window can be done directly with the mouse or indirectly using the keyboard. The next exercise asks you to move a window using a mouse. Exercise 1-10 asks you to move a window using the keyboard.

EXERCISE 1-9
Moving and sizing using the mouse

For this exercise, use the EAST.XLS worksheet once again and do the following:

1. With a blank display screen in front of you (if Sheet1 is showing, click on the Document control icon and close it), select **F**ile (ALT+f) and drag to **O**pen (press o).

2. Select EAST.XLS (type *EAST.XLS*).

3. Choose OK (press ENTER).

4. Place the mouse pointer on the left-edge of EAST.XLS. This edge is marked by a gray line.

5. Select the edge (the gray line turns to black) and drag the edge to the left (on a color monitor the new position of the window is outlined by the color red). **Figure 1-20** shows were the worksheet should now be located.

6. Click on the Document control menu icon (ALT+-) and drag to **C**lose (press c). This should remove all worksheets from your display screen.

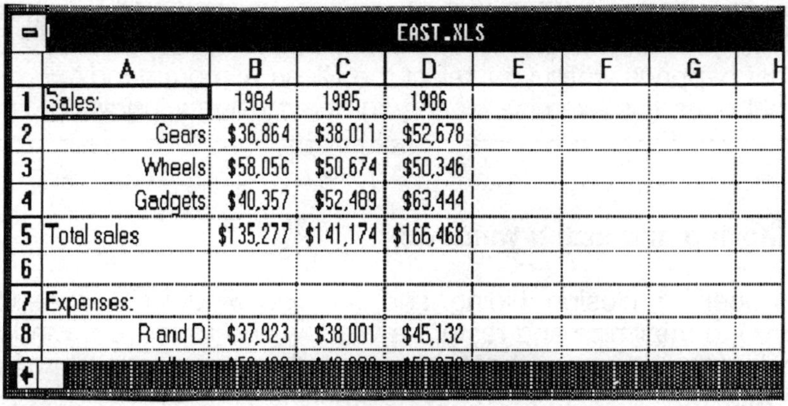

Figure 1-20 Moving the EAST.XLS worksheet to the left

Questions:

1. What happens to the worksheet as you begin to drag it to the left?
2. Suppose you wanted to return the worksheet to the location of the right-hand side of the display screen. How would you do this?

EXERCISE 1-10
Moving and sizing using the keyboard

Using the keyboard to move and size a worksheet requires the use of the Control Move and the Control Size commands. We will repeat the last exercise to demonstrate the use of these commands.

1. With a blank display screen in front of you (if Sheet1 is showing, close it), select **F**ile (ALT+f) and drag to **O**pen (press o).

2. Select EAST.XLS (type *EAST.XLS*).

3. Choose OK (press ENTER).

4. Select the Document Control menu icon (ALT+-) and drag to **M**ove (press m). This step highlights the worksheet, indicating that Microsoft Excel is waiting for you to reposition the window on the screen.

5. Use the LEFT and UP keys to move the worksheet to the left-hand side of the display screen (see Figure 1-20).

6. Press ENTER.

7. Select the Document Control menu icon (ALT+-) and drag to **S**ize (press s). This step also highlights the border of the worksheet; however, note the size icon. This means that Microsoft Excel is waiting for you to change the size of the worksheet.

8. Use the RIGHT key to increase the size of the right-hand side of the worksheet and press ENTER.

9. Click on the Document control menu icon (ALT+-) and drag to **C**lose (press c). A dialog box will open asking you, "Save changes in EAST.XLS?" Click on **N**o. This should remove all worksheets from your display screen.

Questions:

1. When might it be more important to use the keyboard with the size command, rather than to move the worksheet with the mouse? Hint: use the Size command and the mouse to find out the difference.
2. Suppose you wanted to return the worksheet to the same location and size when you started this exercise. How would you do this with the keyboard?

EXERCISE 1-11
Splitting a window into parts

A window can be split into window panes, using the Control Split command. When you choose this command, *split bars* appear as gray lines at the upper-left hand corner of the worksheet. When these gray lines appear, you can use DIRECTION keys or the mouse to move the split bar to the point on the worksheet where you want to divide it into parts.

1. With a blank display screen in front of you (if Sheet1 is showing, close it), select **F**ile (ALT+f) and drag to **O**pen (press o).

2. Select EAST.XLS (type *EAST.XLS*).

3. Choose OK (press ENTER).

4. Select the Document Control menu icon (ALT+-) and drag to Split (press t). This step highlights the split bars, indicating that Microsoft Excel is waiting for you to split the window into panes.

5. Drag the split bar line to row 12 (SHIFT+DOWN).

6. Press ENTER.

7. Scroll on the top-most pane to make the top pane the same as the lower pane (see **Figure 1-21**).

8. Select **F**ile and drag to **C**lose (ALT+f and press c) to close the split window.

9. Click on **N**o when asked if you want to save the changes to EAST.XLS (press n). You should be faced with a blank screen.

Questions:
1. Why is it important to be able to split a screen? Hint: Consider a very large worksheet.
2. What happens when you scroll on the upper scroll bar? What happens when you scroll on the lower scroll bar?

1-5 Exiting From Microsoft Excel

You can exit from Microsoft Excel and return to the DOS operating system by choosing the File Exit command.

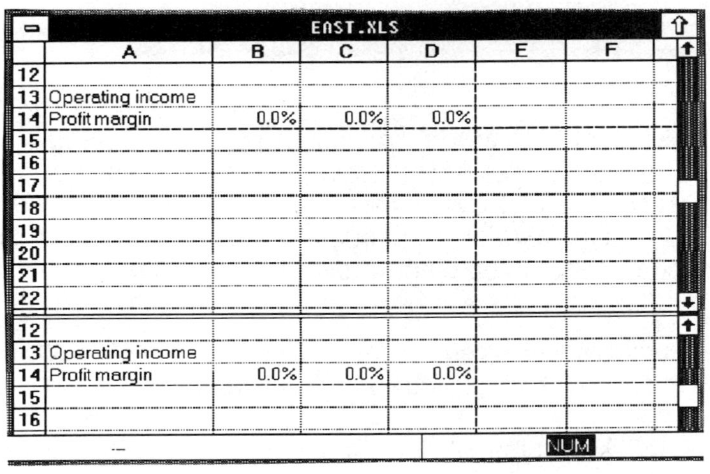

Figure 1-21 A split window showing identical information in two panes

EXERCISE 1-12
Exiting from Microsoft Excel

1. With a blank display screen in front of you (if Sheet1 is showing, close it), select **F**ile (ALT+f) and drag to **O**pen (press o).

2. Select EAST.XLS (type *EAST.XLS*).

3. Choose OK (press ENTER).

4. Move EAST.XLS to the right.

5. Select **F**ile and drag to E**x**it. (ALT+f and press x).

6. You will be asked, "Save changes in EAST.XLS?" Click on **N**o.

Normally, if you have made changes to a worksheet that you want to save, and plan to return to use the worksheet at a time in the future you would want to click on **Y**es to save the worksheet. *This is the normal procedure*. For now, observe that the dialog box offers three choices: yes, which saves the changes to your worksheet on a disk; no, which ignores the changes to your worksheet and does not save these changes on a disk; and cancel, which cancels the File Exit command.

Questions:

1. Why is it important to be faced with yes, no, or cancel decisions when you decide to exit?

1-6 Summary

The main purpose of this chapter is to acquaint you with the layout of the worksheet display screen, the main sets of worksheet commands, and several file and window commands. The layout features many important concepts. These include three different types of bars---the worksheet menu bar, the formula bar, and the status bar----and several different types of icons.

By now we expect that you will know how to open and close a drag-down menu, how to work within a dialog box, and how to exit from Microsoft Excel, using the mouse or the keyboard.

In working with Microsoft Excel remember that a worksheet is contained within a window. As a window, a position of the worksheet can be displayed, the worksheet can be moved and sized, and can be hidden and unhidden. It is also possible to arrange several windows on the same display screen. Finally, you can close a window using the File Close or the Document Control Close commands.

In working through this chapter you should realize that if you get into trouble, Microsoft Excel is forgiving. Before taking an action---such as the decision to exit---Microsoft Excel often asks if you wish to save a worksheet or to cancel the action. In addition, Microsoft Excel is designed to help you get out of trouble. You can press ESC to close a drag-down window, click to close a dialog box (TAB to cancel), and read the status bar to determine where you are in processing.

The next chapter asks you to produce and print a worksheet. We use the terms and techniques from this chapter to make these next exercises easy to understand.

KEY TERMS

Active cell
Application control menu
Cell
Dialog box
Document control menu
Drop-down menu
File commands
Formula bar
Icon
Menu bar
Split bars
Status bar
Window commands
Worksheet window

COMMAND REFERENCE

File Open: File menu. Opens an existing file. You must specify the drive from which you wish to retrieve and the file name.

File Close: File menu. Closes the active file.

File Close All: File menu. Closes all active files. Activated by holding the SHIFT key and the File Close command.

File Exit: File menu. Exits Microsoft Excel. If changes have been made to files and not saved, you will be asked, "Do you wish to save file changes?"

Options Display: Options menu. Controls screen display options, including gridline color, row and column headings, and gridlines. Removing row and column headings and gridlines with this command does not remove them when you print. The File Page Setup command is used to remove both headings and gridlines.

Window Activate: Window menu. Allows you to change the active window when more than one window is open.

Window Arrange All: Window menu. Arranges all open windows on the display screen, displaying at a minimum, a portion of the open document.

Document Control Maximize: Document control menu. Maximizes the size of the active window on the display screen.

Document Control Restore: Document control menu. Restores a window to its original size.

Document Control Close: Document control menu. Closes the active window, prompting you to save changes.

Document Control Move: Document control menu. Allows you to move the active window using the DIRECTION keys.

Document Control Size: Document control menu. Allows you to change the size of the active window using the DIRECTION keys.

Document Control Split: Document control window. Divides the active window. The size of the split window is controlled by the DIRECTION keys.

ON YOUR OWN

1. Microsoft Excel includes all of the following except:
   a) Worksheets
   b) Databases
   c) Macros
   d) Charts
   e) Clip art

2. Which of the following does not appear on the worksheet menu bar?
   a) File
   b) Options
   c) Macro
   d) Graph
   e) Formula

3. The __________ is the basic unit of the worksheet.
   a) row
   b) window
   c) document window
   d) application window
   e) cell

4. A(n) ____ is a graphic symbol used to show a function to be performed.
   a) icon
   b) cell
   c) mouse
   d) menu
   e) formula

5. If a command ends in a(n) _______, Microsoft Excel will display a _____ that requires more information.
   a) ellipsis, menu
   b) question mark, menu
   c) ellipsis, dialog box
   d) question mark, dialog box
   e) colon, dialog box

6. The _____ command is used to access a file already saved to a disk.
   a) File Save
   b) File New
   c) File Close
   d) File Open
   e) File Close All

7. ___________ will always move you to the upper left corner of your worksheet.
   a) Home
   b) Control+End
   c) Page up
   d) Control+Home
   e) Control+Direction key

8. The _____ extension is added to all Microsoft Excel worksheets.
   a) .XLW
   b) .XLS
   c) .XLC
   d) .XLM
   e) .XLR

9. The ________ command allows you to divide a single worksheet into panes.
   a) Window Arrange All
   b) Control Move
   c) Control Size
   d) Control Split
   e) Control Restore

10. The ________ command allows you to look at all open windows at one time.
    a) Window Arrange All
    b) File View
    c) File Open
    d) File Arrange All
    e) Window Hide

MORE PRACTICE

At the end of each chapter you will find additional practice exercises to help you practice what you have learned. These exercises assume that you have worked through the tutorial exercises in the chapter. They do not always specify which commands you should use to complete them and do not proceed in a step-by-step manner.

I. Open REPORT.XLS stored on the Microsoft Excel Promotion diskette and answer the following questions:
   1. How many cogs were sold in May?
   2. Which cell(s) contains the entry **cogs**?

II. With a blank SHEET1 worksheet facing you,
   1. Open ANNUAL.XLS first and SALES.XLS second.
   2. Arrange the windows so you can see the three worksheets.
   3. Close SHEET1 and answer the questions below.
      a) After you arranged all the windows, which window appeared in the upper left side of the screen?
      b) Why didn't Microsoft Excel ask you if you wanted to save changes in SHEET1.XLS?

III. With a blank SHEET1 worksheet facing you,
   1. Open all files with the extension .XLS.
   2. Arrange all of the windows.
   3. Maximize SALES.XLS.

4. Hide SALES.XLS.
5. Press SHIFT+File Close to close all of the open worksheets. Do not save any changes. Then answer the questions below.
   a) How many files are displayed?
   b) After you hide SALES.XLS, which window becomes the active window?

CHAPTER 2 - ENTERING AND EDITING WORKSHEET INFORMATION

By now you should be comfortable moving around the Microsoft Excel worksheet using either the mouse and/or the keyboard. You should be able to open, close, and change a worksheet window, open and close a worksheet saved as a file, enter commands, and be able to work with drop-down menus and dialog boxes. The next step is to ask you to enter and edit (meaning to modify) information on a worksheet. Once you are satisfied with how your worksheet looks, we will ask you to print it, using your computer printer.

When you complete this chapter you should be able to:

* Create a new worksheet and save it.
* Enter information into a cell and a cell range.
* Edit information in a cell and a cell range.
* Insert and delete cells in a worksheet.
* Enter and edit a worksheet formula.
* Format numbers and text.
* Print a worksheet.

2-1 Opening a Worksheet

Before you can create a new worksheet, an empty worksheet window must be open. With Microsoft Excel, an empty worksheet is opened automatically, each time you start the program. This worksheet is given the default name Sheet1. Let's suppose, however, that you closed Sheet1, using the windowing command discussed in the last chapter. You can open additional new worksheets using the File New command and selecting Worksheet.

EXERCISE 2-1
Opening a new worksheet

For this exercise, start the software so that Sheet1 is facing you.

1. Select **F**ile and drag to **N**ew (ALT+f and press n).

2. When the dialog box opens, click on OK (press ENTER). Since the default is a worksheet, this will open a new worksheet.

3. Repeat steps 1 and 2 again.

4. Repeat steps 1 and 2 one more time.

5. Select **F**ile and drag to **C**lose (ALT+f and press c). Do not save changes.

6. Repeat step 5 again.

7. Exit Microsoft Excel at this time, or continue by doing the next exercise.

Questions:
1. What is the name of the second worksheet? The third worksheet?
2. Suppose you wanted to close all three new worksheets at the same time. How do you do this? (Review the materials in Chapter 1 if you cannot remember this command sequence.)

2-2 Saving a New Worksheet

Worksheets are saved using the commands File Save As and File Save. The *File Save As* command is used when saving a worksheet for the first time. If you select File Save instead, this command will prompt or ask you for a name at that time. As shown by **Figure 2-1**, selecting the File Save As command opens a dialog box which contains a worksheet name box. This name can be changed by typing in the name you decide to use. For example, if you want to save this worksheet as NPV1, as required in the next exercise, you would type *NPV1* and click on OK (press ENTER). Microsoft Excel then saves this new worksheet on drive C, using the filename NPV1.XLS. The XLS extension is automatically added.

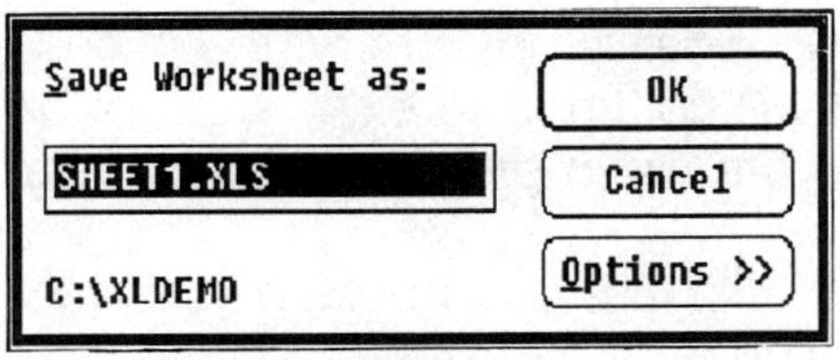

Figure 2-1 The File Save dialog box

Let's suppose you want to save a file on drive A, instead of drive C. Using the last example, to change the drive, type *A:NPV1* and click on OK (press ENTER). Microsoft Excel would save the worksheet as NPV1.XLS on drive A of your computer.

The *File Save* command is much easier to use than the File Save As command. Once a file has been named and saved once, it can be opened, worked on, and saved again and again. To save a previously named file, simply select File and drag to Save.

As a final illustration, let's suppose you want to make a copy of a worksheet, storing the worksheet under two different names. In this case, open the worksheet, saved under one name and use the File Save As command to store the worksheet under a different name. This method also allows you to make a backup copy of all your valuable worksheets.

2-3 Entering Worksheet Information

Worksheets accept three types of information: text, numbers, and formulas. As shown in the last chapter, *text* consists of descriptive entries, such as names, abbreviations, and expressions. Text entries can include numbers, such as *1-2-3-4 off we go*. In contrast, *numbers* are restricted to combinations of 0 through 9. After a number has been typed on a worksheet, it can be *formatted*, which means to change the looks of a number by setting the decimal point and adding commas, or a dollar sign ($) or pound sign (#). Numbers can also be used in *formulas*---arithmetic expressions designed to calculate other values. For example, the formula = *5 * 6 + 2* tells Microsoft Excel to multiply 5 times 6 (where * is the times sign) and add 2 to the product. This yields the value 32 using Microsoft Excel. Section 2.5 explains how to build and use formulas.

2-3-1 Entering text

Text is entered on a worksheet by selecting a cell, typing the text, and pressing ENTER, or one of the DIRECTION keys (LEFT, RIGHT, UP, or DOWN). If the number of text characters exceeds the width of the cell, and the right adjacent cell is empty, excess text will appear to be placed in the space to the right. If, however, the right-most cell is not empty, the excess characters will be hidden from view (they will continue to exist, but not be displayed). Formatting is used to change the width of a cell. Section 2.6 deals with this topic.

Text is aligned by default to the left in a cell. If this is not how you want text to appear, formatting commands are required once again. In this case, you might design to align text to the right, or center text in a cell.

The fastest way to enter text in a row is to move from left to right, pressing the RIGHT key after text has been typed in a cell. This follows the direction we use when we read. Likewise, the fastest way to enter text in a column is to move from top to bottom, pressing the DOWN key after text has been typed in a cell. Moving quickly to a cell located some distance from where you are on a worksheet is best accomplished with the *Formula Goto* command. This command asks you to type in the name of the cell and click on OK (press ENTER). Microsoft Excel goes directly to the name of the referenced cell.

EXERCISE 2-2
Entering text information

For this exercise, start so that Sheet1 is facing you. You will be asked to add the text shown on **Figure 2-2**. This worksheet represents the beginnings of a net present value analysis table. In this and the next chapter, we will ask you to complete this table. Since many of you may not know what is meant by Net Present Value, let us briefly explain. Net Present Value is a formula that expresses dollars earned several years from today in today's dollars (since the value of a dollar depreciates over time---due to the time value of money and inflation in our society). For example, a dollar earned 1 year from today, is not worth a dollar today. Rather it is worth a smaller amount such as 90 cents. Given this difference, financial theory tells us that we would be willing to receive 90 cents today, or a dollar one year from today, since both represent the same dollar amount.

In this initial exercise, you are asked to type in the headings important to the first twenty-five rows of the table shown on Figure 2-2. You might think of the problem to be solved as follows:

You are a financial analyst at Timberware, a software development company that writes specialty software to trace reforestation. You are deciding whether or not to go ahead with a development project. First you list the benefits of the project. These include cost savings and the dollar savings that result from better service. You compare these benefits to the costs of development---the one time development cost and the continuing

	A	B	C	D	E	F
1					Year Effective	
2	BENEFITS					
3						
4	Cost Savings					
5	Direct labor					
6	Indirect labor					
7	Total					
8						
9	Better Service					
10	Better Information					
11						
12	TOTAL BENEFITS					
13						
14	COSTS					
15						
16	Development					
17	Operating					
18						
19	TOTAL COSTS					
20						
21	Net Value					
22	Discount rate					
23	Present value					
24						
25	NET PRESENT VALUE					

Figure 2-2 The row and column headings for the net present value analysis worksheet

operating costs. The difference between benefits and costs is called Net Value. After Net Value is determined, it is applied to a Discount Rate. This returns the Present Value. The value of the Net Value expressed in today's dollars. Finally, you must sum the Present Value totals to arrive at the Net Present Value.

To begin this analysis do the following:

1. Select cell E1 (press RIGHT four times).

2. Type *Year Effective*. If you make a typing mistake and wish to make a change, use the BACKSPACE key. Once you are satisfied with your entry press ENTER.

3. Move to cell A2 using the mouse (press DOWN once and LEFT four times).

4. Type (in lower case letters) *benefits* and press DOWN.

5. Press DOWN again to skip a space.

6. In cell A4 type *Cost Savings* and press DOWN.

7. Move to cell A2 once again (Press UP twice).

8. To change benefits to BENEFITS, type *BENEFITS* and press ENTER.

9. Select Fo**r**mula and drag to **G**oto (ALT+r and press g).

10. Type *A5* in the reference box and press ENTER.

11. Type *Direct labor* in cell A5 and press DOWN.

12. Complete the remaining text entries shown on Figure 2-2. If you make a mistake, use the BACKSPACE key, or retype the heading.

13. To save this worksheet, select **F**ile and drag to Save **A**s (ALT+f and press a).

14. Type *a:npv1* to save this worksheet on drive A. Remember to change the drive number if necessary. The worksheet will be saved as NPV1.XLS on drive A.

Questions:
1. How do direction keys save you time when entering information on a worksheet?
2. When is the Formula Goto command the most useful?
3. Why is it wise to save a worksheet even when it is not completed?

2-3-2 Entering numbers

Numbers are added to a worksheet in the same way as text, with the following exceptions. Using the normal cell width, Microsoft Excel will only accept 8 digits, including the decimal point. If more digits are typed, the number will be rounded and displayed in scientific notation. Another difference is that numbers are automatically aligned to the right (remember that text is aligned to the left). Formatting commands must be used to change the alignment.

EXERCISE 2-3
Entering different types of numbers

For this exercise, you are asked to try several experiments using numbers. Review the questions before starting this exercise.

With a blank worksheet facing you, do the following:

1. Type *50* in cell A1 and press ENTER.
2. Type *50.60* in a different cell, such as A2, and press ENTER.
3. Type *$50* in a different cell and press ENTER.
4. Type *$50.60* in a different cell and press ENTER.
5. Type ten 5's, *5555555555*, in a different cell and press ENTER.
6. Type a minus sign and ten 5's, *-5555555555*, in a different cell and press ENTER.
7. You do not need to save this worksheet.

Questions:
For each case above (50, 50.60, $50, $50.60, 5555555555, and -5555555555)
1. What value is displayed in the cell after typing the number and pressing ENTER?
2. What value is displayed in the formula bar after typing the number and pressing ENTER?
3. What conclusions can you draw?

EXERCISE 2-4
Entering numbers on the present value table

For this exercise, use NPV1.XLS, the worksheet saved for exercise 2-2. You are asked to key in the costs shown on **Figure 2-3**. Do not add dollar signs at this time. Later on, we will show you a quicker way of adding dollar amounts to a worksheet.

1. Select **F**ile and drag to **O**pen (ALT+f and press o).
2. Click on the directory you need if it differs from the current directory. For example, if you are on drive C and your file is on drive A, click on directory A (ALT+d) and press OK (press ENTER). Do this again to list the worksheets on this drive.

	A	B	C	D	E	F	G
1					Year Effective		
2	BENEFITS						
3							
4	Cost Savings						
5	Direct labor		0	15000	15500	16000	17000
6	Indirect labor		0	5000	5500	6000	7000
7	Total						
8							
9	Better Service		0	10000	12000	15000	16000
10	Better Information		0	15000	15000	15000	16000
11							
12	TOTAL BENEFITS						
13							
14	COSTS						
15							
16	Development		50000	20000			
17	Operating		0	30000	35000	40000	45000
18							
19	TOTAL COSTS						
20							
21	Net Value						
22	Discount rate						
23	Present value						
24							
25	NET PRESENT VALUE						

Figure 2-3 Adding numbers to the Net Present Value Analysis worksheet

3. Select NPV1.XLS (ALT+f and press DOWN to NPV1).
4. Click on OK (press ENTER).
5. With NPV1.XLS facing you, move to cell C5 (use DIRECTION keys).
6. Type zero *0* and press RIGHT.
7. Type *1500* and press RIGHT.
8. Continue to add all the numbers shown on Figure 2-3.
9. Select **F**ile and drag to **S**ave (ALT+f and press s). This will save your revised worksheet under the name NPV1.XLS.

Questions:
1. If you make a mistake when typing a number, what should you do?
2. If you want to save the revised worksheet as NPV2, what changes would you make to the exercise procedure?

2-3-3 Entering numbers or dates in a series

A shortcut approach to entering numbers or dates in a series uses the *Data Series* command. This command tells Microsoft Excel how to fill a selected range of cells, where a *range* represents a rectangular section of the worksheet containing two or more cells. Carried to the extreme, a range can refer to all the cells in a row or column or even all the cells in a worksheet.

Figure 2-4 illustrates a range for the cells A4:H6. The notation:

cell reference 1:cell reference 2

is a time-saving way of defining the boundaries of a range. For example, A4:H6 means the same as cells A4, B4, C4, D4, E4, F4, G4, H4, A5, ...G6, H6.

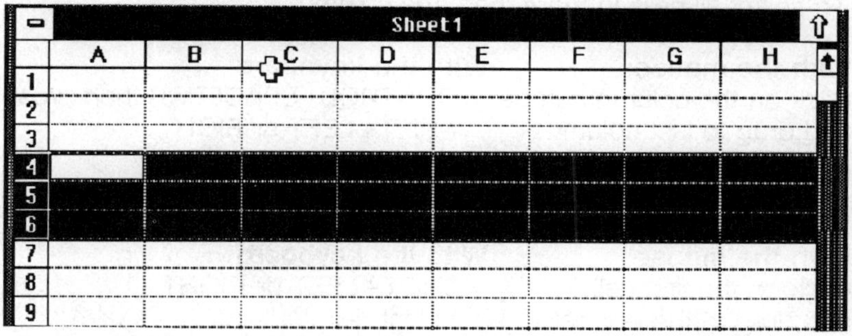

Figure 2-4 A multiple-row range and how it appears on a worksheet

Figure 2-5 shows how a range of cells is selected. This is somewhat complex and will require some practice on your part. As a general rule, it is much easier to use the mouse in defining a range. When using the keyboard, one difficult procedure to remember is how to select an entire column as the range (see step 2). To make this selection you must type CONTROL+SPACEBAR to define all the cells in the column. To select all the cells in several columns, two keyboard procedures are required: first, type CONTROL+SPACEBAR to define the initial column and second, type SHIFT+RIGHT or LEFT to define multiple columns.

The Data Series command requires the definition of a range. To use this command you must initially type in the beginning value in the series. Next, you must tell Microsoft Excel where to fill the numbers in the series. This location is defined by the range.

1. To select all cells in a row:

With the mouse:	**With the keyboard:**
Click on the row number	SHIFT+SPACEBAR

2. To select all cells in a column:

With the mouse:	**With the keyboard:**
Click on the column number	CONTROL+SPACEBAR

3. To select all cells in more than one row:

With the mouse:	**With the keyboard:**
Click on the row number and drag to the last row	SHIFT+SPACEBAR then press SHIFT+LEFT or RIGHT

4. To select all cells in more than one column:

With the mouse:	**With the keyboard:**
Click on the column number and drag to last column	CONTROL+SPACEBAR then press SHIFT+LEFT or RIGHT

5. To select specific cells (but not all) in a row:

With the mouse:	**With the keyboard:**
Click on the first cell and drag to the last cell	SHIFT+LEFT or RIGHT to last cell

6. To select specific cells (but not all) in a column:

With the mouse:	**With the keyboard:**
Click on the first cell and drag to the last cell	SHIFT+UP or DOWN to last cell

7. To select a specific block of cells:

With the mouse:	**With the keyboard:**
Click on the first cell and drag to the last cell	SHIFT+UP or DOWN and TOP or BOTTOM

Figure 2-5 Mouse and keyboard procedures for defining a range

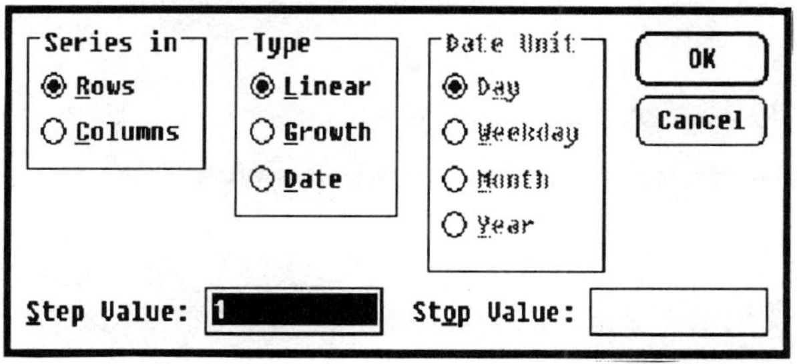

Figure 2-6 The Data Series dialog box

Figure 2-6 illustrates the dialog box for this command. The purpose of each option is as follows:

* **Series in**: Determines whether to fill to the right (rows) or down (columns).

* **Type**: Determines the makeup of the series. A *linear fill* adds the step value to the last number to create a new number, while a *growth fill* multiplies the step value by the last number to create a new number. With a step value of 2 and an old value of 8, linear fill produces a new value of 10 (8 + 2) while a growth fill produces a new value of 16 (8*2). A *date fill* calculates a series of calendar dates.

* **Date unit**: Sets each successive value in a date series. The date unit choices are day, week, month, and year. **Figure 2-7** illustrates a date series by month. After typing 1/1/90 and defining the range as A4:H4, the Data Series command fills the range by month. Observe how this command helps you. It adds seven new values to the worksheet by using a single command.

* **Step value**: Sets the value by which each successive cell in the data series is to be increased (or decreased).

* **Stop value**: Sets the value at which you want the series to stop. This step is optional.

	A	B	C	D	E	F	G	H
1								
2				Date Series				
3								
4	1/1/90	1/2/90	1/3/90	1/4/90	1/5/90	1/6/90	1/7/90	1/8/90

Figure 2-7 Adding dates to a worksheet using the Data Series command

EXERCISE 2-5
Using the Data Series command

For this exercise use NPV1.XLS (or NPV2.XLS), the worksheet saved for Exercise 2-4. **Figure 2-8** shows the revised net present value analysis worksheet.

1. Select **F**ile and drag to **O**pen (ALT+f and press o).

2. Select NPV1.XLS (ALT+f and press DOWN to NPV1).

3. Click on OK (press ENTER).

4. Type *1* in cell C2 and press ENTER.

	A	B	C	D	E	F	G
1					Year Effective		
2	BENEFITS		1	2	3	4	5
3							
4	Cost Savings						
5	Direct labor		0	15000	15500	16000	17000
6	Indirect labor		0	5000	5500	6000	7000
7	Total						
8							
9	Better Service		0	10000	12000	15000	16000
10	Better Information		0	15000	15000	15000	16000
11							
12	TOTAL BENEFITS						
13							
14	COSTS						
15							
16	Development		50000	20000			
17	Operating		0	30000	35000	40000	45000
18							
19	TOTAL COSTS						
20							
21	Net Value						
22	Discount rate						
23	Present value						
24							
25	NET PRESENT VALUE						

Figure 2-8 Using the Data Series command to add the year effective information to the net present value analysis worksheet

5. Select the range C2:G2 (press SHIFT+RIGHT 4 times).

6. Select **D**ata and drag to Ser**i**es (ALT+d and press r).

7. Choose the default values---**R**ows, **L**inear, and a **S**tep Value of 1---by clicking OK (press ENTER).

8. Select **F**ile and drag to **S**ave (ALT+f and press s). This will save your revised worksheet as NPV1.XLS.

Questions:
1. What are the main advantages in using the Data Series command?
2. How would you change the exercise if you decided to fill the "Year Effective" row with dates rather than with linear numbers?

2-3-4 Entering formulas

Entering a formula on a worksheet is more difficult than entering text or numbers. With formulas, a syntax must be followed. An important part of this syntax is to begin each formula with an equal (=) sign. Second, each value in a formula must be joined to another by a *formula operator*. As shown by **Figure 2-9**, formula operators include range, exponentiation, all arithmetic operators, and all comparison operators. Collectively, these operators form a *precedence hierarchy*---an ordering which gives some operators a greater importance than others. As shown by the table,

This Operator	Means
:	Range
space	Intersection
,	Union
-	Negation
%	Percent
^	Exponentiation
* and /	Multiplication and division
+ and -	Addition and subtraction
&	Add text
= < > <= >= <>	Comparison operators

Figure 2-9 Operator precedence hierarchy

multiplication has a higher precedence (importance) than addition. Thus, the formula: *=12+2*2*, yields a value of 16 (multiply 2 by 2 first and add the product to 12). This precedence can be overridden by using parentheses. The formula: *=(12+2)*2*, yields a value of 28 (add twelve to two and multiply the sum by two). Whenever two operators are at the same level, such as * and / this means the precedence is the same. The formula *=10*6/6* would yield 10. In this example, the formula is processed from left to right, multiplying 10 by 6 first and dividing by 6 second, since both operators have the same precedence.

A formula usually contains cell references rather than numbers. The formula: *=A1+B1*, entered in cell C1, adds the numbers stored in cells A1 and B1 and stores the sum in cell C1.

2-3-5 The Edit Fill commands

After a formula has been added to a cell, it can be copied to the next cell using one of four *Edit Fill* commands. These commands are:

Command	Is Used To
Edit Fill Down:	Copies the contents and formats in the top row of a cell into the rest of the rows in the defined range.
Edit Fill Up:	Copies the contents and formats in the bottom row of a cell into the rest of the rows in the defined range.
Edit Fill Right:	Copies the contents and formats in the right column of a cell into the rest of the columns in the defined range.
Edit Fill Left:	Copies the contents and formats in the left column of a cell into the rest of the columns in the defined range.

The Edit Fill Down and Edit Fill Right commands appear on the Edit drop-down menu. To activate the Edit Fill Up and Edit Fill Left commands, hold down the SHIFT key when using the mouse. (With the keyboard, hold down SHIFT+ALT and press e; then press w to fill up or h to fill left.) As a caution: these commands are powerful. Any contents or formats in the fill range are completely replaced by the fill command.

EXERCISE 2-6
Simple formulas and the Edit Fill command

For this exercise use NPV1.XLS, the worksheet saved for Exercise 2-4. **Figure 2-10** shows the revised net present value analysis worksheet. As shown, you are asked to determine the Net Value (Total Benefits less Total Costs) of the software development project.

1. Select **F**ile and drag to **O**pen (ALT+f and press o).
2. Select NPV1.XLS (ALT+f and press DOWN to NPV1).
3. Click on OK (press ENTER).

	A	B	C	D	E	F	G
1					Year Effective		
2	BENEFITS		1	2	3	4	5
3							
4	Cost Savings						
5	Direct labor		0	15000	15500	16000	17000
6	Indirect labor		0	5000	5500	6000	7000
7	Total		0	20000	21000	22000	24000
8							
9	Better Service		0	10000	12000	15000	16000
10	Better Information		0	15000	15000	15000	16000
11							
12	TOTAL BENEFITS		0	45000	48000	52000	56000
13							
14	COSTS						
15							
16	Development		50000	20000			
17	Operating		0	30000	35000	40000	45000
18							
19	TOTAL COSTS		50000	50000	35000	40000	45000
20							
21	Net Value		-50000	-5000	13000	12000	11000
22	Discount rate						
23	Present value						
24							
25	NET PRESENT VALUE						

Figure 2-10 Adding column totals to the Net Present Value Analysis worksheet

4. Type *=C5+C6* in cell C7 and press DOWN. This adds direct labor costs and indirect labor costs and shows the sum as the total cost savings.

5. Type *=C7+C9+C10* in cell C12 and press DOWN. This adds the total cost savings to the savings from better service and better information and stores the sum as the Total Benefits.

6. Type *=C16+C17* in cell C19 and press DOWN. This adds the total costs of development and the total costs of operating the software and stores the sum as the Total Costs.

7. Type *=C12-C19* in cell C21 and press ENTER. This subtracts the total costs from the total benefits, which in the first year leads to a negative value.

8. Select the range C7:G7 (press SHIFT+RIGHT 4 times).

9. Select **E**dit and drag to Fill Rig**h**t (ALT+e and press h).

10. Select the range C12:G12, select **E**dit and drag to **R**epeat Fill Right (ALT+e and press r).

11. Select the range C19:G19 and repeat fill right again.

12. Select the range C21:G21 and repeat fill right again.

13. Select **F**ile and drag to **S**ave (ALT+f and press s). This will save your revised worksheet as NPV1.XLS.

Questions:

1. What are the main advantages in using the Edit Fill command?
2. Compare the formula in cell C7 to the formula stored in cell C8. How do the formulas differ? What does this difference mean?

2-4 Editing Worksheet Information

After a worksheet is created, it is often necessary to edit cell entries. *Editing* is the revising of a worksheet to add or subtract from its contents, to correct errors, or to improve its layout. As shown by the Edit drop-down menu (see **Figure 2-11**), there are twelve edit commands, beginning with the Edit Undo command and ending with Edit Fill Right and Edit Fill Down, the two commands discussed in the last section.

In this section we consider eight more edit commands: Edit Clear, Edit

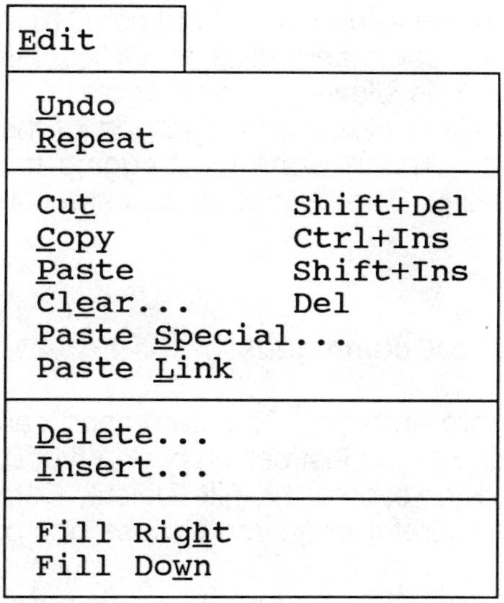

Figure 2-11 The Edit drop-down menu

Undo and Edit Repeat, Edit Copy and Edit Paste, Edit Cut, and Edit Insert and Edit Delete.

2-4-1 The Edit Clear command

The Edit Clear command is used when you want to clear the old entry from a cell and start again. The shortcut key for this command is the DELETE key. When the formula bar is inactive, Edit Clear or DELETE clears the contents, formats, notes, or all three from selected cells. When this command is selected, the dialog box shown on **Figure 2-12** appears. The four choices mean the following:

Clear	Means To
All	Clears everything from the selected cells.
Formats	Clears only the formats of the selected cells.
Formulas	Clears formulas, text, and numbers from selected cells.
Notes	Clears only notes from selected cells.

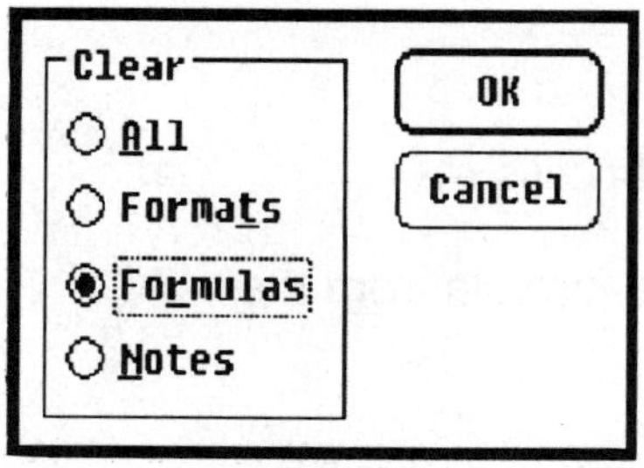

Figure 2-12 The Edit Clear dialog box

As an example, suppose you wish to clear the value 50000 from cell C16 in Figure 2-10. After selecting the Edit Clear command, click on OK (press ENTER) to clear the contents of the cell. This allows you start again.

When the formula bar is active, Edit Clear clears only that part of the formula, text, or number that is selected. This is done by dragging the insertion bar to highlight the range to delete. The next exercise asks you to make this type of change.

2-4-2 The Edit Undo and the Edit Repeat commands

The Edit Undo command is used to restore an entry. This command can only reverse the last command you choose or the last cell entry you typed, however. In addition, it cannot be used to reverse the File Delete, Data Delete, or Data Extract commands, so be careful when you choose one of these.

The Edit Repeat command is used to repeat a command. In this case, the command only works for reasonable cases. It cannot be used for commands such as File Close All or File Exit, for example. This next exercise asks you to test the Edit Undo command; Exercise 2-8 asks you to use the Edit Repeat command.

EXERCISE 2-7
Making Edit Clear changes

For this exercise, use NPV1.XLS, the worksheet saved for the last exercise. Figure 2-10 will not be changed by this exercise.

1. Select **F**ile and drag to **O**pen (ALT+f and press o).

2. Select NPV1.XLS (ALT+f and press DOWN to NPV1).

3. Click on OK (press ENTER).

4. Select cell C12.

5. Select **E**dit and drag to Cl**e**ar (ALT+e and press e).

6. Choose OK (press ENTER) to remove this formula from the worksheet.

7. Select **E**dit and drag to **U**ndo Clear (ALT+e and press u).

8. Repeat steps 5 through 7, but use the DELETE key in place of Edit Clear.

9. While in cell C12, press F2 to activate the formula bar.

10. Position the insertion bar (|) after the first plus sign (press LEFT to position the insertion bar) and drag to the number 9 (press RIGHT). The selected area is shown below:

```
=C7 + C9 + C10
```

11. Press the DELETE key.

12. Select **E**dit and drag to **U**ndo Clear (ALT+e and press u).

13. Select **E**dit and drag to **R**edo Clear (ALT+e and press u).

14. Select **E**dit and drag to **U**ndo Clear (ALT+e and press u). Press ENTER.

15. Do not save this worksheet. When asked, do not save changes to this worksheet.

Questions:

1. What happens to the formula bar when you drag the mouse (or press LEFT)?
2. What is the difference between Edit Undo and Edit Redo?
3. What is the difference between Edit Clear with the formula bar active and Edit Clear with the formula bar inactive?

2-4-3 The Edit Insert and Edit Delete commands

Edit commands can also be used to add rows or columns to a worksheet or to delete rows and columns. The Edit Insert command allows you to insert a blank cell, a range of cells, or a new row or column of cells. When this command is selected, the dialog box shown on **Figure 2-13** opens. When inserting new cells, you must decide whether to Shift Cells Right or

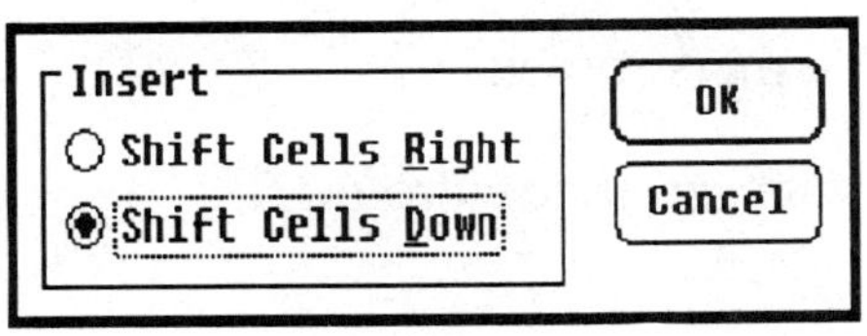

Figure 2-13 The Edit Insert dialog box

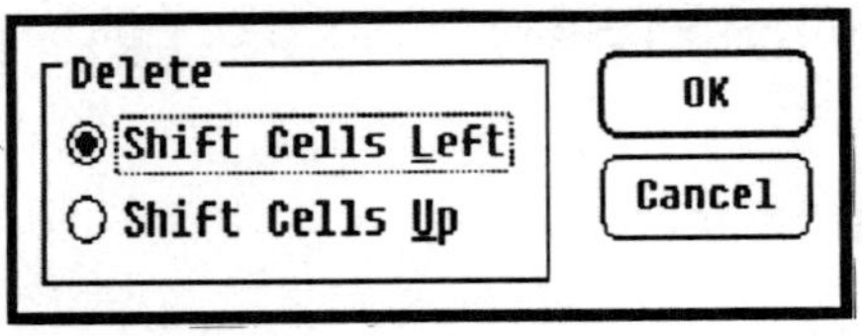

Figure 2-14 The Edit Delete dialog box

Shift Cells Down. The exception is when you decide to insert an entire row or column. In these cases, Microsoft Excel shifts cells automatically, since there is only one direction to shift the other cells.

The Edit Delete command allows you to delete a cell, a specified range of cells, or a row or column of cells. It differs from the Edit Clear command in an important way: Edit Delete removes the contents of the cell *and the cell*. Edit Clear removes only the contents of the cell.

Figure 2-14 shows the dialog box for the Edit Delete command. With this command, you must decide whether to Shift Cells Left or Shift Cells Up. Once again the exception is when you decide to delete an entire row or column---in which case this is done automatically for you.

EXERCISE 2-8
Inserting and deleting cells

For this exercise, use NPV1.XLS, the worksheet saved for Exercise 2-6. **Figure 2-15** illustrates the revised worksheet. The white area of the worksheet shows the numbers we would like to have you add in this exercise. The next exercise asks you to add headings to these new rows.

1. Select **F**ile and drag to **O**pen (ALT+f and press o).

2. Select NPV1.XLS (ALT+f and press DOWN to NPV1).

3. Click on OK (press ENTER).

4. Click on row number 8 to indicate that the range is the entire row (move to row 8 and press SHIFT+SPACEBAR).

5. Select **E**dit and drag to **I**nsert (ALT+e and press i).

6. Select **E**dit and drag to **R**epeat (ALT+e and press r).

7. Select A8 and drag to G8 to define a limited range (from A8, SHIFT+RIGHT to G8).

	A	B	C	D	E	F	G
1					Year Effective		
2	BENEFITS		1	2	3	4	5
3							
4	Cost Savings						
5	Direct labor		0	15000	15500	16000	17000
6	Indirect labor		0	5000	5500	6000	7000
7	Total		0	20000	21000	22000	24000
8							
9							
10			0	15000	15500	32000	34000
11			0	1000	2500	3000	4000
12			0	16000	18000	35000	38000
13							
14	Better Service		0	10000	12000	15000	16000
15	Better Information		0	15000	15000	15000	16000
16							
17	TOTAL BENEFITS		0	45000	48000	52000	56000
18							
19	COSTS						
20							
21	Development		50000	20000			
22	Operating		0	30000	35000	40000	45000
23							
24	TOTAL COSTS		50000	50000	35000	40000	45000
25							
26	Net Value		-50000	-5000	13000	12000	11000
27	Discount rate						
28	Present value						
29							
30	NET PRESENT VALUE						

Figure 2-15 Inserting new rows and adding additional cost savings to the Net Present Value Analysis Worksheet

8. Select **E**dit and drag to **I**nsert (ALT+e and press i).

9. Select **E**dit and drag to **R**epeat (ALT+e and press r).

10. Select **E**dit and drag to **R**epeat again (ALT+e and press r).

11. In row C10:G10, add the numbers shown.

12. In row C11:G11, add the numbers shown.

13. In cell C12 type *=C10+C11*.

14. Select the range C12:G12 (press SHIFT+RIGHT 4 times).

15. Select **E**dit and drag to Fill Rig**h**t (ALT+e and press h).

16. Select **F**ile and drag to **S**ave (ALT+f and press s). This will save your revised worksheet as NPV1.XLS.

Questions:
1. What are the main advantages in using the Edit Repeat command?
2. Why is it important to be able to insert new cells in a worksheet? To delete cells?

2-4-4 The Edit Copy, Edit Cut, and Edit Paste commands

Two sets of time-saving edit commands are Edit Copy and Edit Paste and Edit Cut and Edit Paste. The first set---Edit Copy and Edit Paste---allows you to select an area on a worksheet and to paste a copy of the area on another worksheet area. After the range to be copied has been defined, the Edit Copy command tells Microsoft Excel to highlight this area, using a *marquee* (or boxed dotted line). The Edit Paste command, in turn, tells Microsoft Excel where to place the area outlined by the marquee.

The second set---Edit Cut and Edit Paste---allows you to select an area on a worksheet and to paste it to another area, while deleting or cutting the area indicated by the marquee. The Edit Cut command defines the area to be deleted; the Edit Paste command tells Microsoft Excel where to place the area outlined by the marquee.

EXERCISE 2-9
Copying and pasting text

For this exercise, use NPV1.XLS once again. **Figure 2-16** shows the revised worksheet. As illustrated, you are to add labels to the numbers added in the last exercise. These labels show that additional cost savings, called *cost avoidance*, have been identified. This type of savings reflects costs that will be avoided in the future as a direct result of the new development. For example, with the new software, the expenses for additional clerical help will not be needed in the next six months. The costs of employing the clerical help will be avoided.

This exercise is also designed to introduce you to cut and paste and copy and paste. Initially, you are do cut and paste.

	A	B	C	D	E	F	G
1					Year Effective		
2	BENEFITS		1	2	3	4	5
3							
4	Cost Savings						
5	Direct labor		0	15000	15500	16000	17000
6	Indirect labor		0	5000	5500	6000	7000
7	Total		0	20000	21000	22000	24000
8							
9	Cost Avoidance						
10	Direct labor		0	15000	15500	32000	34000
11	Indirect labor		0	1000	2500	3000	4000
12	Total		0	16000	18000	35000	38000
13							
14	Better Service		0	10000	12000	15000	16000
15	Better Information		0	15000	15000	15000	16000
16							
17	TOTAL BENEFITS		0	45000	48000	52000	56000
18							
19	COSTS						
20							
21	Development		50000	20000			
22	Operating		0	30000	35000	40000	45000
23							
24	TOTAL COSTS		50000	50000	35000	40000	45000
25							
26	Net Value		-50000	-5000	13000	12000	11000
27	Discount rate						
28	Present value						
29							
30	NET PRESENT VALUE						

Figure 2-16 Using the Edit Copy and Edit Paste commands to add headings to the Net Present Value Analysis worksheet

To add these labels and to practice with cut and paste and copy and paste, do the following:

1. Select **F**ile and drag to **O**pen (ALT+f and press o).

2. Select NPV1.XLS (ALT+f and press DOWN to NPV1).

3. Click on OK (press ENTER).

4. Define the range A4:A7 (SHIFT+DOWN and press DOWN).

5. Select **E**dit and drag to Cu**t** (ALT+e and press t).

6. Select cell A9.

7. Select **E**dit and drag to **P**aste (ALT+e and press p).

8. Select **E**dit and drag to **U**ndo (ALT+e and press u).

9. Define the range A5:A7 (SHIFT+DOWN and press DOWN).

10. Select **E**dit and drag to **C**opy (ALT+e and press c).

11. Select cell A9.

12. Select **E**dit and drag to **P**aste (ALT+e and press p).

13. Select cell A9 and press F2 to activate the formula bar.

14. Change the word Savings to *Avoidance*.

15. Select **F**ile and drag to **S**ave (ALT+f and press s). This will save your revised worksheet as NPV1.XLS.

Questions:
1. After you select the Edit Cut or the Edit Paste commands, what happens to the display screen?
2. Why is it important to be able to paste sections on a worksheet?

EXERCISE 2-10
Editing formulas

When rows or columns are inserted into worksheets, formulas that reference cells are changed to correspond to the new cell locations. For example, the total benefits, total costs, and net value totals shown on Figure 2-15 are the same as those shown on Figure 2-10, *even though new rows have been added to the worksheet*. Close inspection of the totals shown, however, indicate that some are incorrect. Cost avoidance totals are not included in Total Benefits.

Figure 2-17 shows the correct net value totals. To make these corrections, do the following:

1. Select **F**ile and drag to **O**pen (ALT+f and press o).

2. Select NPV1.XLS (ALT+f and press DOWN to NPV1).

	A	B	C	D	E	F	G
1					Year Effective		
2	BENEFITS		1	2	3	4	5
3							
4	Cost Savings						
5	Direct labor		0	15000	15500	16000	17000
6	Indirect labor		0	5000	5500	6000	7000
7	Total		0	20000	21000	22000	24000
8							
9	Cost Avoidance						
10	Direct labor		0	15000	15500	32000	34000
11	Indirect labor		0	1000	2500	3000	4000
12	Total		0	16000	18000	35000	38000
13							
14	Better Service		0	10000	12000	15000	16000
15	Better Information		0	15000	15000	15000	16000
16							
17	TOTAL BENEFITS		0	61000	66000	87000	94000
18							
19	COSTS						
20							
21	Development		50000	20000			
22	Operating		0	30000	35000	40000	45000
23							
24	TOTAL COSTS		50000	50000	35000	40000	45000
25							
26	Net Value		-50000	11000	31000	47000	49000
27	Discount rate						
28	Present value						
29							
30	NET PRESENT VALUE						

Figure 2-17 Editing worksheet formulas to show the correct totals

3. Click on OK (press ENTER).

4. Select cell C17.

5. Press F2 to activate the formula bar.

6. Insert C12 in the equation, as in:

```
=C7 + C12 + C14 + C15
```

Press ENTER when done.

7. Select C17:G17 (press SHIFT+RIGHT 4 times).

8. Select **E**dit and drag to Fill Rig**h**t (ALT+e and press h).

9. Save this worksheet as NPV1.XLS.

Questions:
1. Why is row 17 the only row in need of change? Why not rows 24 and 26?
2. How do cost avoidance totals change the net value totals? Why is this the case?

2-5 Formatting Worksheet Information

After a worksheet has been edited, it is often necessary to format text and numbers. As shown by the Format drop-down menu (see **Figure 2-18**), there are eight format commands. These commands mean the following:

Format Command	Is used to
Number	Changes the appearance of a number in a cell or in a range of cells. Allows you to display numbers in a variety of formats such as $50.00, or 50%.
Alignment	Changes the position of text in a cell or in a range of cells.
Font	Changes the font used in displaying numbers and text, and in printing numbers and text provided your printer supports the change.
Border	Changes the borders and shading on a worksheet.
Cell	Prevents others from changing the contents of a worksheet.
Row Height	Adjusts the height of a row.
Column Width	Adjusts the number of characters in a column.
Justify	Rearranges text to display text of approximately the same width.

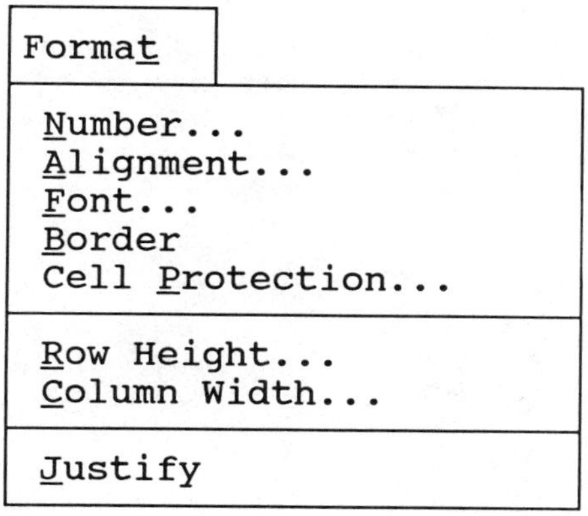

Figure 2-18 The Format drop-down menu

For now we ask you to become familiar with five of these commands. The next two chapters consider other topics important to formatting.

2-5-1 The Format Number command

This command is used to list all available numeric formats. As shown below, there are twelve possible choices. For example, to format 5000 in dollars, you might choose $#,##0.00;($#,##0.00) or $#,##0;($#,##0).

Numeric Format	Change to .5	Change to 5000
General	0.5	5000
0	1	5000
0.00	0.50	5000.00
#,##0	1	5,000
#,##0.00	0.50	5,000.00
$#,##0;($#,##0)	$1	$5,000
$#,##0;[RED]($#,##0)	Negative	Will display red
$#,##0.00;($#,##0.00)	$0.50	$5,000.00
$#,##0.00;[RED]($#,##0.00)	Negative	Will display red
0%	50%	500000%
0.00%	50.00%	500000.00%
0.00E+00	5.00E-01	5.00E+3

Besides these twelve numeric formats, there are nine time and date formats. The default value is m/d/yy, as in 2/2/90. The next table shows all nine formats.

Time/Date Format	Will Display
m/d/yy	2/2/90
d-mmm-yy	2-Feb-90
d-mmm	2-Feb
mmm-yy	Feb-90
h:mmm AM/PM	9:00 AM
h:mmm:ss AM/PM	9:00:22 AM
h:mm	9:00
h:mm:ss	9:00:22
m/d/yy h:mm	2/2/90 9:00

Finally, Microsoft Excel will allow you to create your own formats if these 21 different formats do not meet your needs.

2-5-2 The Format Column Width command

The standard column width is 8.43 characters. The Format Column Width command allows you to change this default value. As shown by the Column Width dialog box (see **Figure 2-19**), the dialog box for this command allows you to enter the desired column width (from 0 to 255 characters).

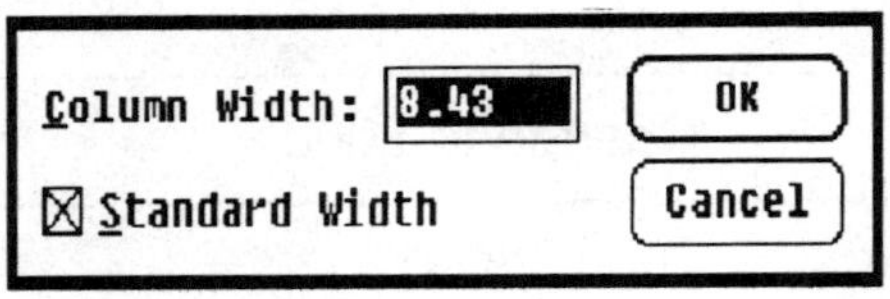

Figure 2-19 The Format Column Width dialog box

2-5-3 The Format Row Height command

The standard row height is defined in terms of *points*, where the larger the point size, the larger the row height. The standard row height is 12.75 points (see **Figure 2-20**). The Row Height text box allows you to enter the

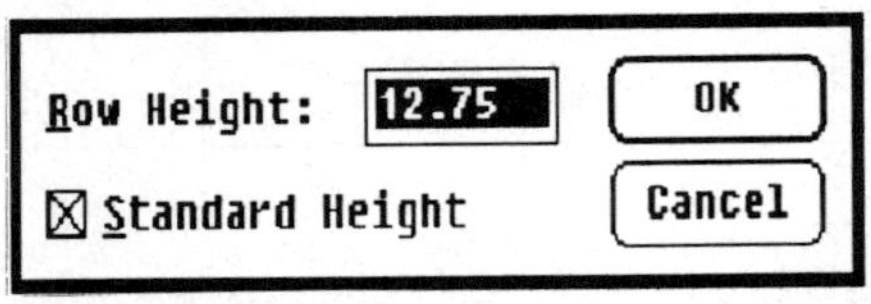

Figure 2-20 The Format Row Height dialog box

desired height (from 0 to the largest point size supported by the display fonts). As with column width, row height can be expressed as a fraction.

2-5-4 The Format Alignment command

This command aligns the contents of selected cells. The dialog box for this command (see **Figure 2-21**) illustrates that the contents can be aligned in five ways, where:

Alignment Choice	Will
General	Align text to the left, numbers to the right, and centers logical and error values.
Left	Aligns all cell contents to the left.
Right	Aligns all cell contents to the right.
Center	Centers all cell contents.
Fill	Repeats the contents of a cell until the cell is full.

2-5-5 The Format Border command

This command allows you to place a solid line on the top, left, right, or bottom of cells; to place a solid line around the entire cell selection; or to shade every cell in a cell selection. **Figure 2-22** shows the dialog box for this command. To place a solid line around all edges of a cell, click on Outline; otherwise, make an edge selection. To add shading to a cell, click on shade.

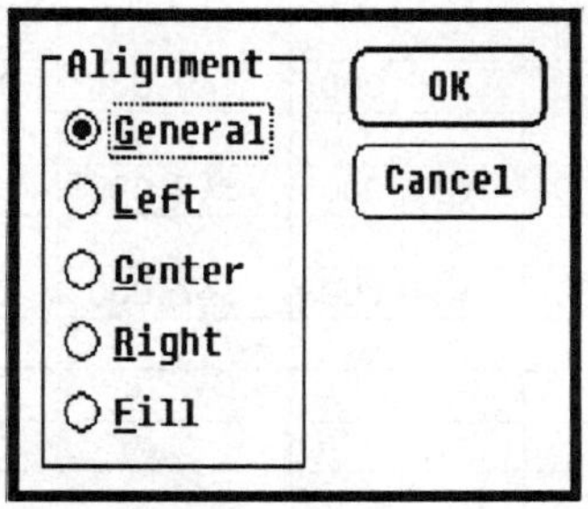

Figure 2-21 The Format Alignment dialog box

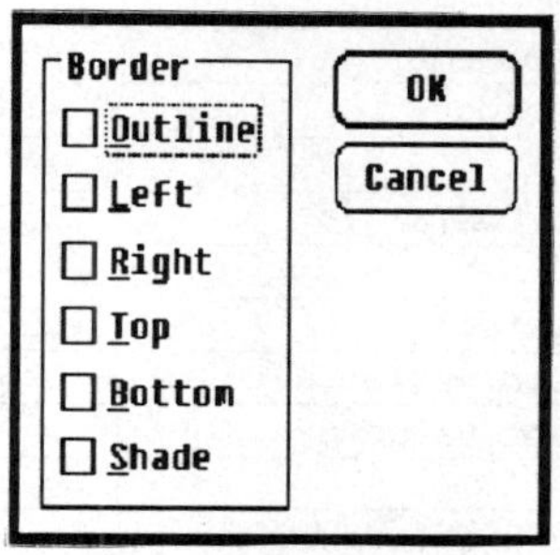

Figure 2-22 The Format Border command

EXERCISE 2-11
Formatting the Net Present Value worksheet

For this exercise, use NPV1.XLS once again. **Figure 2-23** shows how the worksheet should look when you complete this exercise.

1. Select **F**ile and drag to **O**pen (ALT+f and press o).

2. Select NPV1.XLS (ALT+f and press DOWN to NPV1).

	A	C	D	E	F	G
1				Year Effective		
2	BENEFITS	1	2	3	4	5
3						
4	Cost Savings					
5	Direct labor	$0	$15,000	$15,500	$16,000	$17,000
6	Indirect labor	$0	$5,000	$5,500	$6,000	$7,000
7	Total	$0	$20,000	$21,000	$22,000	$24,000
8						
9	Cost Avoidance					
10	Direct labor	$0	$15,000	$15,500	$32,000	$34,000
11	Indirect labor	$0	$1,000	$2,500	$3,000	$4,000
12	Total	$0	$16,000	$18,000	$35,000	$38,000
13						
14	Better Service	$0	$10,000	$12,000	$15,000	$16,000
15	Better Information	$0	$15,000	$15,000	$15,000	$16,000
16						
17	TOTAL BENEFITS	$0	$61,000	$66,000	$87,000	$94,000
18						
19	COSTS					
20						
21	Development	$50,000	$20,000			
22	Operating	$0	$30,000	$35,000	$40,000	$45,000
23						
24	TOTAL COSTS	$50,000	$50,000	$35,000	$40,000	$45,000
25						
26	Net Value	($50,000)	$11,000	$31,000	$47,000	$49,000
27	Discount rate					
28	Present value					
29						
30	NET PRESENT VALUE					

Figure 2-23 Formatting the Net Present Value Analysis worksheet

3. Click on OK (press ENTER).
4. Select column A.
5. Select Forma**t** and drag to **C**olumn Width (ALT+t and press c).
6. Type *20* and click on OK (press ENTER).
7. Select column B.
8. Select Forma**t** and drag to **C**olumn Width (ALT+t and press c).
9. Type *zero* and click on OK (press ENTER).
10. Select range C5:G28 (SHIFT+DIRECTION keys).
11. Select Forma**t** and drag to **N**umber (ALT+t and press n).
12. Select $#,##0;($#,##0) and click on OK (press ENTER).
13. Select A5:A8 (SHIFT+DOWN 3 times).
14. Select Forma**t** and drag to **A**lignment (ALT+t and press a).
15. Select **R**ight (press r) and click on OK (press ENTER).
16. Select A10:A12 (SHIFT+DOWN 3 times).
17. Select **E**dit to **R**epeat Alignment (ALT+e and press r).
18. Select C2:G2 (SHIFT+RIGHT 4 times).
19. Select Forma**t** and drag to **A**lignment (ALT+t and press a).
20. Select **C**enter (press c) and click on OK (press ENTER).
21. Save this worksheet as NPV1.XLS.

Questions:

1. What is the value in formatting a worksheet?
2. Why are only 6 rows in column A aligned to the right?
3. If you needed to restore column B to standard width, how would you do it?

2-6 Printing a Finished Worksheet

Once you are happy with the content and layout of a worksheet, you will most likely want to print a copy of it. Three commands are important to printing a worksheet: the File Printer Setup command, the File Page Setup command, and the File Print command.

2-6-1 The File Printer Setup command

In Chapter 1, you were introduced to the File Printer Setup command and the dialog box important to this command (see Figure 1-10). To check on the printer designated for printing, select **F**ile and drag to P**r**inter Setup (ALT+f and press r). If you have told Microsoft Excel that you will be printing on an HP LaserJet printer, the dialog box shown on **Figure 2-24** will confirm this information. If a printer is not shown, click on **S**etup and define the printer you intend to use. Remember, this promotional version of Microsoft Excel supports only the Epson and the HP LaserJet printer families.

2-6-2 The File Page Setup command

Besides defining the printer, you must also indicate how you want your worksheet page to appear. As shown by **Figure 2-25**, the dialog box for the File Page Setup command, page setup involves indicating whether or not you want to print a header or a footer, specifying the margins for your worksheet, and telling Microsoft Excel whether or not you want to print the row and column headings and gridlines.

A page *header* specifies the contents and position of information appearing on the head of each worksheet page. Special codes are used

Figure 2-24 The File Printer Setup dialog box

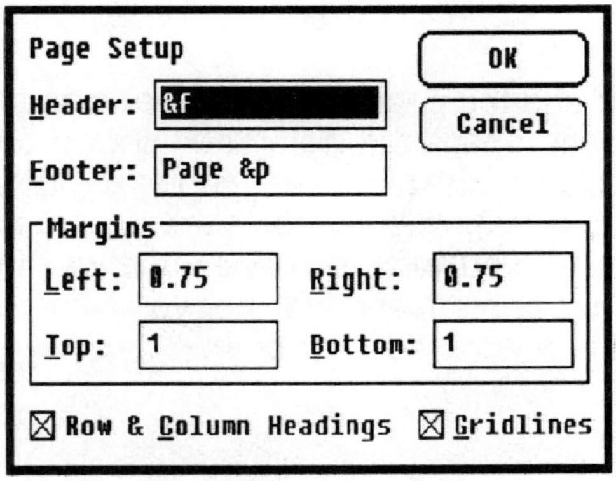

Figure 2-25 The File Page Setup dialog box

to modify the default, shown as &f (which prints the name of the document). These codes are as follows:

Use this	to
&F	Print the name of the document.
&L	Left-align the characters that follow.
&C	Center the characters that follow.
&R	Right-align the characters that follow.
&B	Print the header or footer in bold.
&I	Print the header or footer in italic.
&D	Print the current date.
&T	Print the current time.
&P	Print the page number.
&P+number	Add number to page number and print it.
&P-number	Subtract number from page number and print it.
&&	Print an ampersand.

As an example, the header &CNet Present Value&R&D will print "Net Present Value" centered and add the date to the right-hand side of the worksheet.

A page *footer* specifies the contents and the position of information at the foot of each worksheet page. A footer uses the same list of codes as a header; however, with this promotion version, a footer cannot be printed on a page.

2-6-3 The File Print command

Once you are satisfied with the printer and the page setup, the decision to print can begin. Selecting this command opens the dialog box shown on **Figure 2-26**. In this case, you can decide on the number of copies to print, whether you want to print all pages (or some), whether you want to print in draft quality (or finished quality), whether you wish to preview the way in which your worksheet will look when it is printed, and whether you want to print the worksheet, notes appended to a worksheet, or both.

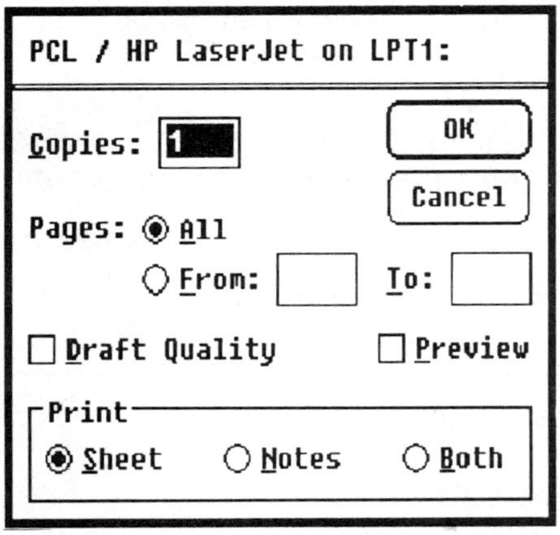

Figure 2-26 The File Print dialog box

EXERCISE 2-12
Printing the Net Present Value worksheet

For this exercise, you are asked to add a header to the worksheet NPV1.XLS and to remove row and column and gridline markings. **Figure 2-27** shows how you printed worksheet should look.

1. Select **F**ile and drag to **O**pen (ALT+f and press o).

2. Select NPV1.XLS (ALT+f and press DOWN to NPV1).

3. Click on OK (press ENTER).

4. Select **F**ile and drag to Pr**i**nter Setup (ALT+f and press r) to determine if your printer is setup properly. If not, click on **S**etup (ALT+s) and define the correct printer (see Chapter 1 for instructions).

Net Present Value Worksheet

			Year Effective		
BENEFITS	1	2	3	4	5
Cost Savings					
Direct labor	$0	$15,000	$15,500	$16,000	$17,000
Indirect labor	$0	$5,000	$5,500	$6,000	$7,000
Total	$0	$20,000	$21,000	$22,000	$24,000
Cost Avoidance					
Direct labor	$0	$15,000	$15,500	$32,000	$34,000
Indirect labor	$0	$1,000	$2,500	$3,000	$4,000
Total	$0	$16,000	$18,000	$35,000	$38,000
Better Service	$0	$10,000	$12,000	$15,000	$16,000
Better Information	$0	$15,000	$15,000	$15,000	$16,000
TOTAL BENEFITS	$0	$61,000	$66,000	$87,000	$94,000
COSTS					
Development	$50,000	$20,000			
Operating	$0	$30,000	$35,000	$40,000	$45,000
TOTAL COSTS	$50,000	$50,000	$35,000	$40,000	$45,000
Net Value	($50,000)	$11,000	$31,000	$47,000	$49,000
Discount rate					
Present value					
NET PRESENT VALUE					

Figure 2-27 Printing the Net Present Value Analysis worksheet

5. Click on Cancel (TAB and press ENTER).

6. Select **F**ile and drag to Page Se**t**up (ALT+f and press t).

7. Click the Row & **C**olumn Heading box to remove the X (ALT+c and press ENTER).

8. Click the **G**ridlines box to remove the X (TAB and press ENTER).

9. In the header box, type *&CNet Present Value Worksheet&R&D*.

10. Click on OK (press ENTER).

11. Select **F**ile and drag to **P**rint (ALT+f and press p).

12. Click on **P**review to turn it on (ALT+p).

13. When the preview box is opened, select Zoom to expand the page to show its full size.

14. Select Zoom again to turn the page to the preview size.

15. Select Print to print the worksheet on your printer.

16. Do not save the changes made to this worksheet, but do not delete the worksheet either. In the next chapter, you will make further modifications to NPV1.XLS.

Questions:
1. What is purpose of the Preview option?
2. What are the advantages of adding headings to your worksheet?

2-7 Summary

The main purpose of this chapter is to introduce you to building worksheets. When you have completed this chapter, you should be familiar with ten of the twelve file commands, ten of the twelve edit commands, and four of the eight format commands.

File commands are essential to building worksheets. The File New, File Save, and File Save As commands (together with the File Open and File Close commands) are vital to starting and saving a worksheet. The File Print, File Page Setup, and File Printer Setup commands, in contrast, are vital to printing a finished worksheet.

There is no better way of learning how to build a worksheet than to do so. Entering text, numbers, and formulas are all essential to worksheet construction. When entering these types of information, it becomes important to remember input shortcuts. These include: use the Data Series command to enter a series of numbers or dates; the Edit Fill Down and Edit Fill Right commands to copy text, numbers, or formulas to adjacent cells; the Edit Cut and Paste or Edit Copy and Paste commands to move one area of a worksheet to another area; and edit formatting commands to change the way in which text and numbers look.

Once worksheet information has been entered, editing and formatting become important for revising the worksheet. Besides the Edit Fill Right, Edit Fill Down, Edit Cut, Edit Copy, and Edit Paste commands, five other editing commands are important: The Edit Clear command is used to clear an entry from a cell, the Edit Undo is used to restore an entry (in case you made a mistake), the Edit Repeat command is used to repeat a command, and the Edit Insert and Edit Delete commands are used to add or remove rows and columns from a worksheet.

Formatting commands allow you to change the appearance of text and numbers on a worksheet. The Format Number command allows you to change the way numbers look, the Format Alignment command allows you to change the position of text and numbers in a cell, the Format Row Height and Format Column Width commands allow you to adjust the height and width of worksheet cells, and the Format Border command allows you to add solid edges or shading to a cell selection.

KEY TERMS

Cutting and Pasting
Editing
Footer
Formatting
Header
Precedence hierarchy
Range

COMMAND REFERENCE

Data Series: Data menu. Fills a selected range of cells with a numerical or date time series.

Edit Clear: Edit menu or delete key. Clears formats and formulas from a cell or a cell range without deleting the cells. Contrasts with Edit Delete. Click on Formulas to clear numbers or alphanumeric entries.

Edit Copy: Edit menu. Specifies the cell or cell range to be moved to another worksheet location. Use with Edit Paste. Updates cell references unless otherwise specified.

Edit Cut: Edit menu. Specifies the cell or cell range to be erased from one worksheet location and moved to another location. Use with Edit Paste.

Edit Delete: Edit menu. Deletes entire cell or cell range and adjusts worksheet accordingly.

Edit Fill Down: Edit menu. Copies cell contents downwards to an adjacent selected range. Quickest way to copy a cell or cell range.

Edit Fill Right: Edit menu. Same as Fill Down but copies to the right.

Edit Insert: Edit menu. Inserts a cell(s), row(s) or column(s). Adjusts worksheet references based on cell insertion.

Edit Paste: Edit menu. Used after the Edit Cut or Edit Copy commands to paste values to a new location.

Edit Repeat: Edit menu. Repeats last command.

File New Command: File menu. Opens new worksheets, charts or macro files (not ones you have previously saved).

File Page Setup: File menu. Allows you to change page setup options for printing including: gridlines, row & column headings, margins, footers and headers.

File Print: File menu. Allows you to specify print options before printing, including: number of copies, whether or not you wish to preview before printing, draft quality, and what to include in printing sheets, notes, or both.

File Printer Setup: File menu. Specifies printer setup options including: portrait vs. landscape orientation, resolution, memory, printer type and cartridges. Used to add a new printer type.

Format Alignment: Format menu. Specifies alignment in a cell range as general(default), left, right, or center.

Format Border: Format menu. Allows you to place a solid line or edges around a cell or to add shading to a cell.

Format Column Width: Format menu. Specifies column width in terms of number of characters. To change column width it is necessary to select one cell in that column. 8.43 is the default width.

Format Number: Format menu. Specifies number format including date, time, percentage, and dollar signs. You can design your own format by inserting it in the format box.

Formula Row Height: Format menu. Specifies row height in terms of size of font. 12.75 is the default.

Formula Goto: Formula menu. Shortcut function key is F5. Quickest way to go to a cell or defined name if you know exactly where you want to go.

ON YOUR OWN

1. The term _______ is used to refer to a group of cells.
   a) range
   b) selection
   c) data series
   d) formula
   e) menu

2. The _______ command removes formats, formulas and notes from a cell, but doesn't delete the actual cell.
   a) Edit Delete
   b) Edit Clear
   c) Edit Undo
   d) File New
   e) Format Border

3. The Edit Undo will undo all of the following commands **except**:
   a) Edit Clear
   b) Edit Delete
   c) Edit Cut
   d) File Delete
   e) File Page Setup

4. The _______ command can be used to add rows or columns to a worksheet.
   a) Edit Paste
   b) Edit Copy
   c) Edit Insert
   d) Edit Delete
   e) Edit Fill Down

5. The _______ command is used to remove values from one cell range and copy them to another whereas the _______ command is used to duplicate values from one cell range to another.
   a) Edit Cut, Edit Fill Down
   b) Edit Copy, Edit Cut
   c) Edit Cut, Edit Copy
   d) Edit Paste, Edit Insert
   e) Edit Fill Right, Edit Fill Left

6. Which of the following **is not** a choice offered by the Alignment command?
   a) Center
   b) Left

c) Right
d) General
e) Shade

7. Rows are measured in _______, columns are measured in _______.
   a) characters, points
   b) inches, inches
   c) points, characters
   d) fonts, points
   e) width, height

8. The command **&C** will _______ the header when printing.
   a) capitalize
   b) center
   c) cut
   d) control
   e) compute

9. The _______ command is used to turn gridlines off and on before printing.
   a) Options Display
   b) File Print
   c) File Printer Setup
   d) Format alignment
   e) File Page Setup

10. If cell A1 contains the value 10, cell B1 contains the value 5, and cell C1 contains the value 3; the formula =A1-B1*C1 will yield the value:
    a) 15
    b) -15
    c) 5
    d) -5
    e) 10

MORE PRACTICE

I. Open East.XLS and make the following changes:
   1. Insert a new row between rows 1 and 2.
   2. Insert a new row between rows 8 and 9.
   3. Use Format Border to shade the cell ranges A2:D2 and A9:D9.
   4. In cell B15, enter the formula that will compute Operating Income by subtracting Expenses from Sales.
   5. Use Edit Fill Right to copy your formula to cells C16:D16.
   6. Save your worksheet as EAST2.XLS.

   Answer the following:
   a) What was the operating income for 1984?

b) What formula would you use to compute operating income for 1984-5?

II. Open West.XLS and make the following changes:
1. In cell E1, type *Totals to Date*.
2. In cell E2, enter the formula that will compute the total sales of widgets during the years 1984-6.
3. Use Edit Fill Down to copy the formula to cells E3:E5.
4. Use Edit Copy to copy the formula to cells E8:E11 and cell E13 (but not E12!!).
5. Change the column width of column E to 12.
6. Format the numbers in column E so they match the formats used in the rest of the worksheet.
7. Save your worksheet as WEST2.XLS.

Answer the following:
a) Why couldn't you have used Edit Fill Down instead of Edit Copy to copy all of the formulas?
b) What was the total Operating Income for the Western region during the years 1984-6?

III. Your little brother, David, is studying economic history in his high school American History class and has come to you with a problem. He needs to write a report on the history of the Stock Market, has collected the data, but doesn't have a way to analyze his findings. Help him out by creating a worksheet as follows:

1. Make the following cell entries:

A1:A16	**B1:B16**
Year	Average
1/1/62	735
1/1/66	995
1/1/67	744
1/1/69	985
1/1/70	631
1/1/71	951
1/1/73	952
1/1/75	578
1/1/76	1015
1/1/78	742
1/1/79	908
1/1/81	1024
1/1/83	777
1/1/84	1287
1/1/88	2722

2. Center the values in cells A1:B1.
3. Using Format Number, format the years in cells A2:A16 so they appear only as years (for example, 1962, 1966, and so forth). Hint: Remember to select all of the cells before formatting. Since Microsoft Excel doesn't have a standard format for dates as only years, you will have to use ALT+f at the Format Numbers Dialog box and enter your own format.
4. Print your worksheet with gridlines, but without row and column headings.
5. Save your worksheet as STOCK.XLS.

Answer the following:

a) What did you enter to change to the year-only format?
b) Which year had the lowest Dow Jones average?

CHAPTER 3 - USING FUNCTIONS AND NAMES

The last chapter was written to provide you with the basic skills needed to prepare, edit, format, and print a worksheet. This chapter builds on these skills to allow you to explore some of the more advanced properties of Microsoft Excel. You will be asked to become familiar with some of the built-in functions provided by the software, to use names in place of formulas, and to link one worksheet to another. In addition, we will describe some useful techniques for working with complex worksheets. We will show you how to save a workspace, add a note to a worksheet, protect a document, and protect a cell within a document.

When you complete this chapter you will be expected to be able to do several new tasks. These include the following:

* Use functions in formulas.

* Paste a function into a formula.

* Use names in functions and formulas.

* Understand the difference between a relative reference and an absolute reference.

* Define, create, and paste names.

* Link one worksheet to another.

* Understand techniques for preserving your workspace and protecting your worksheet.

3-1 Functions

Functions are built-in formulas provided by Microsoft Excel to simplify the writing of formulas. Each function is written to perform specific operations on a value or range of values and then return a result. Microsoft Excel groups functions into the following eleven major categories: database functions, date functions, financial functions, information functions, logical functions, lookup functions, mathematical functions, matrix functions, statistical functions, text functions, and trigonometric functions. In this section, we examine the three most used functions: statistical, logical, and financial.

3-1-1 Statistical functions

Figure 3-1 lists the fourteen built-in statistical functions provided by Microsoft Excel. The key to using functions lies in understanding their *structure* or *syntax*. For example, the syntax for the function SUM is:

SUM(number 1,*number 2,...number N)*

This indicates that only number 1 is required and that numbers 2 through N are optional. Four features of the syntax are important: the name of the function (SUM, in our case), the parentheses that enclose the argument list, the commas that separate each argument, and the required and optional arguments. How does the SUM() function work? The equation:

=SUM(100,200,300)

returns a value of 600. You might compare this function to the COUNT() function. The equation:

=COUNT(100,200,300)

counts the number of arguments and returns a value of 3.

A main advantage in using functions compared to mathematical equations is their simplicity. For example, the equation:

=SUM(G5:G15)

Statistical Functions	
This function	returns
AVERAGE(number1,number2,...)	Average of numbers
COUNT(value1,value2,...)	Count of numbers in values
COUNTA(value1,value1,...)	Count of values in values
GROWTH(old_y's,old_x's,new_x's)	Values on exponential trend
LINEST(old_y's,old_x's)	Parameters of linear trend
LOGEST(old_y's,old_x's)	Parameters of exponential trend
MAX(number1,number2,...)	Maximum number in numbers
MIN(number1,number2,...)	Minimum number in numbers
STDEV(number1,number2,...)	Standard deviation based on a sample
STDEVP(number1,number2,...)	Standard deviation based on entire population
SUM(number1,number2,...)	Sum of numbers
TREND(old_y's,old_x's,new_x's)	Values of linear trend
VAR(number1,number2,...)	Variance based on a sample
VARP(number1,number2,...)	Variance based on entire population

Figure 3-1 Built-in statistical functions

sums the values stored in these eleven cells. Compare this to the equation:

=G5+G6+G7+G8+G9+G10+G11+G12+G13+G14+G15

3-1-2 Logical functions

Figure 3-2 illustrates the six logical functions provided by Microsoft Excel. As an example of how one of these functions works, consider the following:

Suppose you wanted to display one value in cell D10 provided the total in another cell, say cell D9, is 10,000 or greater, or another value in cell D10 if the total is less than 10,000. Using the IF() function, you would type in cell D10:

=IF((D9>=10000),2000,D9*.20)

This equation states:

IF the cell D9 total is greater than or equal to 10,000
THEN assign 2,000 to cell D10
OTHERWISE multiply the value stored in D9 by .20 and assign this value to cell D10.

Besides simple IF() function expressions, the IF() function can be combined with the AND() and OR() functions to create compound logical statements. For example, if you want to place 2,000 in cell D10 if the value

Logical Functions	
This function	returns
AND(logical1,<u>logical2</u>,...)	TRUE if every argument is TRUE; otherwise FALSE
FALSE()	Logical value FALSE
IF(logical_test,value_if_true,<u>value_if_false</u>)	Value_if_true if logical is TRUE; otherwise null or FALSE
NOT(logical)	TRUE if logical is FALSE; FALSE if logical is TRUE
OR(logical1,<u>logical2</u>,...)	TRUE if any argument is TRUE; otherwise FALSE
TRUE()	Logical value TRUE

Figure 3-2 Built-in logical functions

in cell D9 is more than 10,000 *and* less than 15,000, you might type in cell D10:

=IF(AND(D9>10000,D9<15000),2000,"")

This equation states:

IF D9 is greater than 10,000 AND less than 15,000
THEN assign 2,000 to cell D10
OTHERWISE assign nothing (since "" means a null value).

The rule to remember when working the AND() function is that all logical arguments must be TRUE for the expression as a whole to be TRUE. The evaluation table works as follows:

Logical Argument 1	Logical Argument 2	Yields	Returns
FALSE	no evaluation	FALSE	0
TRUE	FALSE	FALSE	0
TRUE	TRUE	TRUE	1

Thus, the AND() function only returns a 1 if both arguments are TRUE.

The logical OR() function is the reverse of the logical AND() function. In this instance, only 1 argument needs to be TRUE for the expression as a whole to be TRUE. The evaluation table is:

Logical Argument 1	Logical Argument 2	Yields	Returns
FALSE	FALSE	FALSE	0
TRUE	no evaluation	TRUE	1
FALSE	TRUE	TRUE	1

Thus, finding the first argument to be TRUE, no further evaluation is required.

As an example of a logical OR() function, we might type in cell D15:

=IF(OR(D9< =5000,D12>12000),2000,"")

This equation means:

IF the value in cell D9 is less than or equal to 5,000
OR the value in cell D12 is greater than 12,000
THEN assign 2,000 to cell D15
OTHERWISE assign no value.

3-1-3 Financial functions

Figure 3-3 shows the thirteen financial functions provided by Microsoft Excel. Of these, three---DDB(), SLN(), and SYN()---treat methods of depreciating an asset; three---IRR(), MIRR(), and RATE()---concern the return on an investment; and the remaining seven determine the present and future value of an investment. In all cases, the importance of "time" and how it changes the value of money is important. For example, suppose you were asked: What would you rather have, $20,000 in fifteen years, or $1,000 each year for the next 15 years, invested at 8.5 percent interest.

Financial Functions	
This function	returns
DDB(cost,salvage,life,period)	Double-declining balance depreciation for an asset
FV(rate,nper,pmt,pv,type)	Future value of investment
IPMT(rate,per,nper,pv,fv,type)	Interest payment for an investment
IRR(values,guess)	Internal rate of return of values
MIRR(values,finance_rate, reinvest_rate)	Modified internal rate of return of values
NPER(rate,pmt,pv,fv,type)	Number of payments of investment
NPV(rate,value1,value2,...)	Net present value of values
PMT(rate,nper,pv,fv,type)	Periodic payment of investment
PPMT(rate,per,nper,pv,fv, type)	Payment on the principle for an investment
PV(rate,nper,pmt,fv,type)	Present value of investment
RATE(nper,pmt,pv,fv,type, guess)	Rate returned on investment
SLN(cost,salvage,life)	Straight-line depreciation for an asset
SYD(cost,salvage,life,per)	Sum-of-years' digits depreciation for an asset

Figure 3-3 Built-in financial functions

Your choice is the latter, provided you used the future value of an investment equation to determine the dollar difference. The future value of $1,000 each year for the next 15 years at a rate of 8.5% is computed as follows:

=FV(8.5%,15,-1000)

where the $1,000 is entered as a negative cash flow amount. This equation returns $28,232.27, which is considerably more than $20,000.

3-1-4 The Formula Paste Function command

The command used frequently with functions is the Formula Paste Function command. While a function such as SUM() or FV() can be typed directly, it is often helpful to paste a function. By pasting a function, the function name and its arguments can be displayed.

Figure 3-4 displays the dialog box for this command. To paste a function, select the function name from the list box and choose OK. To display the arguments for the function turn the paste arguments check box on.

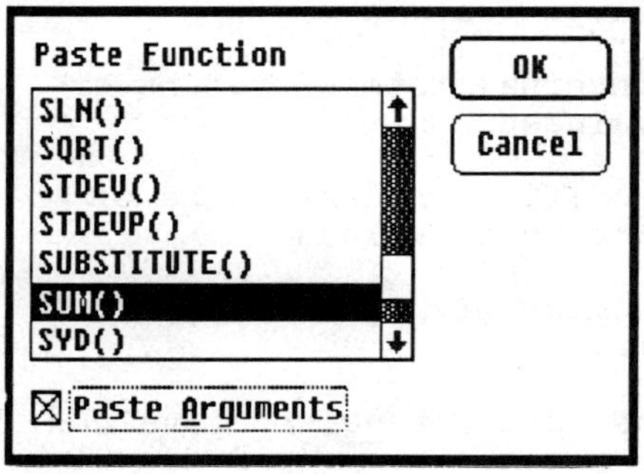

Figure 3-4 The Formula Paste Function dialog box

EXERCISE 3-1
Depreciating an asset

For this exercise, you are asked to build a worksheet to show how financial functions can be used to depreciate an asset. *Depreciation* means something quite special. It is the amount you are allowed to deduct each year to reflect the reduced value of business property.

Let's suppose once again that you are a financial analyst employed by Timberware. Your assignment is to determine the difference in depreciation using three alternative methods: straight line, double declining balance, and sum-of-years-digits. With straight line, the same amount can be written off each year. The other two methods represent *accelerated methods of depreciation*. These two methods allow greater deductions during the early years in the life of an investment.

The data used in comparing these three methods involve the use of a truck by Timberware. The truck cost $60,000 and has an expected life of 10 years. The salvage value of the truck after 10 years is $20,000.

Figure 3-5 shows how your worksheet should look when you complete this exercise. As indicated, straight-line depreciation allows a much lower deduction during the early years in the 10-year life of the asset.

With Sheet1 or a blank worksheet facing you, do the following:

1. In cell C1 type *TABLE OF DEPRECIATION*.

2. In cells B4, B6, and B8 type *Cost*, *Salvage value*, and *Life*.

3. In cells E4, E6, and E8 type *60000*, *20000*, and *10*.

4. In cells B11:E12 type the headings, *Year*, *Straight-line Depreciation*, Double-declining Depreciation, and *Sum-of-years' Depreciation*.

	A	B	C	D	E
1			TABLE OF DEPRECIATION		
2					
3					
4		Cost			60000
5					
6		Salvage value			20000
7					
8		Life			10
9					
10			Straight-line	Double-declining	Sum-of-years'
11		Year	Depreciation	Depreciation	Depreciation
12					
13		1	4000	12000	7272.727273
14		2	4000	9600	6545.454545
15		3	4000	7680	5818.181818
16		4	4000	6144	5090.909091
17		5	4000	4576	4363.636364
18		6	4000	0	3636.363636
19		7	4000	0	2909.090909
20		8	4000	0	2181.818182
21		9	4000	0	1454.545455
22		10	4000	0	727.2727273
23					
24		Total	40000	40000	40000

Figure 3-5 Using financial functions to determine the amount to depreciate

5. Click on column C and drag to column E (while in column C, CONTROL+SPACEBAR then SHIFT+RIGHT).

6. Select Forma**t** and drag to **C**olumn Width (Alt+t and press c).

7. Type *15* and click on OK (press ENTER).

8. In cell B13, type *1*.

9. Select the range B13:B22.

10. Select **D**ata and drag to Se**r**ies (ALT+d and press r).

11. In the open dialog box choose the default values: **C**olumns, **L**inear, and a **S**tep value of 1.

12. Click on OK (press ENTER).

13. Select cell C13.

14. Select Fo**r**mula and drag to Pas**t**e Function (ALT+r and press t).

15. Turn the Paste **A**rguments check box on (ALT+a).

16. Scroll to SLN() and choose OK (ALT+f, DOWN and press ENTER). In the formula bar, the SLN() equation should read: =SLN(cost,salvage,life)

17. Replace these arguments with dollar values. Replace cost with *60000*, salvage with *20000*, and life with *10*. The revised equation should read: =SLN(60000,20000,10)

18. Select C13:C22.

19. Select **E**dit and drag to Fill Do**w**n (ALT+e and press w).

20. Select cell D13.

21. Select Fo**r**mula and drag to Pas**t**e Function (ALT+r and press t).

22. Scroll to DDB() and choose OK.

23. In the formula bar type *60000*, *20000*, *10*, and *B13*, replacing cost, salvage, life, and period.

24. Select D13:D22.

25. Select **E**dit and drag to Fill Do**w**n (ALT+e and press w).

26. Select cell E13.

27. Select Fo**r**mula and drag to Pas**t**e Function (ALT+r and press t).

28. Scroll to SYD() and choose OK.

29. In the formula bar type *60000*, *20000*, *10*, and *B13*, replacing cost, salvage, life, and period.

30. Select E13:E22.

31. Select **E**dit and drag to Fill Do**w**n (ALT+e and press w).

32. In cell B24 type *Total*.

33. In cell C24 type *=SUM(C13:C22)*.

34. Select the range C24:E24.

35. Select **E**dit and drag to Fill Rig**h**t (ALT+e and press h).

36. Save this worksheet. Select **F**ile and drag to Save **A**s (ALT+f and press a). Call this worksheet DEPR.XLS.

Questions:

1. Suppose the cost of the truck increased to $65,000. How would this change the three formulas written for this exercise?
2. With a double-declining balance method of depreciation, first year depreciation is twice that of straight line depreciation. Does the built-in function return the correct value?
3. With the sum-of-years' depreciation, the first year is the life divided by the sum of the lives, or in our example 10 divided by 55 (1+2+3...+10). What equation would you write to determine if this is the correct value?

EXERCISE 3-2
Completing the Net Present Value worksheet

For this exercise use NPV1.XLS, the worksheet prepared for the last chapter. This exercise will complete this worksheet. **Figure 3-6** shows how your worksheet will look when you complete this exercise.

In working through this exercise, you will use the equation
=(1/(1+10%)^(C2)).

This equation means: divide one by 1.10, raised to the power indicated by the value stored in cell C2, which is the year of the investment. Thus for

	A	C	D	E	F	G
1				Year Effective		
2	BENEFITS	1	2	3	4	5
3						
4	Cost Savings					
5	Direct labor	$0	$15,000	$15,500	$16,000	$17,000
6	Indirect labor	$0	$5,000	$5,500	$6,000	$7,000
7	Total	$0	$20,000	$21,000	$22,000	$24,000
8						
9	Cost Avoidance					
10	Direct labor	$0	$15,000	$15,500	$32,000	$34,000
11	Indirect labor	$0	$1,000	$2,500	$3,000	$4,000
12	Total	$0	$16,000	$18,000	$35,000	$38,000
13						
14	Better Service	$0	$10,000	$12,000	$15,000	$16,000
15	Better Information	$0	$15,000	$15,000	$15,000	$16,000
16						
17	TOTAL BENEFITS	$0	$61,000	$66,000	$87,000	$94,000
18						
19	COSTS					
20						
21	Development	$50,000	$20,000			
22	Operating	$0	$30,000	$35,000	$40,000	$45,000
23						
24	TOTAL COSTS	$50,000	$50,000	$35,000	$40,000	$45,000
25						
26	Net Value	($50,000)	$11,000	$31,000	$47,000	$49,000
27	Discount rate	0.90909091	0.82644628	0.7513148	0.68301346	0.62092132
28	Present value	($45,455)	$9,091	$23,291	$32,102	$30,425
29						
30	NET PRESENT VALUE	($45,455)	($36,364)	($13,073)	$19,029	$49,454

Figure 3-6 Using financial functions to complete the Net Present Value Analysis worksheet

year 1, the equation becomes: (1/1.10). For year 2, the equation becomes (1/1.21), where 1.21 is the value of 1.10 squared.

Do the following:

1. Select **F**ile and drag to **O**pen (ALT+f and press o).
2. Select NPV1.XLS (ALT+f and press DOWN to NPV1).
3. Click on OK (press ENTER).
4. Select cell C27.
5. Type *=(1/(1+10%)^(C2))*
6. Select the range C27:G27.
7. Select **E**dit and drag to Fill Rig**h**t (ALT+e and press h).
8. Select cell C28.
9. Type *=C26*C27*
10. Select the range C28:G28.
11. Select **E**dit and drag to Fill Rig**h**t (ALT+e and press h).
12. Select cell C30.
13. Select Fo**r**mula and drag to Pas**t**e Function (ALT+r and press t).
14. Turn Paste Arguments check box on.
15. Scroll to NPV() and choose OK. The formula =NPV(rate, value1, value2,...) should appear in the formula bar.
16. In the formula bar type *10%* to replace rate and *C26* to replace value1. The revised formula should read: =NPV(10%,C26).
17. Select cell D30.
18. Repeat steps 13 to 16, except in the formula bar, type *10%, C26:D26*. To save typing, use Edit Copy and Edit Paste to transfer the formula placed in cell C30 to D30; then edit to add C26.
19. Select cell E30.

20. Repeat steps 13 to 16, except in the formula bar type *10%, C26:E26.* To save time, use Edit Copy and Paste or Edit Fill Right. Edit to add C26.

21. Select cell F30.

22. Repeat steps 13 to 16, except in the formula bar type *10%, C26:F26.*

23. Select cell G30.

24. Repeat steps 13 to 16, except in the formula bar type *10%, C26:G26.*

25. Select the range C28:G30.

26. Select Forma**t** and drag to **N**umber (ALT+t and press n).

27. Select $#,##0;($#,##0) and click on OK (press ENTER).

28. Save this worksheet as NPV1.XLS.

Questions:
1. Net present value could have been computed a different way. What formula would you type? Test your formula. Are the answers the same?
2. What is the difference between present value and net present value?
3. What is the advantage in using the built-in function in computing net present value, compared to typing the actual formula?

3-2 Using Names

Microsoft Excel lets you assign English names to individual cells, cell ranges, constants, and formulas. These names are used in place of cell references when building formulas. For example, instead of the formula, =SYD(E4,E6,E8), names can be defined and used in place of these references. The new formula might read: =SYD(cost,salvage,life). This second version is easier to read and understand.

Three commands are important in using names: Formula Define Name, Formula Create Names, and Formula Paste Names. Before we consider each command, we need to know how to define an absolute cell reference and to change a relative cell reference to an absolute one. The important command to use when working with changing cell references is the Formula Reference command.

3-2-1 Defining an absolute reference

With Microsoft Excel, there are three types of cell references: relative, absolute, and mixed. A *relative reference*, such as E4, is direction specific. It is like giving directions to an address, such as go over five columns to E street and down four rows to 4th avenue. With a relative address the cells referenced in a formula will change as the formula is copied to a new cell.

An *absolute reference* is cell specific. It tells Microsoft Excel to go to a specific cell, even though new rows and cells might have been added to a worksheet. The syntax for an absolute reference is $column$row, as in $E$4. The dollar signs make the address absolute.

A *mixed reference* is part cell specific and part direction specific, as in $E4 (an absolute column, but relative row) or E$4 (a relative column, but absolute row). Mixed references provide flexibility when designing worksheets.

3-2-2 The Formula Reference command

The Formula Reference command is a quick way to change the type of reference assigned to a cell. By selecting this command several times, the following change sequence is followed:

Change reference type	To reference type
relative (A6)	absolute ($A$6)
absolute ($A$6)	mixed (A$6, absolute row)
mixed (A$6, absolute row)	mixed ($A6, absolute column)
mixed ($A6, absolute column)	relative (A6)

The Formula Reference command requires that the formula bar be active, indicating the cell reference to be changed. Unless this is done, the command appears as a grayed option on the drop-down menu.

EXERCISE 3-3
Changing a cell reference

For this exercise, use worksheet DEPR.XLS, the worksheet prepared for Exercise 3-1.

1. Select **F**ile and drag to **O**pen (ALT+f and press o).

2. Select DEPR.XLS (ALT+f and press DOWN to DEPR).

3. Click on OK (press ENTER).

4. Select cell C13.

5. Edit cell C13 to read SLN(E4,2000,10), replacing 60000 with cell reference E4.

6. Select the range C13:C22.

7. Select **E**dit and drag to Fill Do**w**n (ALT+e and press w). Note the problems that result.

8. While in cell C13, press F2.

9. Within the formula bar, drag to highlight E4 (SHIFT+RIGHT, two times).

10. Select Fo**r**mula and drag to **R**eference (ALT+r and press r).

11. Press ENTER.

12. Repeat steps 6 and 7.

13. Do not save this revised worksheet.

Questions:
1. Why does step 7 lead to incorrect results?
2. Could a mixed reference be used for this exercise? If so, what mixed reference should be placed in cell C13? How can the Formula Reference command be used to change a relative reference to a mixed reference?

3-2-3 The Formula Define Name command

Names are placed on a worksheet in place of cell references to simplify remembering what cells are supposed to accomplish. Once you decide to use a name in place of a cell reference, cell range, a constant, or a formula, absolute references become important. Consider the Define Name dialog box shown on **Figure 3-7**. The name, *cost*, refers to an absolute cell E4. If you transfer the value stored in this cell to another location (without editing

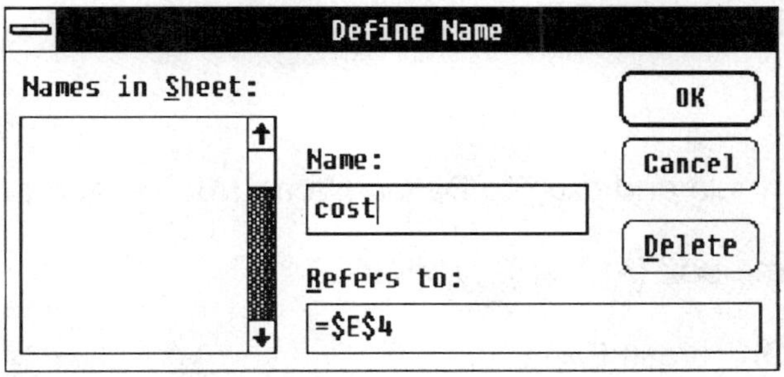

Figure 3-7 The Formula Define Name dialog box

the refers-to box), the command will return whatever value is stored in cell E4, or return an error. The next exercise illustrates the usefulness of placing a name in a worksheet.

EXERCISE 3-4
Defining a name

For this exercise, use worksheet DEPR.XLS, the worksheet prepared for Exercise 3-1.

1. Select **F**ile and drag to **O**pen (ALT+f and press o).
2. Select DEPR.XLS (ALT+f and press DOWN to DEPR).
3. Click on OK (press ENTER).
4. Select E4.
5. Select Fo**r**mula and drag to **D**efine Name (ALT+r and press d).
6. In the **N**ame box (ALT+n), type *cost*.
7. Click on OK (press ENTER).
8. Select E6.
9. Select Fo**r**mula and drag to **D**efine Name (ALT+r and press d).
10. In the **N**ame box (ALT+n), type *salvage*.

11. Click on OK (press ENTER).

12. Select E8.

13. Select Formula and drag to **D**efine Name (ALT+r and press d).

14. In the **N**ame box (ALT+n), type *life*.

15. Click on OK (press ENTER).

16. Select cell D13.

17. Press F2.

18. Edit the formula to read: =DDB(cost,salvage,life,B13)

19. Select the range D13:D22.

20. Select **E**dit and drag to Fill Do**w**n (ALT+e and press w).

21. Copy and paste the DDB() formula from cell D13 to cell E13.

22. Edit the formula to read: =SYD(cost,salvage,life,B13)

23. Select the range E13:E22.

24. Select **E**dit and drag to Fill Do**w**n (ALT+e and press w).

25. Save this revised worksheet as DEPR.XLS. You will use it again in the next exercise.

Questions:
1. When you complete this exercise, how many names are in the Names in Sheet list box?
2. What are the main advantages in using names rather than cell references in the design of a worksheet?

3-2-4 The Formula Create Names command

An alternative to the Define Name command is the Create Names command. With this command, Microsoft Excel defines a name for you, provided the name exists in an adjacent row or column. This method is important if you want to assign names that are identical to worksheet

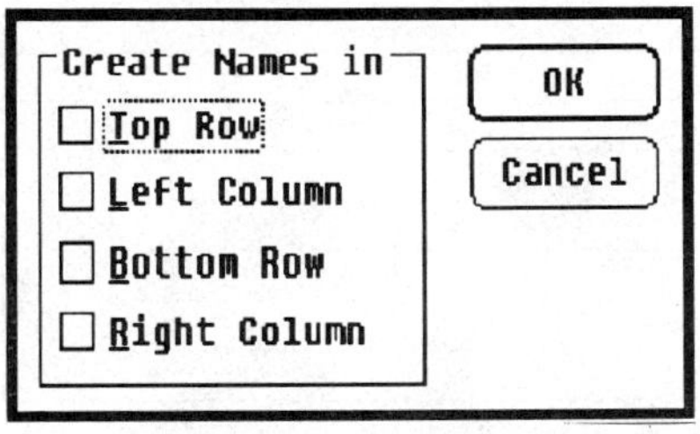

Figure 3-8 The Formula Create Names dialog box

column and row headings. **Figure 3-8** illustrates the dialog box for this command. By selecting Top Row, the text in the top row of the range is used to name the cell or cells in each column of the range. The Left Column choice works the same way. This selection assigns the text in the left-most column to the cell or cells in each row. The next exercise will clarify this procedure.

EXERCISE 3-5
Creating names

For this exercise, use worksheet DEPR.XLS, the worksheet prepared for Exercise 3-1 and revised and saved in Exercise 3-4. **Figure 3-9** illustrates how your worksheet will look when you complete this exercise.

1. Select **F**ile and drag to **O**pen (ALT+f and press o).
2. Select DEPR.XLS (ALT+f and press DOWN to DEPR).
3. Click on OK (press ENTER).
4. Select Fo**r**mula and drag to **D**efine Name (ALT+r and press d).
5. Select **Cost** (ALT+s) (see **Figure 3-10**) and click on **D**elete (ALT+d).
6. Click on Salvage (SHIFT+RIGHT) to highlight.
7. Click on **D**elete (ALT+d).
8. Repeat steps 6 and 7 to delete Life.
9. Click on OK (press ENTER) and observe what happens to the depreciation totals on your worksheet.

	A	B	C	D	E
1			TABLE OF DEPRECIATION		
2					
3					
4				Cost	60000
5					
6				Salvage	20000
7					
8				Life	10
9					
10			Straight-line	Double-declining	Sum-of-years'
11		Year	Depreciation	Depreciation	Depreciation
12					
13		1	4000	12000	7272.727273
14		2	4000	9600	6545.454545
15		3	4000	7680	5818.181818
16		4	4000	6144	5090.909091
17		5	4000	4576	4363.636364
18		6	4000	0	3636.363636
19		7	4000	0	2909.090909
20		8	4000	0	2181.818182
21		9	4000	0	1454.545455
22		10	4000	0	727.2727273
23					
24		Total	40000	40000	40000

Figure 3-9 Using the Formula Create Names command to add names to a worksheet

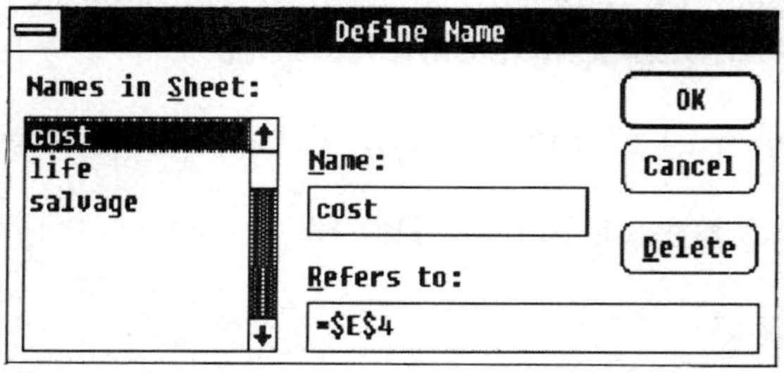

Figure 3-10 Names contained in the worksheet

10. Select the range B4:B8.

11. Select **E**dit and drag to Cl**e**ar (press DEL).

12. Click on OK (press ENTER).

13. In cells D4, D6, and D8, type *Cost*, *Salvage*, and *Life*.

14. Select the range D4:E4.

15. Select Formula and drag to **C**reate Names (ALT+r and press c).

16. Click on **L**eft Column (TAB).

17. Choose OK.

18. Select the range D6:E6.

19. Select Formula and drag to **C**reate Names (ALT+r and press c).

20. Click on **L**eft Column (TAB).

21. Choose OK.

22. Select the range D8:E8.

23. Select Formula and drag to **C**reate Names (ALT+r and press c).

24. Click on **L**eft Column (TAB).

25. Choose OK and observe what happens to your worksheet.

26. Select Formula and drag to **D**efine (ALT+r and press d).

27. Note the names in the Names in Sheet box and press Cancel.

28. Save this worksheet as DEPR.XLS.

Questions:

1. When you delete the names from the worksheet what message appears in the table? What does this message mean?
2. What names are in the Names in Sheet box?
3. What are the main advantages in using the Create Names command in place of the Define Names command?

3-2-5 The Paste Names command

A third helpful command to use with names is the Paste Names command. Similar to the Paste Function command, this command permits you to add a name to a formula rather than typing an entire expression. The next exercise shows you how this is done.

EXERCISE 3-6
Pasting a name

For this exercise, use worksheet DEPR.XLS, the worksheet prepared for Exercise 3-5. **Figure 3-11** shows how the Names in Sheet box should look when you complete step 15.

1. Select **F**ile and drag to **O**pen (ALT+f and press o).
2. Select DEPR.XLS (ALT+f and press DOWN to DEPR).
3. Click on OK (press ENTER).
4. Select the range C13:C22.
5. Select Fo**r**mula and drag to **D**efine Name (ALT+r and press d).
6. In the **N**ame box (ALT+n), type *range1*
7. Click on OK (press ENTER).
8. Select the range D13:D22.
9. Select Fo**r**mula and drag to **D**efine Name (ALT+r and press d).
10. In the **N**ame box (ALT+n), type *range2*
11. Click on OK (press ENTER).
12. Select the range E13:E22.
13. Select Fo**r**mula and drag to **D**efine Name (ALT+r and press d).
14. In the **N**ame box (ALT+n), type *range3*

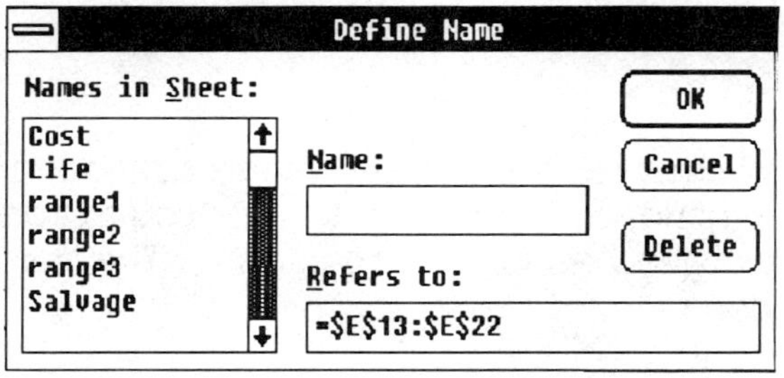

Figure 3-11 Revised Names in Sheet box

15. Click on OK (press ENTER).

16. Select the range C24:E24.

17. Select **E**dit and drag to Cl**e**ar (ALT+e and press c or DEL).

18. Click on OK. This clears all the equations from the three depreciation totals.

19. Select cell C24.

20. Select Fo**r**mula and drag to Pas**t**e Function (ALT+r and press t).

21. Select SUM() and click on OK.

22. With the formula bar active---waiting for you to supply an argument--select Fo**r**mula and drag to Paste **N**ame (ALT+r and press n).

23. Select range1 and click on OK.

24. Your formula should read: SUM(range1). Press ENTER.

25. Select cell D24.

26. Select Fo**r**mula and drag to Pas**t**e Function (ALT+r and press t).

27. Select SUM() and click on OK.

28. Select Fo**r**mula and drag to Paste **N**ame (ALT+r and press n).

29. Select range2 and click on OK.

30. Press ENTER.

31. Select cell E24.

32. Select Fo**r**mula and drag to Pas**t**e Function (ALT+r and press t).

33. Select SUM().

34. Select Fo**r**mula and drag to Paste **N**ame (ALT+r and press n).

35. Select range3 and click on OK.

36. Press ENTER.

37. Select Formula and drag to **G**oto.

38. Select range1.

39. Save this worksheet as DEPR.XLS.

Questions:
1. When you paste a name to a worksheet, what action is performed by Microsoft Excel?
2. What happens when you use Formula Goto and select range1?

3-3 Linking Worksheets

Linking worksheets allows you to combine information from more than one worksheet. This feature is especially useful if you need to look up a single value from a table of values and to add it to the active cell.

3-3-1 Table lookup

Before linking two worksheets, the way in which a lookup function works should be understood. Two built-in functions that are commonly used to link documents are VLOOKUP() and HLOOKUP(). Both represent different forms of lookup tables---VLOOKUP() searches through a table to find a value by following a vertical orientation, HLOOKUP() searches through a table to find a value by following a horizontal orientation.

Figure 3-12 illustrates how a lookup table works. As shown, taxable income and the tax at this income level are listed for the range 8000 to 20000. If you want to determine the tax for an income table, the VLOOKUP() function is typed as follows: =VLOOKUP(C17,A3:C15,3). This formula tells Microsoft Excel to search through the values in the first column of the range (A3:C15) to find the nearest value to the value stored in the lookup cell (C17). Once the nearest value is found, Microsoft Excel is further instructed to return the value in the column number indicated (column 3).

EXERCISE 3-7
Using the lookup function

Enter the tax information shown on Figure 3-12 on a blank worksheet. To save time and to improve on accuracy, use the Data Series command in building the table. Then, do the following:

	A	B	C
1	Taxable Income		Tax
2			
3	8000		1200
4	9000		1350
5	10000		1500
6	11000		1650
7	12000		1800
8	13000		1950
9	14000		2100
10	15000		2250
11	16000		2400
12	17000		2550
13	18000		2700
14	19000		2850
15	20000		3000
16			
17	Taxable income is		19000
18	Tax is		2850

Figure 3-12 The taxable income table

1. In cell C18, type *=VLOOKUP(C17,A3:C15,3)*
2. In cell C17, type *19000*
3. In cell C17, type *19001*
4. In cell C17, type *18999*
5. Select **F**ile and drag to Save **A**s (ALT+f and press a).
6. Call this new file TAX. You will use this worksheet in the next exercise.

Questions:

1. After typing 19001, does the VLOOKUP() function round to 20000 or stay at 19000? After typing 18999 does the function round to 19000 or stay at 18000? What does this tell you about the VLOOKUP() function?
2. Suppose taxable income is stored in column B and tax is stored in column D. What is the new VLOOKUP() equation?

3-3-2 Linking two worksheets

Next, we ask you to use the table lookup function to link two worksheets. In order to link worksheets, you must use a formula in one worksheet that refers to (or calls) a cell or a range of cells in a second worksheet. The syntax used in linking two worksheets is:

=*file_name,!,cell_range*, as in =TAX.XLS!$A3$C15

In this example,

* TAX.XLS is the name of the worksheet to be linked. This worksheet is also called the *supporting worksheet.*

* ! indicates that this is an external reference.

* $A3$C15 is the cell range on a worksheet that is referred to.

The next exercise asks you to write a linking statement using this syntax.

EXERCISE 3-8
Linking a tax form to a tax table

For this exercise you are asked to complete the worksheet shown on **Figure 3-13** and to link the abbreviated 1040 Federal tax form to the tax table built for the last exercise. Besides adding the table lookup function, the most difficult part of this exercise is the computation of the IRA for a person and his or her spouse. IRAs are based on total income for both individuals and income for each individual. If individual income is equal or greater than $10,000 but less than a combined income of $50,000, the maximum IRA deduction for an individual is $2,000. If individual income is less than $10,000 and combined income is less than $50,000, the maximum IRA deduction for an individual is 20% of that person's income.

1. To begin this exercise, open worksheet TAX.XLS, the worksheet saved for the last exercise and a clean worksheet, such as Sheet1.

2. Click on Sheet1 or select **W**indow and drag to Sheet**1** (ALT+w and press 1) to hide the TAX.XLS worksheet from view. (Note: for this exercise you are asked to keep two worksheets open, TAX.XLS and a new worksheet.)

3. In cells D1, E1, and G1 type *Yourself*, *Your Spouse*, and *TOTALS*.

4. Type all headings shown in column A, beginning with *6. Personal Exemptions* in cell A2 and ending with *65. Account you owe* in cell A27.

	A	B	C	D	E	F	G
1				Yourself	Your Spouse		TOTALS
2	6. Personal exemptions			1	1		2
3							
4	Income						
5	7. Wages and salary			15000	6000		21000
6	8. Interest income			400	500		900
7	9. Dividend income			500	800		1300
8	10. State tax refund			100	200		300
9	23. Total income			16000	7500		23500
10							
11	Adjustments						
12	24a and b IRAs			2000	1500		3500
13							
14	31. Adjusted gross income						20000
15							
16	Tax Computations						
17	34. Standard deductions						5000
18	36. Personal exemptions						4000
19	37. Taxable Income						11000
20	38. Tax to pay (from tax table)						1650
21							
22	Payments						
23	54. Federal tax withheld			1800	300		2100
24							
25	Refund or Amount you owe						
26	63. Refund						450
27	65. Amount you owe						0

Figure 3-13 The 1040 tax planning worksheet

5. Type *1* in cell D2 and *1* in cell E2.
6. Type *15000* in cell D5 and *6000* in cell E5.
7. Type *400* in cell D6 and *500* in cell E6.
8. Type *500* in cell D7 and *800* in cell E7.
9. Type *100* in cell D8 and *200* in cell E8.
10. In cell D9 type *=SUM(D5:D8)*
11. Select the range D9:E9.
12. Select **E**dit and drag to Fill Rig**h**t (ALT+e and press h).
13. In cell G5 type *=D5+E5*.

14. Select the range G5:G9.

15. Select **E**dit and drag to Fill Do**w**n (ALT+e and press w).

16. Select cell D12.

17. Type the following logical formula:
    *=IF(AND(D9>10000,$G$9<50000),2000,0.2*D9)*
    to compute the individual IRA. This formula is complex. It computes the IRA for the first person as follows:

    IF the amount in cell D9 is greater than 10000
    AND the amount in cell $G$9 is less than 50000,
        THEN enter 2000.
        ELSE enter 20 percent of D9.

18. Select the range D12:E12.

19. Select **E**dit and drag to Fill Rig**h**t (ALT+e and press h).

20. In cell G12 type *=D12+E12*. This represents the total IRA adjustment.

21. In cell G14 type *=G9-G12* to compute adjusted gross income. This is the amount of income on which tax computations are made.

22. Type *5000* in cell G17.

23. Type *4000* in cell G18.

24. In cell G19 type *=G14-G17-G18* to determine taxable income. This is the amount of income on which taxes are to be paid.

25. In cell G20 type *=VLOOKUP(G19,TAX.XLS!$A$3:$C$15,3)* to lookup the tax on taxable income and to return the tax to pay. (An alternative method is to use Edit Copy to transfer the lookup formula stored in cell C18 of worksheet TAX and Edit Paste to place the formula in cell G20 of the new worksheet. At this time, the formula must be edited.)

26. In cell D23 type *=0.12*D5*. We have assumed that 12 percent of your wages and salary were withheld by your employer for payment of Federal tax.

27. In cell E23 type *=0.05*E5*. In this case, since income was lower, only 5 percent of wages and salary were set aside.

28. In cell G23 type *=D23+E23*

29. In cell G26 type *=IF((G23-G20)>0,G23-G20,0)*

30. In cell G27 type *=IF((G23-G20)>0,0,G20-G23)*

31. Test your completed worksheet by trying several values.

32. Save this new worksheet. Select **F**ile and drag to Save **A**s (ALT+f and press a). Call this new worksheet *1040.XLS*.

33. Save TAX.XLS at this time, too, unless you plan to begin work on the next exercise.

Questions:
1. In step 17 what happens later on if you type G9 instead of $G$9?
2. What is the IRA adjustment if both parties in this exercise each earn $26,000? Each earn $7,500?
3. Why it is better to place the tax table on a separate worksheet?
4. Why must both worksheets be stored in the memory of your computer for this exercise to work? What would happen if TAX.XLS were not stored in memory?

3-4 Useful Techniques For Working With Complex Worksheets

It is often difficult to remember all the steps to take when building a multiple-window arrangement, such as the 1040.XLS and the TAX.XLS arrangement. Four useful techniques for working with complex worksheets feature the File Save Workspace command, the Formula Note command, the Options Protect Document command, and the Format Cell Protection command.

3-4-1 The File Save Workspace command

This command is used to save a multiple window worksheet arrangement. When you select the File Save Workspace command, Microsoft Excel asks you to name the worksheet (see **Figure 3-14**). After you have indicated

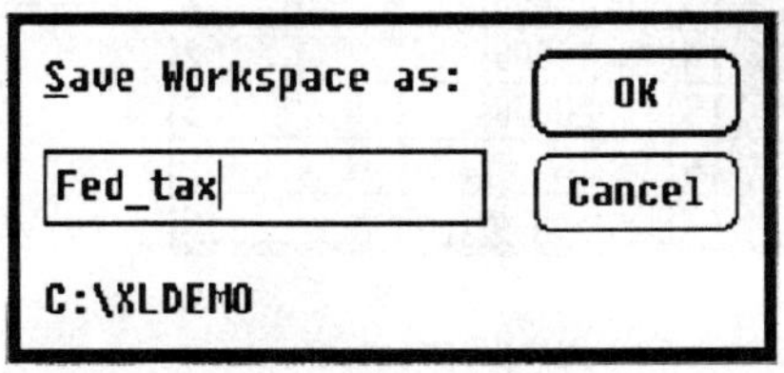

Figure 3-14 The File Save Workspace command

OK, Microsoft Excel saves all open worksheets, adding a .XLW extension to the new file. When the worksheet is opened, using the File Open command, Microsoft Excel checks the workspace file to determine which documents are to be opened, loads these documents into memory, and arranges the windows on the screen as you left them.

EXERCISE 3-9
Saving a workspace

For this exercise, use the TAX.XLS and the 1040.XLS worksheets. **Figure 3-15** shows how your workspace should look when you complete this exercise.

1. Open TAX.XLS, if this file is closed.

2. Open 1040.XLS, if this file is closed.

3. Drag **W**indow to **A**rrange All (ALT+w and press a).

4. Click on Sheet1 (press the number assigned to Sheet1).

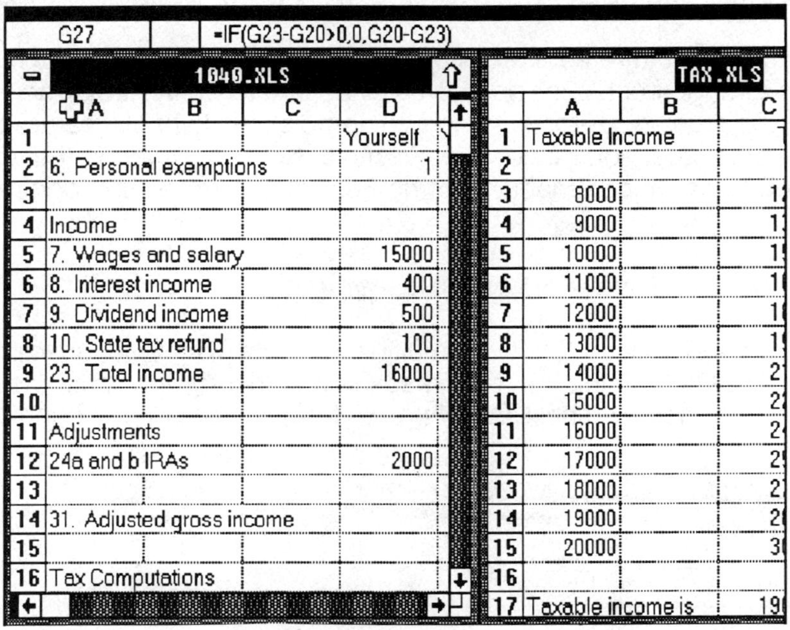

Figure 3-15 The arrangement to save as a workspace

5. Drag **W**indow to **H**ide (ALT+w and press h) Sheet1, leaving only 1040.XLS and TAX.XLS.

6. Drag **W**indow to **A**rrange All (ALT+w and press a).

7. Drag **F**ile to Save **W**orkspace (ALT+f and press w).

8. In the dialog box type *FED_TAX*.

9. Click on OK (press ENTER).

10. Click on Yes (press ENTER) when asked, "Save changes in 1040.XLS?"

11. Press SHIFT and select **F**ile. Drag to **C**lose All (SHIFT+ALT+f and press c).

12. Select **F**ile and drag to **O**pen (ALT+f and press o).

13. Select FED_TAX.XLW (ALT+f and DOWN).

14. Click on OK (press ENTER).

15. Click on Yes (press ENTER) when asked, "Update references to unopened documents?"

16. Select **F**ile and drag to E**x**it, unless you want to begin the next exercise.

17. Click on Yes when asked, "Save changes in 1040.XLS?"

Questions:
1. How does the File Save Workspace save you time?
2. What is the difference between the File Save As command and the File Save Workspace command?

3-4-2 The Formula Note command

This command allows you to add notes to a worksheet. A *note* is a message or comment about a specific cell or cell range. Notes are useful for describing how complicated functions and equations work, for documenting data sources, and for explaining underlying assumptions used in constructing a worksheet.

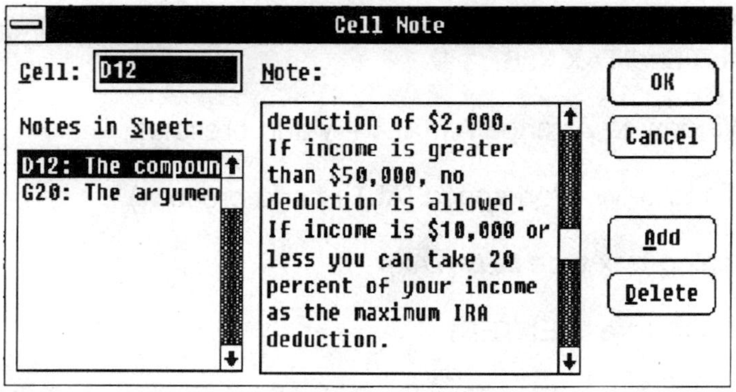

Figure 3-16 The Formula Note dialog box

Figure 3-16 shows the dialog box for the Formula Note command. The *Note box* contains the message describing your worksheet. After typing a note, press the Add button to add the note to the worksheet. The *Cell box* indicates the cell for which you are assigning the note. Each note must have an absolute cell reference. The *Notes in Sheet* box lists all notes prepared for a worksheet.

Notes and their location can be displayed and printed. The *Formula Select Special* command instructs Microsoft Excel to search the entire worksheet for notes and to display their location. **Figure 3-17** illustrates the dialog box for this command. Select *Notes* to begin the search.

The *Window Show Info* command displays the notes for a single cell. In addition, the *Window Arrange All* command displays one note at a time for a single worksheet.

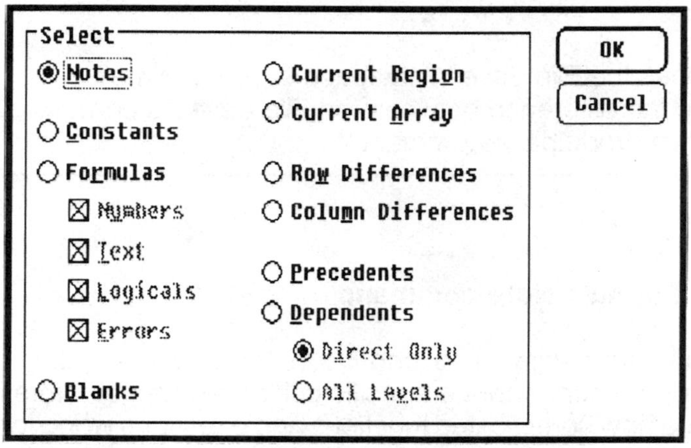

Figure 3-17 The Formula Select Special dialog box

Printing a note is done using the File Print command. As shown in Chapter 2 (see Figure 2-25), you can print the worksheet only (Sheet), notes only (Notes), or both the worksheet and notes (Both).

EXERCISE 3-10
Adding notes to a worksheet

For this exercise, use the FED_TAX.XLW workspace. **Figure 3-18** shows how your notes will look when they are printed.

1. Open workspace FED_TAX.XLW, if it is closed. Click on **Y**es (ALT+y) when asked, "Update references to unopened documents?"

2. Activate worksheet 1040.XLS (ALT+w and press 1).

3. Select Fo**r**mula and drag to **G**oto (ALT+r and press g).

4. Type *G20* and click on OK (press ENTER).

5. Select Fo**r**mula and drag to **N**ote (ALT+r and press n).

6. In the Note box (ALT+n) type:
   The arguments of the Vlookup() function mean the following: the first is a value to search for, the second is the range of the search and where the search will be conducted, and the third is the column to return a value from.

7. Click on **A**dd (ALT+a).

8. Click on OK (TAB and press ENTER).

```
Cell: D12
Note: The compound IF statement requires total income to be greater than $10,000 for yourself and less than $50,000
      for you and your spouse for you to take a maximum IRS deduction of $2,000.  If income is greater than $50,000,
      no deduction is allowed.  If income is $10,000 or less you can take 20 percent of your income as the maximum
      IRA deduction.

Cell: G20
Note: The arguments of the Vlookup() function mean the following:  the first is a value to search for, the second is
      the range of the search and where the search will be conducted, and the third is the column to return a value
      from.
```

Figure 3-18 Notes added to the FED_TAX.WLW workspace and the 1040.XLS worksheet

9. Select Formula and drag to **G**oto (ALT+r and press g).

10. Type *D12* and click on OK (press ENTER).

11. Select Formula and drag to **N**ote (ALT+r and press n).

12. In the Note box (ALT+n) type:
The compound IF statement requires total income to be greater than $10,000 for yourself and less than $50,000 for you and your spouse for you to take a maximum IRA deduction of $2,000. If income is greater than $50,000, no deduction is allowed. If income is $10,000 or less you can take 20 percent of your income as the maximum IRA deduction.

13. Click on **A**dd (ALT+a).

14. Click on OK (TAB and press ENTER).

15. Select Formula and drag to **S**elect Special (ALT+r and press s).

16. Click on OK (press ENTER).

17. Use the scroll bars to position the 1040.XLS worksheet so you can see cells D12 and G20.

18. Select cell G20.

19. Select **W**indow and drag to **S**how Info (ALT+w and press s).

20. Select cell D12.

21. Select **W**indow and drag to **S**how Document (ALT+w and press s) to escape from Show Document.

22. Select **W**indow and drag to **A**rrange All (ALT+w and press a).

23. With the 1040.XLS worksheet still active, select **F**ile and drag to **P**rint (ALT+f and press p).

24. Click on **N**otes (ALT+n).

25. Click on OK (press ENTER) to print the notes you have added to the worksheet.

26. Save the revised workspace. Select **F**ile and drag to Save **W**orkspace (ALT+f and press w).

27. Click on OK (press ENTER) to close the dialog box.

28. Click on Yes (press ENTER) to save changes to 1040.XLS.

29. Click on OK (press ENTER) to replace existing FED_TAX.XLW.

30. Select **F**ile and drag to E**x**it unless you want to begin work on the next exercise.

Questions:
1. What happens to 1040.XLS when the Formula Select Special command is selected?
2. What is the main purpose of the Window Show Info command?
3. Why is it important to add notes to a worksheet?
4. How can you delete a note from a worksheet?

3-4-3 The Options Protect Document command

This command allows you to protect a document, to prevent it from being moved, sized, or revised. **Figure 3-19** shows the dialog box for this command. To provide protection, you must type in a *password*---a name of your choice, such as your middle name. If you cannot remember your password, the worksheet protection cannot be reversed. So be careful when using this command.

To protect the cell contents of a worksheet, turn on the contents check box. In a protected worksheet, you cannot change the contents or format of locked cells. To protect the worksheet from being moved, sized, or hidden, turn the windows check box on.

Figure 3-19 The Options Protect Document dialog box

EXERCISE 3-11
Protecting a cell

For this exercise use worksheet TAX.XLS and 1040.XLS once again.

1. Open workspace FED_TAX.XLW, if it is not in memory. Answer **Y**es (press ENTER) when asked, "Update references to unopened documents?"
2. With worksheet 1040.XLS active, select **O**ptions and drag to **P**rotect Document (ALT+o and press p).
3. Type *Password* in the Password text box.
4. Turn the Contents check box on (if an X is missing) and the Windows check box on (if an X is missing).
5. Click on OK (press ENTER).
6. In worksheet 1040.XLS, attempt to edit the formula in G20 by typing =
7. Click on OK.
8. Select Fo**r**mula and drag to **N**otes (ALT+r and press n).
9. Type *The* to edit the note in cell G20.
10. Click on **A**dd (ALT+a).
11. Click on OK (press ENTER).
12. Click on Cancel (TAB plus ENTER).
13. Select **O**ptions and drag to Un**p**rotect Document (ALT+o and press p).
14. Type *Password* in the Password text box. Remember, you must type the password exactly as you entered it, including upper- and lower-case letters.
15. Click on OK (press ENTER).
16. Select **F**ile to E**x**it, if you want to quit. Otherwise, begin the next exercise.

17. Click on **N**o (ALT+n) when asked "Save changes in 1040.XLS?"

Questions:
1. What message appears when you type the equal sign?
2. What message appears when you attempt to add the revised note to the worksheet?
3. What is the value in protecting a worksheet with the Options Protect Document command?

3-4-4 The Format Cell Protection command

A second command that allows you to protect a document is the Format Cell Protection command. This command is recognized when the Options Protect Document command is selected. It is ignored at other times.

The dialog box for this command (see **Figure 3-20**) illustrates that it is possible to lock or hide a cell. A *locked cell* cannot be edited. Use this option to protect a cell from being changed. A *hidden cell* prevents others from displaying your formulas. Use this cell to hide your work from the view of others.

EXERCISE 3-12
Locking and hiding a cell

For this exercise use worksheet TAX.XLS and 1040.XLS once again.

1. Open workspace FED_TAX.XLW, if it is not in memory. Answer **Y**es (press ENTER) when asked, "Update references to unopened documents?"

2. With worksheet 1040.XLS active, select the range G9:G20.

3. Select Forma**t** and drag to Cell **P**rotection (ALT+t and press p).

Figure 3-20 The Format Cell Protection dialog box

4. Turn the **L**ocked (ALT+l) check box on (if an X is missing) and the **H**idden (ALT+h) check box on (if an X is missing).

5. Click on OK (press ENTER).

6. Select **O**ptions and drag to **P**rotect Document (ALT+o and press p).

7. Type *Password* in the Password text box.

8. Turn the Contents check box on (if an X is missing) and the Windows check box on (if an X is missing).

9. Click on OK (press ENTER).

10. In worksheet 1040.XLS, attempt to review the formulas stored in cells G9:G20. Try G22.

11. Select **O**ptions and drag to Un**p**rotect Document (ALT+o and press p).

12. Type *Password* in the Password text box.

13. Click on OK (press ENTER).

14. Select **F**ile to E**x**it, if you want to quit. Otherwise, begin the next exercise.

15. Click on **N**o (ALT+n) when asked "Save changes in 1040.XLS?"

Questions:
1. What happens when you try to review the formulas in the protected range? Outside the protected range?
2. Compared to the Options Protect Document command, what additional protection is provided by the Format Cell Protection command?

3-5 Summary

This chapter introduces you to some of the more advanced worksheet commands in Microsoft Excel. You should know how to use a built-in function, how to replace a formula with a name, and understand ways of working with complex worksheets and workspaces.

Functions simplify the performing of worksheet operations. Statistical functions allow you to quickly determine the properties of data, while logical functions enable you to write formulas which contain IF-THEN-ELSE conditions. Financial functions consider the time value of money and determine such things as present and future value.

The Formula Paste Function command is helpful in entering the arguments for functions. The syntax for each function appears in the formula bar.

By using formula commands that feature names, it is possible to use English names to reference cells, constants, and formulas. With English names, absolute references are often necessary. This type of reference is cell specific, while a relative reference is direction specific.

Names can be defined by you, using the Formula Define Name command, or defined by Microsoft Excel, using the Formula Create Names command. The Formula Paste Names command is used to add a name directly to a formula, rather than typing the entire expression.

Linking worksheets involves creating a formula in one worksheet that calls another worksheet. The important table lookup functions are VLOOKUP() and HLOOKUP().

Four useful techniques for preserving and protecting a worksheet or worksheet arrangement are the File Save Workspace command, the Formula Note command, the Options Protect Document command, and the Format Cell Protection command. The first of these simplifies the loading of a complex worksheet arrangement, while the second allows you to add documentation to a worksheet. The Options Protect Document and Format Cell Protection commands work in combination. The Protect Document command is required to protect the contents and/or a worksheet window; the Cell Protection command is required to block the change and display of worksheet formulas in individual cells.

KEY TERMS

Absolute reference
Financial functions
Functions
Linking
Logical functions
Lookup table
Password
Relative reference
Statistical reference
Supporting worksheet

COMMAND REFERENCE

File Save Workspace: File Menu. Saves a group of open windows/files under one name with the extension .XLW.

Format Cell Protection: Format Menu. Protects or hides entries in a cell or cell range. Usually used in tandem with the Options Protect Document command to prevent accidental alteration of your worksheet by yourself or someone else.

Formula Create Names: Formula Menu. Assigns names to a cell or cell range automatically by looking in a direction you specify for the name.

Formula Define Name: Formula Menu. Allows you to assign a name to a cell or cell range to help simplify your worksheet. Also used to delete previously assigned names.

Formula Paste Function: Formula Menu. Automatically pastes a function onto the formula bar for editing and insertion into a cell.

Formula Paste Names: Formula Menu. Automatically pastes a name you have created using Formula Define Name into the insertion bar for direct insertion into a formula or cell.

Formula Note: Formula Menu. Adds or deletes an annotation for a cell. Useful in documenting your worksheet for other users.

Formula Reference: Formula Menu. Changes the reference of a cell. Acts as toggle between four different reference formats: for example, A6, $A$6, A$6, and $A6.

Formula Select Special: Formula Menu. Similar to Formula Goto. Locates special worksheet items like: cell notes, constants, formulas, blanks, precedents, dependents, and row and column differences.

Options Protect Document: Options Menu. Protects a document by allowing you to establish a password to prevent unauthorized entry.

ON YOUR OWN

1. Functions are built-in _______ provided by Microsoft Excel.
   a) cells
   b) formulas
   c) commands
   d) menus
   e) numbers

2. If cells A1,B1,C1,D1 contain the values 34, 25, 37 and 42, the function =COUNT(A1:D1) will return a value of
   a) 3
   b) 138
   c) 0
   d) 4
   e) 6

3. The function =SYN() is an example of a(n) _______ function.
   a) database
   b) logical
   c) statistical
   d) financial
   e) investment

4. If cell A1 contains the value 500, cell B1 contains the value 700 and cell C1 contains the function:
   =IF(AND(A1>300,B1<1000),200,"")
   the value returned in C1 will be:
   a) 300
   b) 1300
   c) 1000
   d) 500
   e) 200

5. In the function =SUM(A1:J1), A1 and J1 are:
   a) arguments
   b) items
   c) references
   d) numbers
   e) equations

6. The _______ command allows you to assign words in place of cell references to help simplify building and understanding formulas.
   a) Formula Apply Names
   b) Formula Select Special
   c) Formula Note
   d) Formula Define Name
   e) Formula Reference

7. Cell C1 contains the formula =$A1+$B$1. If copied to cell C2 the formula would read:
   a) =$A1+$B$1
   b) =$C1+$B$1
   c) =$A2+$C$1
   d) =$B1+$C$2
   e) =$A2+$B$1

8. A(n)________ reference is cell specific, while a(n) ________ reference is direction specific.
   a) absolute, mixed
   b) mixed, relative
   c) relative, absolute

d) mixed, absolute
e) absolute, relative

9. Creating a formula that refers to a cell or cell range in another document is called:
a) linking
b) supporting
c) referencing
d) looking up
e) pasting

10. The _______ command allows you to attach a message or document cells in your worksheet.
a) Formula Define Name
b) Options Protect Document
c) Formula Note
d) File Save Workspace
e) Formula Select Special

MORE PRACTICE

I. Open WEST2.XLS and make the following changes:
1. In cell E14, enter the formula that will compute Overall Profit Margin.
2. Format E14 to 0.00%.
3. Change the reference of cells E5, E11, E13, E14 so they are absolute references.
4. Add the following note to cell E14: *Overall profit margin is good, but fiscal year 87 is critical.*
5. Use Options Protect Document to add a password: Cowboy
6. Save your worksheet as WEST3.XLS.

Answer the following:
a) What command would you use to show your note?
b) Why was it important to protect your document at the end of your changes instead of the beginning?

II. Open STOCK.XLS and a blank worksheet & make the following changes:
1. Arrange the windows so you can see both at once.
2. Add the following headings in the blank worksheet:
A1 Market Analysis A4 Low
A3 High A5 Average
3. In cells B3:B5 of the new worksheet, use the =MAX(), =MIN(), and =AVERAGE() functions to determine the highest and lowest average and the overall average of the stock market for all years. If you

need help with referencing the STOCK.XLS worksheet, review the table lookup examples.

4. Save your new worksheet as MARK.XLS

Answer the following:

a) What formulas did you enter in Cell B3:B5?
b) Why is it helpful to open more than one worksheet?

III. Open EAST2.XLS and make the following changes:

1. In cells E3:E6, E10:E13, add the formula that will compute the total sales for Gears, Wheels, Gadgets, R & D, Mktg, and Admn.
2. Shade cells E2, E9.
3. Format cells E3:E6, E10:E13 to $#,##0
4. Add the heading, *Total* in cells E1, E8.
5. Use Formula Define Name to define cell E6 as *Total_sales* and cell E13 as *Total_expenses*
6. Using Formula Paste Name, enter the formula that will compute Operating Income in cell E15.
7. Format cell E15 as $#,##0
8. Use Formula Define Name to define cell E15 as *Net_Operating_Income*
9. Use Formula Paste Name to help enter the formula that will compute overall profit margin. Hint: A similar formula can be found in cell D16.
10. Format cell E16 to 0.00%
11. Save your worksheet as EAST3.XLS

Answer the following:

a) What formula did you enter in cell E16?
b) When you defined E6 as Total_sales, why didn't it change the figures in cells B16:D16?

CHAPTER 4 - CREATING CHARTS

Besides building worksheets, Microsoft Excel can be used to create charts. As stated in the Getting Started section, a *chart* is a graphic presentation of data. People use charts to make it easier to spot trends, make comparisons, highlight changes, and show percentages.

Microsoft Excel has seven types of charts to choose from: area, bar, column, line, pie, scatter, and combination. These types are available in 44 predefined formats. The purpose of this chapter is to acquaint you with each type of chart. In this and the next two chapters you will be asked to create several different types of charts. When you complete this chapter, you will be able to:

* Create a chart directly.
* Understand basic chart elements and terminology.
* Display each of the seven types of charts.
* Add text to a chart.
* Add arrows and legends to a chart.
* Improve chart appearance.
* Create overlay charts.

4-1 Creating Charts Directly

The initial step in creating a chart is to select the worksheet values you want to chart. Following this, you must select the File New command and select Chart (see **Figure 4-1**). This opens a new chart file and changes the menu bar at the top of the display screen. The menu bar contains two new drop-down menus---Gallery and Chart.

Besides a different menu bar, Microsoft Excel automatically plots preselected worksheet values when a chart is selected, using a column-

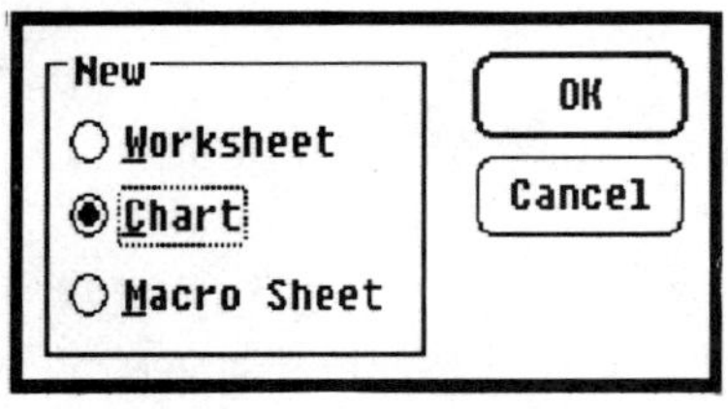

Figure 4-1 The File New dialog box with chart selected

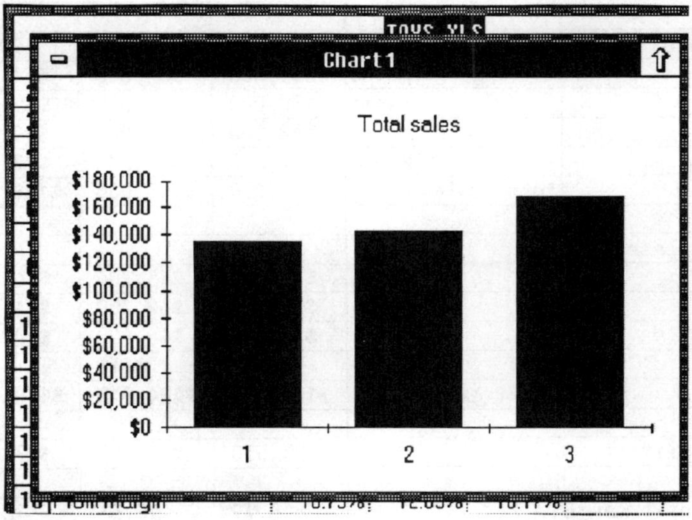

Figure 4-2 Column-style chart showing total sales by period

style chart. **Figure 4-2** illustrates how a display screen might look. Similar to worksheets, each chart is assigned a number, beginning with Chart1. As with a worksheet, you can change this default name using the File Save As command. In addition, each chart contains a document-control icon, located in the upper left-hand corner of the document. Clicking on this icon opens a menu to display commands for moving and sizing a chart.

When Microsoft Excel plots a chart, it checks to determine whether the range selected contains category names and data series names. *Category names* identify the different categories of information to be charted. Category names generally appear along the horizontal axis. The two exceptions are pie charts, that display category names in the legend, and scatter charts, that do not display category names. *Data series names* identifies each data series on a chart. With charts, data series are the values on which charts entries will be scaled. On many types of charts, data series names appear in the chart legend.

EXERCISE 4-1
Constructing a column-style chart

For this exercise, you are asked to initially prepare a new worksheet and save it as TOYS.XLS. **Figure 4-3** shows the worksheet you are to prepare.

	A	B	C	D	E
1	Sales:		1990	1991	1992
2		Trains	$32,000	$34,000	$51,000
3		Planes	$50,000	$45,000	$45,500
4		Autos	$32,000	$36,000	$44,000
5		Boats	$22,000	$28,000	$27,500
6		Total sales	$136,000	$143,000	$168,000
7					
8	Expenses:				
9		R and D	$14,600	$15,200	$16,450
10		Manf.	$58,000	$62,700	$71,300
11		Mktg.	$37,300	$46,400	$52,300
12		Admin.	$550	$645	$781
13		Total expenses	$110,450	$124,945	$140,831
14					
15	Profit:		$25,550	$18,055	$27,169
16					
17	Profit margin		18.79%	12.63%	16.17%

Figure 4-3 The TOYS.XLS worksheet

Type the headings and the data as shown. Next, add the following formulas:

* In cell C6, enter *=SUM(C9:C12)*

* In cell C13, enter *=SUM(C9:C12)*

* In cell C15, enter *=C6-C13*

* In cell C17, enter *=C15/C6*

Use **E**dit, Fill Rig**h**t (ALT+e and press h) to copy the formulas to columns D and E. Set the Column Width of column A to 10 and the Column Width of column B to 14. Following this, do three more things:

* Center the years in cells C1:E1.

* Format all dollar values using $#,##0.

* Add the percent sign to the values in C17:E17.

Save this worksheet as TOYS.XLS! It will be used in other exercises in this chapter.

Once the TOYS.XLS worksheet is completed, it can be used to prepare several types of charts. **Figure 4-4** shows the chart you will be asked to print in the middle of this exercise.

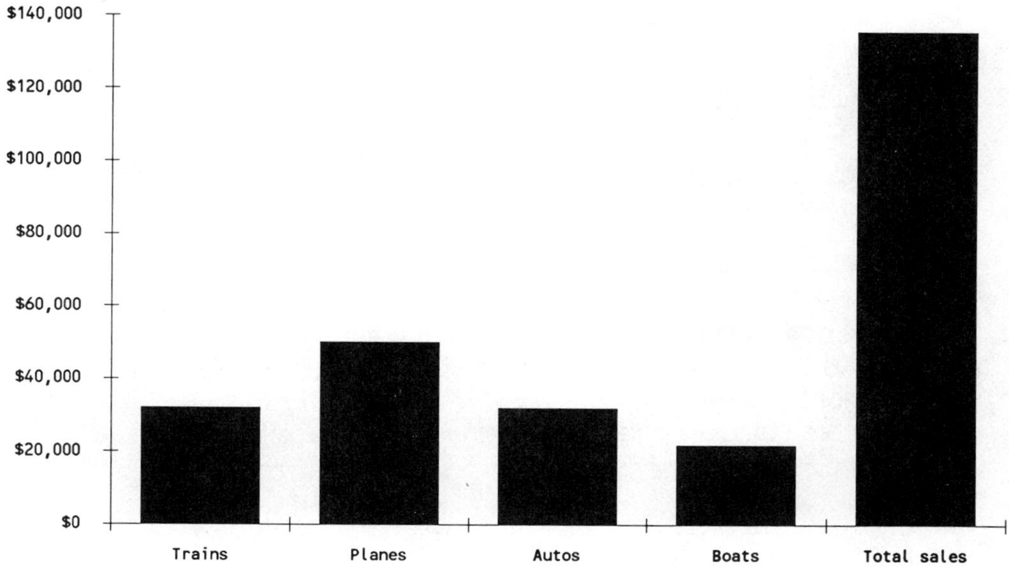

Figure 4-4 Column-style chart showing total sales by product

1. With the TOYS.XLS worksheet facing you, select the range B1:E2.

2. Select **F**ile and drag to **N**ew (ALT+f and press n).

3. Click on **C**hart (ALT+c).

4. Click on OK (press ENTER) to display Chart1. The Category Names will appear on the horizontal axis.

5. Select **W**indow and drag to TOYS.XLS (ALT+w and press the number assigned to the worksheet).

6. Select the range B2:C6.

7. Repeat steps 2, 3, and 4.

8. Select **F**ile and drag to **P**rint (ALT+f and press p).

9. Click on OK (press ENTER).

10. Select **W**indow and drag to TOYS.XLS (ALT+w and press the number assigned to the worksheet).

11. Select the range B1:E6.

12. Repeat steps 2, 3, and 4.

13. Select SHIFT+**F**ile and drag to **C**lose All. Do not save any of the charts or the changes to TOYS.XLS.

14. Select **F**ile and drag to E**x**it if you want to quit. Otherwise, begin the next exercise.

Questions:
1. What does this exercise tell you about creating charts?
2. How is the vertical axis determined by Microsoft Excel? The horizontal axis?
3. How are category names determined by Microsoft Excel?

4-1-1 Changing chart types

With Microsoft Excel you can create seven different types of charts using Gallery commands. **Figure 4-5** shows the drop-down menu for this set of commands. For each type of chart---area, bar, column, and so on---there is a separate command and an associated dialog box. By selecting one of these seven commands, the format of the active chart is changed. Thus, to change a column chart to a pie chart, select the Gallery Pie command.

Figure 4-6 shows the dialog box for the Gallery Pie command. This box identifies six possible pie chart formats: simple pie chart, pie wedges patterned the same with category labels, first pie wedge exploded, all pie wedges exploded, simple pie chart with category labels, and simple pie chart with value labels expressed as percentages. Use the pie chart type whenever you want to show the proportion of each part that makes up the whole. Use the pie wedge options when you want to highlight one or more

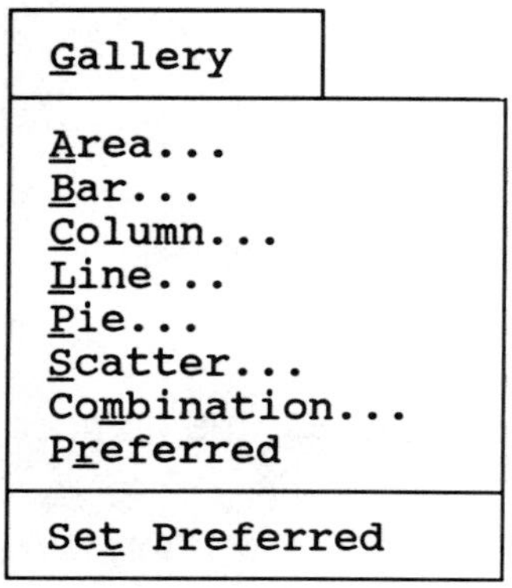

Figure 4-5 The Gallery drop-down menu

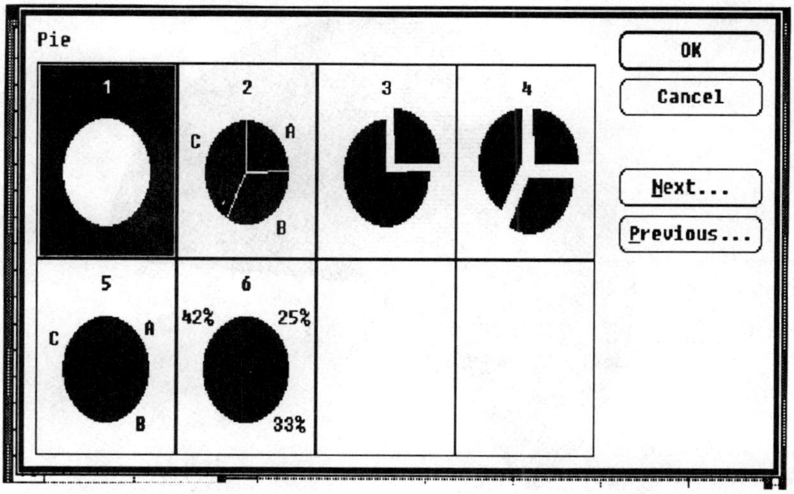

Figure 4-6 The Gallery Pie dialog box

pieces of the pie. To move from one format to the next, click directly on the desired pie chart or use arrow keys.

Besides the six pie chart choices, the Gallery Pie dialog box contains two other actions designed to help you to jump from one type of chart to another: Click on Next to move to the next chart type on the Gallery menu; click on Previous to choose the previous chart type.

Each Gallery chart type command reveals a dialog box. Each dialog box shows the different formats that are available for a specific chart type. Collectively, there are 44 different choices. Likewise, each dialog box contains a Next and a Previous button.

EXERCISE 4-2
Changing chart types

For this exercise, use the TOYS.XLS worksheet once again. **Figure 4-7** shows the pie chart you are asked to create.

1. Open worksheet TOYS.XLS.

2. Select the range B2:C5.

3. Select **F**ile and drag to **N**ew (ALT+f and press n).

4. Click on **C**hart (ALT+c).

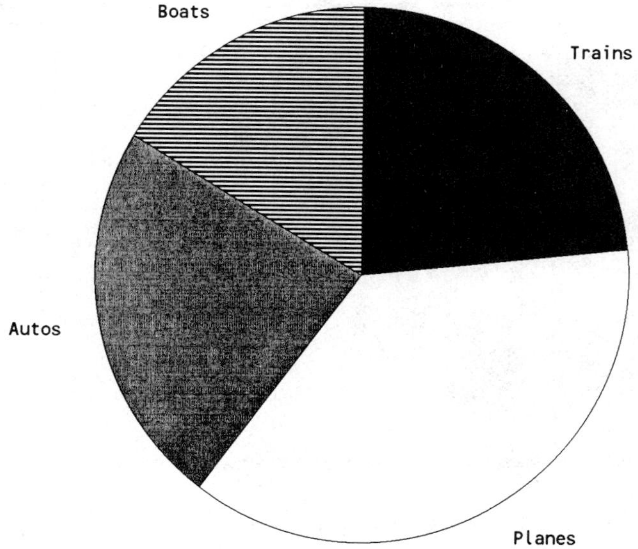

Figure 4-7 A pie chart with category labels

5. Click on OK (press ENTER) to display Chart1.

6. Select **G**allery and drag to **P**ie (ALT+g and press p).

7. Click on **N**ext (ALT+n).

8. Click on **N**ext six more times to examine all chart formats and to return to Pie (ALT+n).

9. Click on pie chart format 5 (RIGHT to 5).

10. Click on OK (press ENTER).

11. Select **F**ile and drag to **P**rint (ALT+f and press p).

12. Click on OK (press ENTER).

13. Select **G**allery and drag to **P**ie (ALT+g and press p).

14. Click on 6 (RIGHT).

15. Click on OK (press ENTER).

16. Experiment by repeating steps 13, 14, and 15 to review the other four pie chart formats.

17. Select **F**ile and drag to E**x**it. Do not save any charts.

Questions:
1. What happens when you click on Next the first time?
2. Why is the range B2:C5 instead of B2:C6?
3. When would a first pie wedge exploded format be the format to use when preparing a chart?

4-1-2 Changing the default chart format

Whenever you create a chart, the default chart format is format1 from the Gallery Column dialog box. The *Gallery Set Preferred* command allows you to change this default to one you like. When the default is changed, the File Save Workspace command must be used to save the preferred chart format. When the workspace is opened, Microsoft Excel automatically uses the perferred chart format.

The *Gallery Preferred* command is the second important command for referencing a chart format of your choice. This command changes the format of the active chart to the format set by the Gallery Set Preferred command.

4-1-3 Saving and printing charts

Charts are saved using the File Save As (for new charts) and File Save (when making revisions to a chart). When saving a chart, Microsoft Excel dynamically links the worksheet used in building the chart to the chart. When you save the chart, Microsoft Excel does not save the values placed on the chart. Instead, it stores a reference to the worksheet containing the chart values.

Charts are printed, like worksheets, using the File Print command. The main difference between charts and worksheets is that charts are sized to fit the pages you are printing on. This often leads to a printed chart that varies in shape from the chart shown on the computer display screen.

With charts, the Page Set Up command provides a different set of printer choices. As shown by **Figure 4-8**, you can determine whether the chart should be printed the same as the size on the screen (screen size), printed as large as possible while retaining height to width ratios (fit to page), or printed to fit the page, regardless of the height to width ratio (full page). Use the *Print Preview* option on the Print dialog box to display how your printed chart will look if you have questions regarding which screen size to choose.

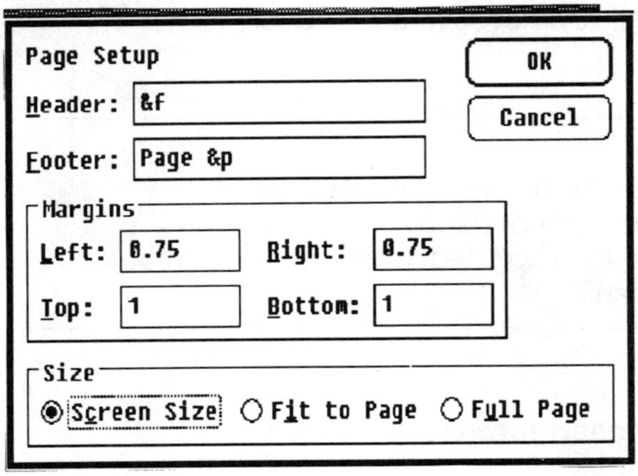

Figure 4-8 The File Page Setup dialog box for charts

EXERCISE 4-3
Changing the chart default

For this exercise, use the TOYS.XLS worksheet again. You are asked to compare the results to those found in earlier exercises and to save and print the Screen Size chart shown on **Figure 4-9**.

1. With a blank worksheet facing you, select **F**ile and drag to **O**pen (ALT+f and press o).

2. Open worksheet TOYS.XLS.

3. On this worksheet, select the range B2:C5.

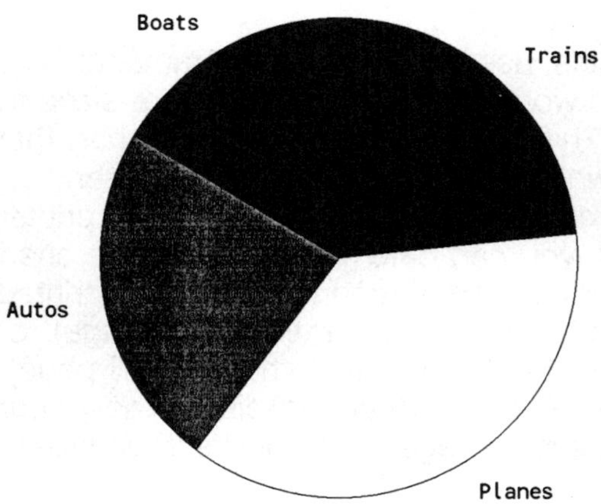

Figure 4-9 A screen size page setup selection

4. Select **F**ile and drag to **N**ew (ALT+f and press n).

5. Click on **C**hart (ALT+c).

6. Click on OK (press ENTER) to display Chart1.

7. Select **G**allery and drag to **P**ie (ALT+g and press p).

8. Click on format5 (RIGHT to 5 and press ENTER).

9. Select **G**allery and drag to Se**t** Preferred (ALT+g and press t). This changes the chart type default.

10. Select **F**ile and drag to Save **A**s (ALT+f and press a).

11. Type *SALES* to save Chart1 under it's new name.

12. Click on OK (press ENTER).

13. Select **F**ile and drag to Save **W**orkspace (ALT+f and press w).

14. Type *PIE* to name the workspace.

15. Click on OK (press ENTER).

16. Select **W**indow and drag to TOYS.XLS (ALT+w and press the number assigned to the worksheet).

17. Select the range B6:E6.

18. Repeat steps 4, 5 and 6.

19. Select **G**allery and drag to **B**ar (ALT+g and press b).

20. Click on format7 and click on OK (RIGHT to 7 and press ENTER).

21. Select **G**allery and drag to P**r**eferred (ALT+g and press r).

22. Select **F**ile and drag to **C**lose (ALT+f and press c).

23. Select **N**o (ALT+n) when asked, "Save changes in 'Chart 2'?"

24. With TOYS.XLS facing you, select **F**ile and drag to **O**pen (ALT+f and press o).

25. Open PIE.XLW.

26. Select **F**ile and drag to Page Se**t**up (ALT+f and press t).

27. Click on S**c**reen Size and click on OK (ALT+c and press ENTER).

28. Select **F**ile and drag to **P**rint (ALT+f and press p).

29. Click on **P**review and click on OK (ALT+p and press ENTER).

30. Click on Prin**t** (within Preview) to print the chart.

31. Select **F**ile and drag to Page Se**t**up (ALT+f and press t).

32. Click on F**i**t to Page and click on OK (ALT+i and press ENTER) to restore the default value.

33. Select **G**allery and drag to **C**olumn (ALT+g and press c).

34. Select Format1 and click on OK (LEFT and press ENTER).

35. Select **G**allery and drag to Se**t** Preferred to restore the default (ALT+g and press t).

36. Select **F**ile and drag to E**x**it (ALT+f and press x).

37. Answer **Y**es (press ENTER) to "Save changes to SALES.XLC?"

Questions:
1. What chart form is automatically provided by Microsoft Excel in creating Chart1? In creating Chart2?
2. What happens when the Gallery Preference command is selected?
3. How does Figure 4-9 differ from Figure 4-7?
4. Why is it important to have different Page Setup options for charts?

4-2 Basic Chart Elements

Several basic chart terms must be understood before chart design can be fully explained. The following list indicates the terms you should be familiar with.

* *Chart* - the entire area inside the chart window, including all chart elements.

* *Plot area* - the central area of the chart window bounded by the horizontal and vertical axes. This is the area where data are plotted.

* *Axes* - the horizontal and vertical lines that provide a reference for plotting data. The *category axis* refers to the horizontal axis and the *value axis* refers to the vertical axis. In bar charts this order is reversed, and pie charts do not contain axes.

* *Tickmarks* - the small marks that separate categories and values on the chart axes.

* *Series markers* - the column, bar, dot, or slice that mark the parts important to the data plot.

* *Chart title* - the text that describes the data in a chart.

* *Legend* - the text that provides the key to the series markers.

4-2-1 Chart commands

Figure 4-10 shows the drop-down menu for the set of special Chart commands. With Chart commands, you can add text, arrows, legends, gridlines, and so on. Once items such as text are added to a chart, chart formatting is done to make the chart more pleasing to the eye. For now, let's review the purpose of each Chart command. The next section explains how the different Chart Format commands are used.

```
Chart
-----------------------
Attach Text...
Add Arrow
Add Legend
Axes...
Gridlines...
Add Overlay
-----------------------
Select Chart
Select Plot Area
-----------------------
Protect Document...
-----------------------
Calculate Now
Short Menus
```

Figure 4-10 Chart drop-down menu

Chart command	is used to
Attach Text	Adds text to the chart title, value axis, category axis, or to series markers. Use the Format Text command to modify the text.
Add Arrow	Adds an arrow to the upper-left corner of the chart. Use the Format Move and Format Size commands to place the arrow where you want it.
Add Legend	Adds legend to the active chart. The plot area becomes smaller when a legend is added. Use the Format Patterns, Format Font, and Format Legend commands to format the Legend.
Axes	Turns on or off the axes on a chart.
Gridlines	Turns on or off the gridlines on a chart.
Add Overlay	Creates an overlay chart and adds it to the active chart. The overlay chart is always plotted as a line chart. Use the Format Overlay command to change this chart type.
Select Chart	Selects the entire chart, rather than part of a chart. Use Format Font, Format Patterns, and Format Main Chart, if there is an overlay chart.
Select Plot Area	Selects only the plot area of a chart, rather than the entire chart. Use Format Patterns to control the changes to this area.
Protect Document	Protects a chart from being altered. It is similar to the Options Protect Document command.
Calculate Now	Calculates all open worksheets and redraws charts following the settings in the Options Calculation command.
Short Menus	Changes the chart menu bar to show those commands that are used most frequently.

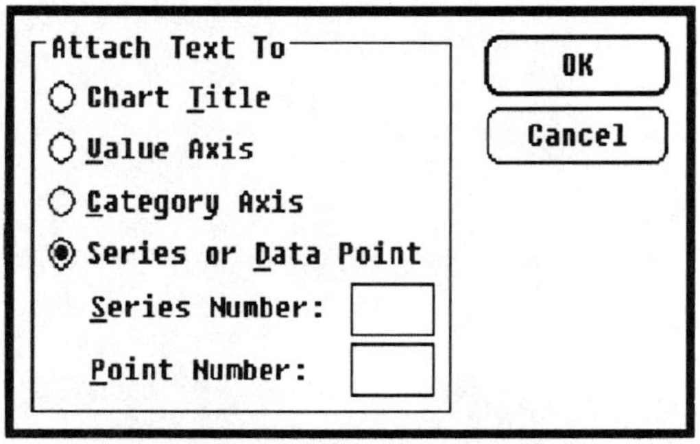

Figure 4-11 Format drop-down menu for charts

4-2-2 Adding text to a chart

Both attached text and unattached text can be added to a chart. *Attached text* is related to one of the following chart objects: chart title, value axis label, category axis label, and series marker label. *Unattached text* is not attached to any chart object and can be added anywhere in the chart area.

Figure 4-11 shows the dialog box for the Chart Attach Text command. This command is used for adding attached text to a chart. Two steps are required for adding text to a data series: type the series number followed by the data point number (for example, data series 1, point number 5). The only time you do not have to type both numbers is when you want to attach text to an area in an area chart.

For unattached text, there is no special dialog box. Instead, type the text in the formula bar and press RETURN. Microsoft Excel will display the text on the chart and surround it with small black boxes. You can use the mouse to move the text box on the display screen. From the keyboard, use the Chart Size and Chart Move commands to size and move the text as desired.

4-3 Chart Formatting

Six Format commands are commonly used with the Chart Attach Text command. These six commands are: Format Patterns, Text, Font, Scale, Move, and Size (see **Figure 4-12**). Three of these commands provide direct access to one another. For example, (1) from the Format Patterns command, it is possible to select either the Format Text or Font commands; (2) from the Format Text command, it is possible to select either the Format Patterns or Font commands; and (3) from the Format Font command, it is possible to select either the Format Patterns or Text commands. Another feature of these commands is that the chart object must be selected *before* the command is selected. The general procedure is: select the object, select the format command to change the object, and press ENTER.

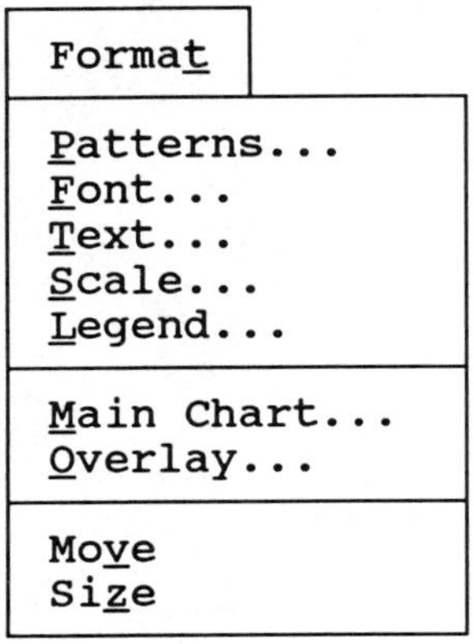

Figure 4-12 The Chart Attach Text dialog box

4-3-1 Format Patterns command

The Format Patterns command is is one of the most interesting commands to work with. As shown by **Figure 4-13**, the dialog box for this command permits you to add a border to text on a chart, to change the color of the border, and change the line weight of the border. Besides the type of border, this command allows you to change an area on a chart. It is possible to change the pattern of an area, the foreground color of an area, and the background color of an area.

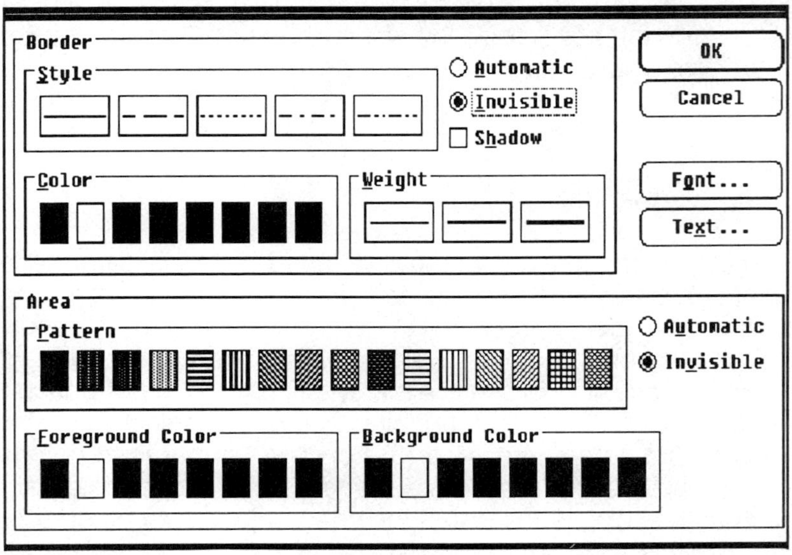

Figure 4-13 The Format Patterns dialog box

4-3-2 Format Text command

This command allows you to adjust the alignment of text placed on a chart. As shown by **Figure 4-14**, you can control horizontal and vertical text alignment, change horizontal text to vertical text, restore edited text, and make a border fit exactly around text, no matter how the text is changed.

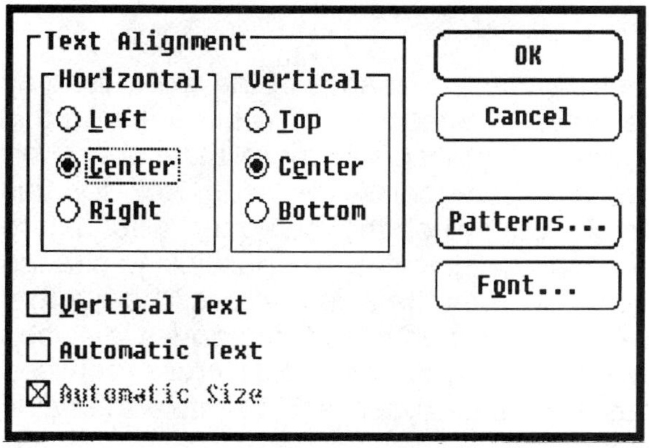

Figure 4-14 The Format Text dialog box

4-3-3 Format Font command

This command is similar to the Format Patterns command---it allows you to perform a variety of changes to text on a chart (see **Figure 4-15**). The Font box permits you to change the type of font, the size of the font (the Promotional Edition of Microsoft Excel does not support this function), and the type style, including such options as bold, italic. Click on Printer Fonts

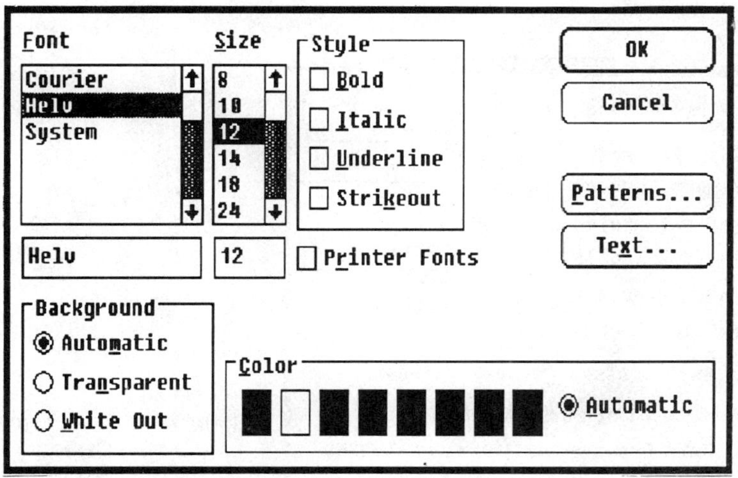

Figure 4-15 The Format Font dialog box

to determine which fonts are supported by your computer printer. Click off Printer Fonts to determine which fonts are supported by your display monitor. The Background box allows you to change the appearance of area behind the text and the color of the text. Set to Automatic color, the text will always print black.

4-3-4 Format Scale command

The Format Scale command controls the appearance of the axes, the way axes cross each other, and the order of categories or values. Using this command thus allows you to show information in more than one chart quadrant. **Figure 4-16** shows the Category Axis dialog box for this command. This box appears if you select the category axis before choosing the Format Scale command. As indicated, it is possible to change the number of the category where you want the axis to cross, the number of categories between tick labels and the number of categories between tick marks. It is even possible to have the value axis cross between categories, to present categories in reverse order, and to make the value axis cross over on the last category.

The Value Axis dialog box (see **Figure 4-17**) appears when you select the value axis before choosing Format Scale. As shown, this options permits you to alter the values computed automatically by Microsoft Excel. For example, you can set the maximum value in the series, the minimum value, the distance between major and minor tick marks, and where the category axis should cross. You can also turn on a logarithmic scale, display values in reverse order, and when working with scatter charts make the value axis cross the category axis at the last category.

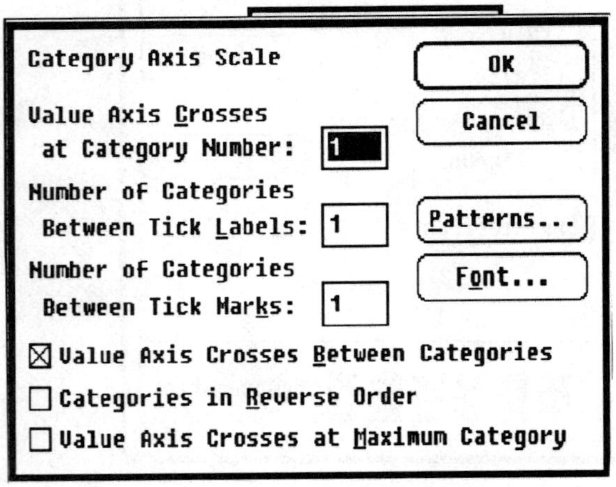

Figure 4-16 The Format Scale Category Axis dialog box

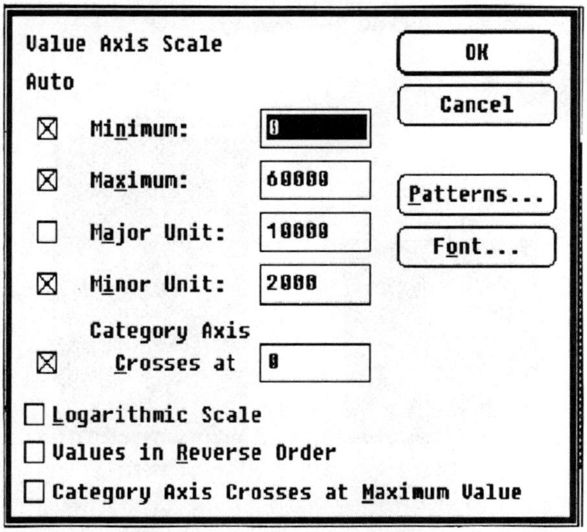

Figure 4-17 The Format Scale Value Axis dialog box

4-3-5 Format Move command

This command permits you to move a chart object with the keyboard. If your computer has a mouse, an object can be moved directly.

4-3-6 Format Size command

The command to complement the Move command is the Size command. It allows you to size a chart object with the keyboard.

EXERCISE 4-4
Adding and changing chart text

For this exercise use TOYS.XLS once again. **Figure 4-18** shows the chart you are asked to create. You are asked to add a title to the chart, to add labels to the axes, to add data-point values to each series marker, to change area and background colors, and to change the font size of the chart title.

1. Open worksheet TOYS.XLS.

2. Select the range B1:E2.

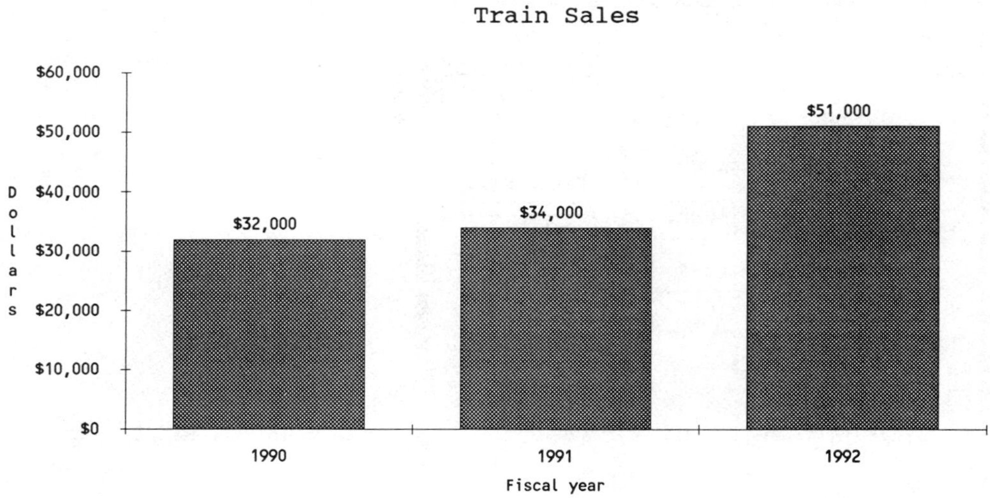

Figure 4-18 TRAIN1, the preliminary three-year sales chart

3. Select **F**ile and drag to **N**ew (ALT+f and press n).
4. Click on **C**hart (ALT+c).
5. Click on OK (press ENTER) to display Chart 1.
6. Select **C**hart and drag to Attach **T**ext (ALT+c and press t).
7. Click on Chart Title and click on OK (press ENTER).
8. Type *Train Sales* and press ENTER.
9. Select **C**hart and drag to Attach **T**ext (ALT+c and press t).
10. Click on **V**alue Axis and click on OK (ALT+v and press ENTER).
11. Type *Dollars*, and press ENTER.
12. Select **C**hart and drag to Attach **T**ext (ALT+c and press t).
13. Click on **C**ategory axis and click on OK (ALT+c and press ENTER).
14. Type *Fiscal year*, and press ENTER.
15. Select **C**hart and drag to Attach **T**ext (ALT+c and press t).
16. Click on Series or **D**ata point (ALT+d).

17. Type *1* and press TAB.

18. Type *1* and click on OK (press ENTER).

19. Repeat steps 16 through 18, except type *2* for the Point number.

20. Repeat steps 16 through 18, except type *3* for the Point number.

21. Click on Dollars (press LEFT 4 times to move the set of the value axis label).

22. Select Forma**t** and drag to **T**ext (ALT+t and press t).

23. Click on the left-most **V**ertical Text and OK (ALT+v and press ENTER).

24. Click on the first column in the plot area (LEFT until the first column is highlighted).

25. Select Forma**t** and drag to **P**atterns (ALT+t and press p).

26. Click on the right-most Area **P**attern (NO. 16)---(ALT+p and press RIGHT until the last pattern is highlighted).

27. Click on the second column, select **E**dit and drag to **R**epeat Patterns (LEFT, ALT+e, and press r).

28. Click on the third column, select **E**dit and drag to **R**epeat Patterns (LEFT, ALT+e, and press r).

29. Click on $32,000, the first series marker (LEFT).

30. Select Forma**t** and drag to **T**ext (ALT+t and press t).

31. Click on **P**atterns (ALT+p).

32. With a color monitor, click on **B**ackground Color 8---the light-blue, right-most background color and click on OK (ALT+p, ALT+b, RIGHT, ENTER).

33. Click on $34,000, the second series marker (LEFT), select **E**dit and drag to **R**epeat Patterns (LEFT, ALT+e, and press r).

34. Click on $51,000, the third series marker (LEFT), select **E**dit and drag to **R**epeat Patterns (LEFT, ALT+e, and press r).

35. Click on the chart title, Train Sales.

36. Select Format and drag to Font (ALT+t and press t).

37. Click on **S**ize 12 and press ENTER (ALT+f, Alt+s, DOWN, ENTER).

38. Select **F**ile and drag to Save **A**s (ALT+f and press a). Call this new chart TRAIN1.

39. Exit or continue on with the next exercise.

Questions:
1. What action is required by you before you select a format command?
2. What is the main purpose of the Format Patterns command? The Format Text command? The Format Font command?
3. What happens after you select Area Color 16? Background Color 8?
4. Why is it helpful to change the font size?

4-4 Using Other Chart Commands

Besides adding text and formatting text, Microsoft Excel allows you to modify charts in other ways. For example, you can add text to a chart, add legends and arrows, size and move charts, change the appearance of a chart, and even overlay one chart on another.

4-4-1 Adding arrows to a chart

The *Chart Add Arrow command* is used to add an arrow to a chart. Once the arrow is placed on the screen, it can be moved and sized using the mouse. Moving an arrow with the keyboard requires two additional commands: the Format Move command and the Format Size command. The *Format Move command* allows you to move an arrow from one location to another. The *Format Size command* permits you to change the size of the arrow. In the exercise that follows you will be advised to use the keyboard for both the Format Move and the Format Size commands. While you can use the mouse to do both functions, it is often more difficult.

EXERCISE 4-5
Adding arrows to a chart

For this exercise use TRAIN1.XLC, the chart built for the last exercise. **Figure 4-19** shows how your revised chart should look. Besides adding

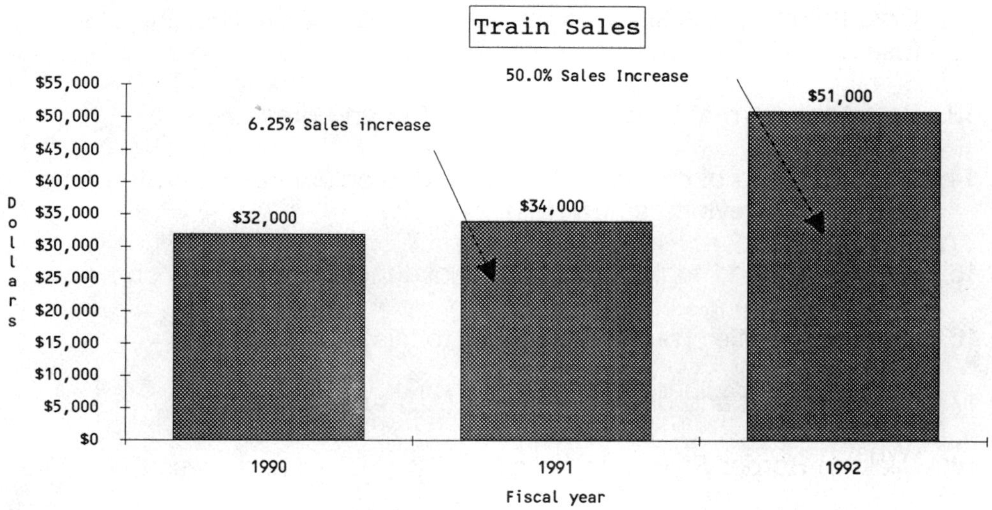

Figure 4-19 TRAIN2, the completed three-year sales chart

two arrows to the chart, you will be asked to add unattached text, change the vertical axis scale, and place a border around the title of the chart.

1. Open TOYS.XLS and TRAIN1.XLC.
2. With TRAIN1.XLC facing you, click on the document control icon and drag to Maximize (ALT+- and press x).
3. Activate the formula bar (press F2).
4. Type *6.25% Sales increase* and press ENTER. If you remove the title, replace it.
5. Select the Format Move command (ALT+t and press v).
6. Drag the text box to the position shown (use DIRECTION keys and press ENTER).
7. Activate the formula bar (press F2).
8. Type *50.0% Sales increase* and press ENTER.
9. Repeat steps 5 and 6 to move the text to the position illustrated.
10. Select Chart and drag to Add Arrow (ALT+c and press r).
11. Select the Format Move command (ALT+t and press v).

12. Drag the tail of the arrow to the text entitled '6.25% Sales increase' (use DIRECTION keys and press ENTER).

13. Select the Forma**t** Si**z**e command (ALT+t and press z).

14. Drag the head of the arrow to the second column as illustrated (use DIRECTION keys press ENTER).

15. Repeat steps 11 to 14 to size and move the second arrow shown.

16. Click on the title 'Train Sales' (LEFT to title).

17. Select Forma**t** and drag to **P**atterns (ALT+t and press p).

18. Click on Border **S**tyle 1 and click on OK (ALT+s and press ENTER).

19. Click on the vertical axis and press ENTER (LEFT to the vertical axis and press ENTER).

20. Select Forma**t** and drag to **S**cale (ALT+t and press s).

21. In the M**a**jor unit box click on 10000 (ALT+a and TAB).

22. Type *5000* and press ENTER.

23. Select **F**ile and drag to Save **A**s (ALT+f and press a). Call this new chart TRAIN2.

24. Exit or continue on with the next exercise.

Questions:
1. How does unattached text differ from attached text?
2. What is the value in placing a border around the title of a report?
3. Why does the vertical axis show the highest value to be $55,000 when TRAIN1 set the highest value at $60,000? How would you change TRAIN2 to set the highest value at $60,000?

4-4-2 Adding a legend to a chart

Adding a legend to a chart is done using the Chart Add Legend command. By selecting this command, Microsoft Excel automatically adds a legend to a chart. Once added, the Format Legend command becomes useful. The first step in using this command is to click on the legend. Following this, select the command to open the dialog box. As shown by **Figure 4-20**, the

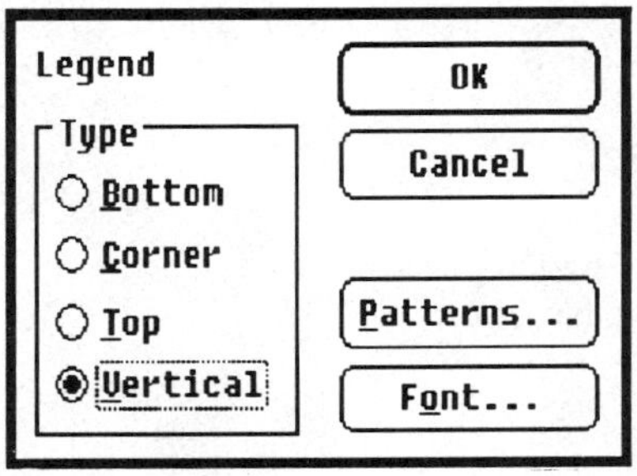

Figure 4-20 The Chart Add Legend dialog box

Format Legend command allows you to position the legend on the bottom, corner, top, or right-hand side (vertical) of the chart. When this command is active, the Format Font and Patterns command can also be selected. These options allow you to alter the appearance of the Legend box.

4-4-3 Adding gridlines to a chart

Besides a legend, gridlines can be added to the plot area of a chart using the Chart Gridlines command. The dialog box for this command (see **Figure 4-21**) controls whether you want gridlines added to the category and/or the value axes. You can also select between major and minor gridlines, where major gridlines conform to the tick marks on the chart. Like other parts of a chart, the appearance of gridlines can be altered using the Format Patterns command.

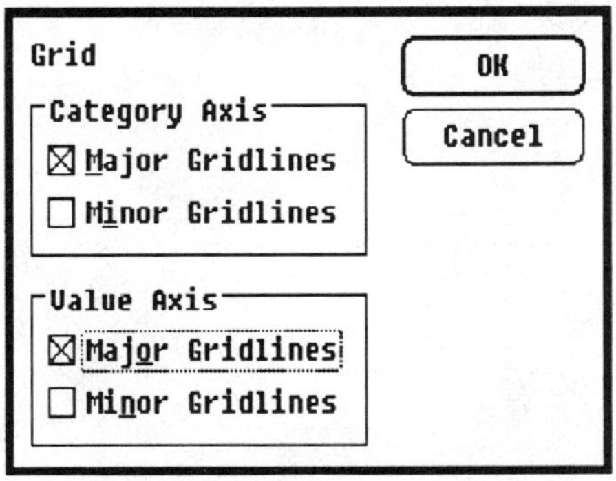

Figure 4-21 The Chart Gridlines dialog box

4-4-4 Changing chart axes

The *Chart Axes command* controls whether the category and value axes are visible. **Figure 4-22** illustrates the dialog box for this command. As indicated, the axes can be turned on or off for the main chart and any chart overlay.

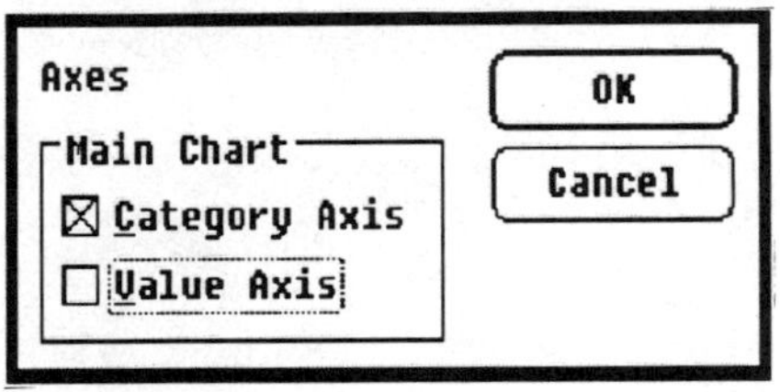

Figure 4-22 The Chart Axes dialog box

EXERCISE 4-6
Adding a legend and gridlines to a chart

For this exercise, use the TOYS.XLS worksheet once again. You are asked to make a product sales comparison (that is, a projected sales comparison) for all product lines. **Figure 4-23** illustrates how your chart should look when you complete this exercise.

1. Open TOYS.XLS.

2. Select the range B1:E5.

3. Select **F**ile and drag to **N**ew (ALT+f and press n).

4. Click on **C**hart and click on OK (ALT+c and press ENTER).

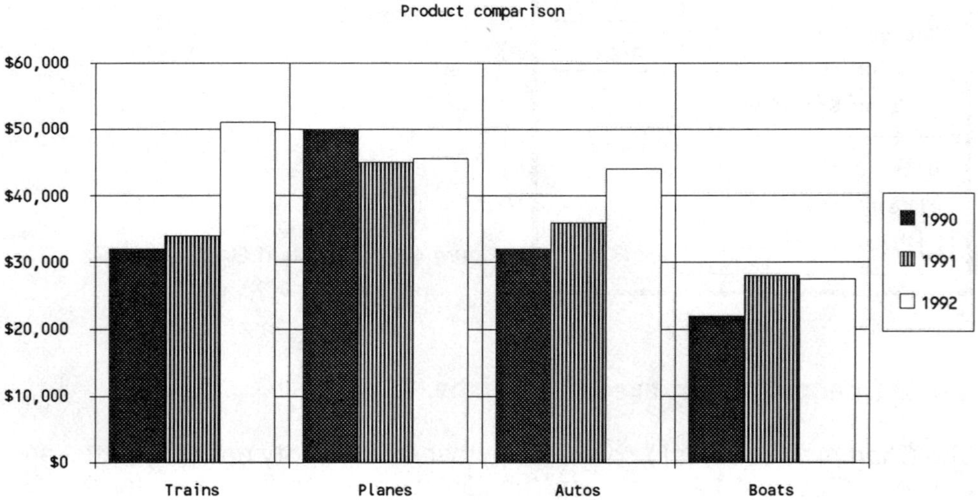

Figure 4-23 A product comparison chart with legend

5. Select **C**hart and drag to Add **L**egend (ALT+c and press l).

6. Click on the 1990 data series---the first column (LEFT until highlighted).

7. Select Forma**t** and drag to **P**atterns (ALT+t and press p).

8. Click on Area **P**attern 10 (ALT+p and RIGHT to 10).

9. Click on OK (press ENTER).

10. Click on the 1991 data series---the second column (RIGHT several times until highlighted).

11. Repeat steps 7, 8, and 9, but select pattern 5.

12. Click on the 1992 data series (RIGHT several times).

13. Click on **F**oreground Color 2 and press OK (ALT+f, RIGHT and press ENTER).

14. Select **C**hart and drag to **G**ridlines (ALT+c and press g).

15. For the category axis, click on **M**ajor Gridlines (ALT+m).

16. For the value axis, click on Maj**o**r Gridlines (ALT+o).

17. Click on OK (press ENTER).

18. Select **C**hart and drag to Attach **T**ext (ALT+c and press t).

19. Click on OK to change Chart **T**itle (press ENTER).

20. Type *Product comparison* and press ENTER.

21. Save this chart. Call it PRODUCT.XLC.

22. Select **F**ile and drag to **P**rint (ALT+f and press p).

23. Click on OK (press ENTER).

24. Exit at this time or begin work on the next exercise.

Questions:

1. What happens to the format box when a pattern is selected for a column?

2. What is the value in placing gridlines on a chart?
3. Why is a legend required for this chart? What can you conclude about using legends when designing charts?

EXERCISE 4-7
Changing the order of categories

The Format Scale command can be used to change the order of values on a chart. **Figure 4-24** shows the Product Comparison chart with the four categories placed in reverse order and the legend moved from the right-hand side to the bottom of the chart. Do the following:

1. Open TOYS.XLS and PRODUCT.XLC if they are closed.

2. Select the horizontal axis (LEFT until the horizontal axis is highlighted).

3. Select Forma**t** and drag to **S**cale (ALT+t and press s).

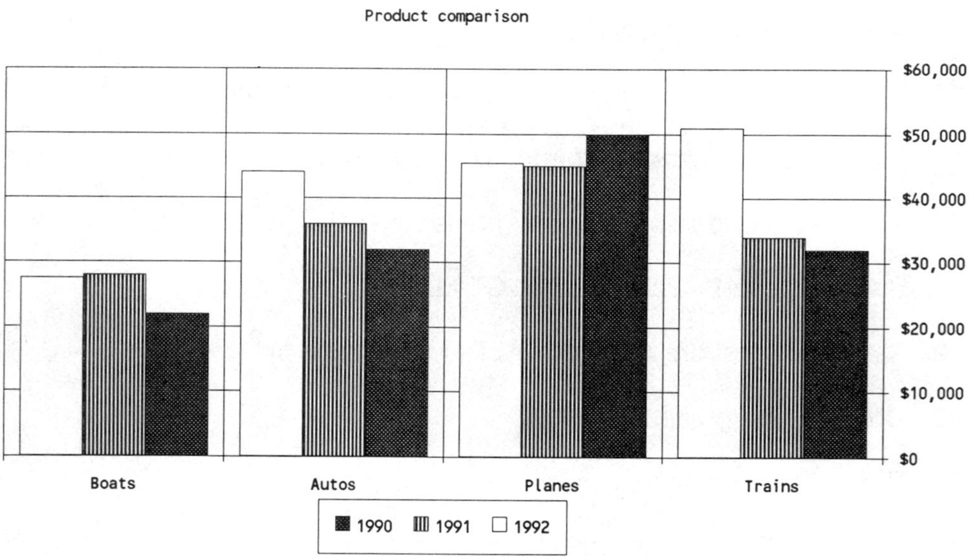

Figure 4-24 A product comparison chart with categories reversed

4. Click on Categories in **R**everse Order and click on OK (ALT+r and press ENTER).

5. Select the legend (LEFT until the legend box is highlighted).

6. Select Forma**t** and drag to **L**egend (ALT+t and press l).

7. Click on **B**ottom and click on OK (ALT+b and press ENTER).

8. Save this chart. Call it PRODUCT2.XLC.

9. Select **F**ile and drag to **P**rint (ALT+f and press p).

10. Click on OK (press ENTER).

11. Exit at this time or close PRODUCT2.XLC and begin work on the next exercise.

Questions:
1. What is the value in changing the layout of information appearing on a chart?
2. When the chart order is reversed how are the various categories altered?

4-5 Multiple Range Selection Charts

At times a single range selection on a worksheet will not provide the information needed for creating a chart. Instead, information from several parts of a worksheet (or from more than one worksheet) must be identified. Fortunately, Microsoft Excel will allow you to select non-adjacent cell ranges in order to create a chart. This procedure is known as *multiple range selection*---different parts of a worksheet form a range. With the mouse, a multiple range selection is done as follows: select the first range, press the CTRL key and hold it down when selecting the second range, and so on. With the keyboard, a multiple range selection is also quite easily done: select the first range, press SHIFT+F8 to tell Microsoft Excel that you wish to add another range segment, use DIRECTION keys to go to the next worksheet location, and select the second range.

Figure 4-25 illustrates how a multiple range selection looks when different range segments are identified. You are asked to define this multiple range in the next exercise.

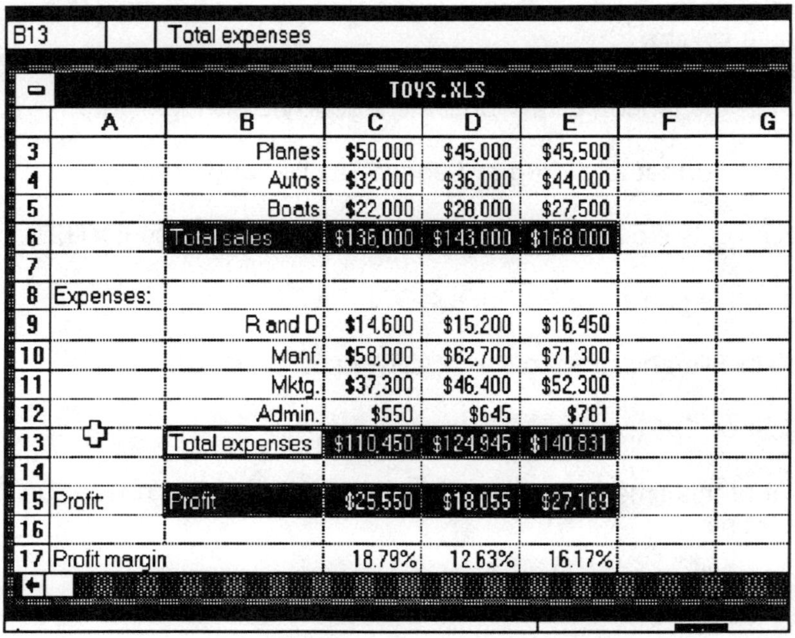

B13 | Total expenses

TOYS.XLS

	A	B	C	D	E	F	G
3		Planes	$50,000	$45,000	$45,500		
4		Autos	$32,000	$36,000	$44,000		
5		Boats	$22,000	$28,000	$27,500		
6		Total sales	$136,000	$143,000	$168,000		
7							
8	Expenses:						
9		R and D	$14,600	$15,200	$16,450		
10		Manf.	$58,000	$62,700	$71,300		
11		Mktg.	$37,300	$46,400	$52,300		
12		Admin.	$550	$645	$781		
13		Total expenses	$110,450	$124,945	$140,831		
14							
15	Profit	Profit	$25,550	$18,055	$27,169		
16							
17	Profit margin		18.79%	12.63%	16.17%		

Figure 4-25 Selecting multiple ranges on a worksheet

EXERCISE 4-8
Creating a chart from several worksheet areas

For this exercise use TOYS.XLS again. **Figure 4-26** shows the completed chart you will be asked to create.

1. Open TOYS.XLS.

2. In cell B15 type *Profit*

3. Select the range B6:E6 (SHIFT+RIGHT).

4. Press CTRL+select the range B15:E15 (SHIFT+F8, DIRECTION keys to B15, SHIFT+RIGHT).

5. Press CTRL+select the range B13:E13 (SHIFT+F8, DIRECTION keys to B13, SHIFT+RIGHT).

6. Select **F**ile and drag to **N**ew (ALT+f and press n).

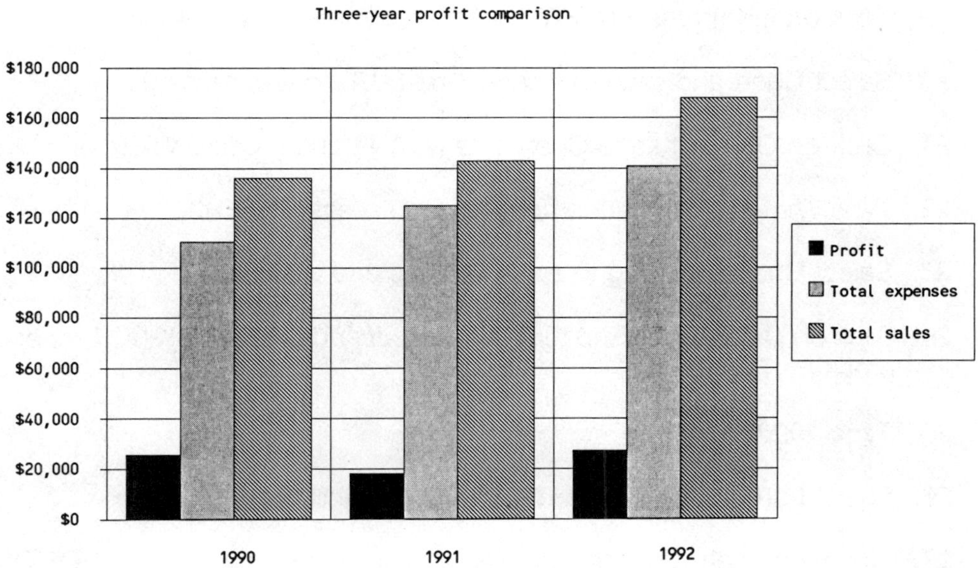

Figure 4-26 A three-year profit comparison chart

7. Click on **C**hart and click on OK (ALT+c and press ENTER).

8. Select **C**hart and drag to Add **L**egend (ALT+c and press l).

9. Click on the profit data series---the first column (LEFT until highlighted).

10. Select Forma**t** and drag to **P**atterns (ALT+t and press p).

11. Click on Area **P**attern 1 and click on OK (ALT+p and press ENTER).

12. Click on the Total expenses data series---the second column (RIGHT several times until highlighted).

13. Repeat steps 10 and 11 but select pattern 4.

14. Click on the Total sales data series (RIGHT several times).

15. Repeat steps 10 and 11 but select pattern 13.

16. Select **C**hart and drag to **G**ridlines (ALT+c and press g).

17. For the category axis, click on **M**ajor Gridlines (ALT+m).

18. For the value axis, click on Maj**o**r Gridlines (ALT+o).

19. Click on OK (press ENTER).

20. Select **C**hart and drag to Attach **T**ext (ALT+c and press t).

21. Click on OK to change Chart **T**itle (ALT+t and press ENTER).

22. Type *Three-year profit comparison* and press ENTER.

23. Select **C**hart and drag to A**x**es (ALT+c and press x).

24. Click on **C**ategory axis to turn this axis off and click on OK (ALT+c and press ENTER).

25. Type *1990*.

26. Select Forma**t** and drag to Mo**v**e (ALT+t and press v).

27. Move the unattached text between gridlines 1 and 2 (use DIRECTION keys).

28. Type *1991* and repeat steps 26 and 27 to position the text between gridlines 2 and 3.

29. Type *1992* and repeat steps 26 and 27 to position the text between gridlines 3 and 4.

30. Save this chart. Call it PROFIT.XLC.

31. Select **F**ile and drag to **P**rint (ALT+f and press p).

32. Click on OK (press ENTER).

33. Exit at this time or close PROFIT.XLC and begin work on the next exercise.

Questions:
1. Why is multiple range selection important when creating a chart?
2. Why would this type of chart be created by a business?

4-6 Creating an Overlay Chart

A combination chart changes the format of the active chart to a main chart and an overlay chart. The *overlay chart*, in this instance, is always placed over the main chart and is treated as a separate chart. In other words one chart is placed on top of another. The main value of an overlay chart is that it often helps in comparing two different types of data, such as sales this year compared to sales last year.

An overlay chart can be created in two ways. If the main chart has not been customized, the Gallery Combination command is the easiest way to create a main chart and an overlay chart. However, if the main chart has been customized, create the overlay chart using the Chart Add Overlay command. In either case, once an overlay chart has been built, it can be customized like any other chart using the Format Patterns, Font, and Overlay commands. These commands can be used to change the overlay chart, but not the main chart.

EXERCISE 4-9
Building a combination chart

For this exercise use TOYS.XLS once again. **Figure 4-27** shows the overlay chart you are asked to build.

1. Open TOYS.XLS.

2. Select the range B1:D5.

3. Select **F**ile and drag to **N**ew (ALT+f and press n).

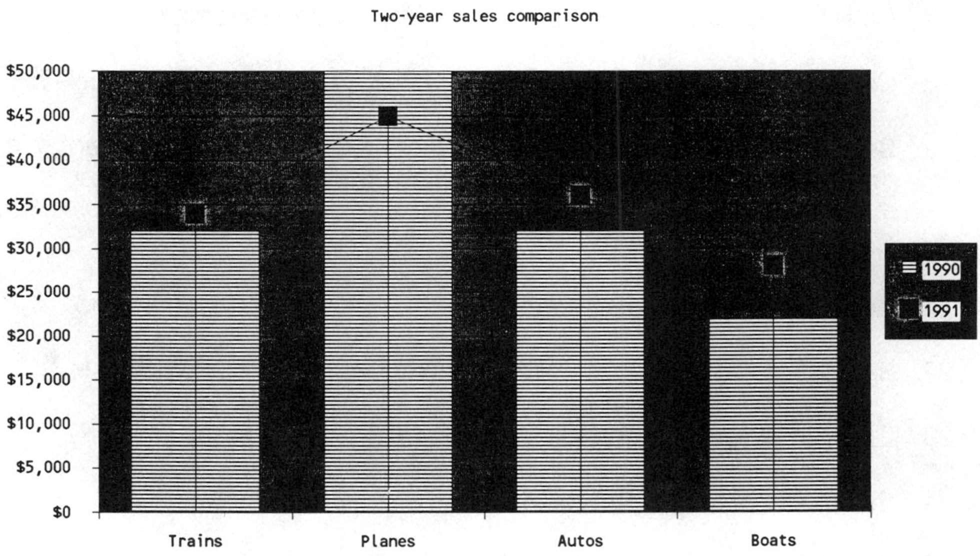

Figure 4-27 Adding a 1991 sales overlay to 1990 sales

4. Click on **C**hart and click on OK (ALT+c and press ENTER).

5. Select **C**hart and drag to Add **L**egend (ALT+c and press l).

6. Select **G**allery and drag to Co**m**bination (ALT+g and press m).

7. Click on OK to select format 1 (press ENTER).

8. Click on the first data point for 1991 (RIGHT to highlight).

9. Select Forma**t** and drag to **P**atterns (ALT+t and press p).

10. Click on **C**olor Black and the **B**ackground color Black and click on OK (ALT+c and press ENTER).

11. Click on the second data point for 1991 (RIGHT).

12. Select **E**dit and drag to Repeat **P**attern (ALT+e and press p).

13. Click on the third data point and repeat the pattern.

14. Click on the fourth data point and repeat the pattern.

15. Click on any chart white space (press ENTER).

16. Click on the first column for 1990 (RIGHT to highlight).

17. Select Forma**t** and drag to **P**atterns (ALT+t and press p).

18. Click on Area **P**attern 11 and click on OK (ALT+p and press ENTER).

19. Select the next column and drag **E**dit to Repeat **P**attern. Repeat this process to change the patterns of the remaining two columns.

20. Click on the legend box.

21. Repeat steps 17 and 18 to change the pattern of the legend box.

22. Select Forma**t** and drag to **O**verlay (ALT+t and press o).

23. Click on **D**rop lines and click on OK (ALT+d and press ENTER).

24. Select **C**hart and drag Plot **A**rea (ALT+c and press a).

25. Select Forma**t** and drag to **P**atterns (ALT+t and press p).

26. Click on Area **P**attern 2 and click on OK (ALT+p and press ENTER).

27. Select **C**hart and drag to **G**ridlines (ALT+c and press g).

28. For the Value Axis, click on Maj**o**r Gridlines and press ENTER (ALT+o and press ENTER).

29. Select **C**hart and drag to Attach **T**ext (ALT+c and press t).

30. Click on OK to change Chart **T**itle (press ENTER).

31. Type *Two-year sales comparison* and press ENTER.

32. Save this chart. Call it OVERLAY.XLC.

33. Select **F**ile and drag to **P**rint (ALT+f and press p).

34. Click on OK (press ENTER).

35. Exit at this time, saving changes to TOYS.XLS.

Questions:
1. Why is an overlay chart helpful when making sales comparisons?
2. What happens when you turn on drop lines?
3. What happens when you select Chart Plot Area?

4-7 Summary

This chapter was written to introduce you to the seven types of charts and the 44 chart formats provided by Microsoft Excel. By completing this chapter, you should be familiar with the nine Gallery commands, eight of the Chart commands, and eight of the special Format commands.

Creating a chart requires you to determine the values to be placed on the chart and, in many cases, the category and value axis names. Microsoft Excel uses these data to create a column-type chart. This chart type can be changed to an area chart, or to a bar, line, pie, scatter, or combination chart.

The column-type chart default can be changed by using Gallery Set Preferred---to redefine the default. Once this is done, the Gallery Preferred command changes the format of the chart you are working on to the default chart type.

Several terms are important when working with charts. These include the chart area, the plot area, the category axis, the value axis, tick marks, series markers, the chart title, and the chart legend. The ways in which you can customize charts include adding text, adding arrows, adding a legend, changing the chart axes, and adding a chart overlay.

Attached text corresponds to adding text to particular chart elements. Unattached text can be placed anywhere on the chart area. Once text is added, it can be customized using Format Patterns, Format Text, and Format Font commands.

Adding arrows to a chart requires the Chart Add Arrows command. The Format Move and Format Size commands are then used to position an arrow on a chart.

The Chart Add Legend command is needed to separate data series. Microsoft Excel determines the names of each series based on worksheet selections.

The Chart Axes command controls the axes of a chart. This command and the Format Scale command permit the axes of a chart to be customized.

Multiple range selections are important when chart information is located on different parts of a worksheet. This is one method of extracting information from various locations on a worksheet to create a chart for comparative purposes.

Creating an overlay chart is an excellent way of separating one data series from another. The Gallery Combination and the Chart Add Overlay commands can be used to plot an overlay on a chart.

KEY TERMS

Attached text
Category axis
Category names
Data series names
Multiple range selection
Overlay chart
Unattached text
Value axis

COMMAND REFERENCE

Chart Add Arrow: Chart menu. Adds an arrow to a chart. Default position is upper left corner.

Chart Add Legend: Chart menu. Adds a legend to your chart based on the category names. Default position is middle right.

Chart Add Overlay: Chart menu. Adds an overlay chart to the active chart. Useful in drawing comparisons for charts based on more than one data series.

Chart Attach Text: Chart Menu. Allows you to create titles, axes, and data series labels for your chart. After selecting the target element and command, you will see "buttons" surrounding the target element. At this point you enter and edit your text.

Chart Axes: Chart menu. Removes or adds category or value axes to your chart.

Chart Gridlines: Chart menu. Adds or deletes gridlines in a chart. Gridlines provide an excellent visual frame of reference when charts contain several data series.

Chart Select Chart: Chart menu. Selects the entire chart. Good for formatting and copying charts.

Chart Select Plot Area: Chart menu. Selects the plot area.

Format Font: Format menu. Specifies font type, size, and format for selected text including bold, underline, strikeout, and italic. Turns printer fonts off and on. You can also access the Format Patterns and Format Text commands format font dialog box.

Format Legend: Format menu. Controls location, pattern, and font of the legend.

Format Move: Format menu. Moves active arrows and unattached text in a chart. It will not move titles or legends.

Format Overlay: Format menu. Controls the overlay portion of an overlay chart. Specifies type of overlay chart (for example, pie, bar, and so on), format of overlay (for example, stacked, cluster, drop lines, hi-lo, angle of first pie slice, and size). Also controls data series of overlay.

Format Patterns: Format menu. Specifies format of selected chart elements including: border color, weight and type, area background, and foreground color and pattern.

Format Scale: Format menu. Formats active chart scale. Specifies minimum and maximum scale values, major and minor values, category axis crossing, and value order. You can access the Format Patterns and Format Text commands with this command.

Format Size: Format menu. Controls size of selected arrows.

Format Text: Format menu. Controls horizontal (left right center) or vertical text alignment (top bottom center).

Gallery Area: Gallery menu. Specifies one of five area chart types. Good for charting trends.

Gallery Bar: Gallery menu. Specifies one of seven bar chart types. Excellent for comparing single categories containing multiple values.

Gallery Column: Gallery menu. Specifies one of eight column chart types. Good for charting comparisons like sales figures.

Gallery Combination: Gallery menu. Specifies one of five combination chart types. Combination charts are excellent for comparing multiple categories with multiple data series. Especially useful when you want to draw distinction between different categories like sales versus costs.

Gallery Line: Gallery menu. Specifies one of eight line chart types. Line charts are the best chart type to graph trends especially those involving dates.

Gallery Pie: Gallery menu. Specifies one of the six pie chart types. Pie charts are useful for showing many categories with one data type.

Gallery Preferred: Gallery menu. Creates the chart you specified as preferred.

Gallery Scatter: Specifies one of five scatter chart types. Good for graphing statistical data like frequency and clustering.

Gallery Set Preferred: Sets current chart type as your default chart while window is active. Setting is lost when you exit Microsoft Excel.

ON YOUR OWN

1. A _______ is a graphic representation of data.
   a) worksheet
   b) file
   c) chart
   d) icon
   e) database

2. In figure 4-2, the chart labels 1,2,3 are examples of
   a) category names
   b) data names
   c) legend annotations
   d) chart titles
   e) sales figures

3. Which of the following is not a default chart type in Microsoft Excel?
   a) Pie
   b) Bar
   c) Combination
   d) Scatter
   e) Font

4. The ________ command is used to create a chart in Microsoft Excel.
   a) File Open
   b) Chart New
   c) Window New
   d) File New
   e) Window Hide

5. In figure 4-19, 6.25% Sales increase is an example of
   a) attached text
   b) a title
   c) a legend
   d) unattached text
   e) value axis

6. Which of the following two commands can be used to create an Overlay Chart?
   a) Gallery Combination, Chart Attach Text
   b) File New, Chart Attach Text
   c) Gallery Combination, Chart Add Overlay
   d) Chart Select Chart, Chart Add Overlay
   e) Chart Axes, Chart Attach Text

7. The _______ command is used to add a title to a chart.
   a) File New
   b) Chart Attach Text
   c) Chart Add Arrow
   d) Format Text
   e) Format Title

8. A _______ selection combines non-adjacent parts of a worksheet to form one cell range.
   a) multiple cell
   b) multiple range
   c) overlay range
   d) multiple overlay
   e) keyboard

9. The 1992 total sales bar in chart 4-26 refers to which cell in 4-25?
   a) C1
   b) B6
   c) D13
   d) E5
   e) E6

10. In figure 4-24, the _______ command was used to reverse the order of categories.
    a) Format Scale
    b) Format Categories
    c) Chart Add Overlay
    d) Chart Axes
    e) Format Text

MORE PRACTICE

I. Open STOCK.XLS and create a line chart that will show the rise and fall of the Dow Jones Average over time. Make the following format changes to your chart:
   1. Edit or add a title, *Dow Jones Average 1962-88*
   2. Shadow the title and change its font to Helvetica 12 Bold.
   3. Reverse the order of the categories.
   4. Move the category axis so it crosses at 1500.
   5. Save your chart as DJA.XLC.

   Answer the following:
   a) After you moved the category axis, how many years were above 1500?
   b) What command did you use to reverse the order of the categories?

II. Open EAST3.XLS and create a chart as follows:
   1. Use the multiple selection technique you learned in this chapter to create a chart that compares total sales to total expenses for all years.
   2. Use Gallery Combination to add an overlay to your chart.
   3. Add a legend.
   4. Add a title, *Sales vs. Expenses*
   5. Save your chart as SALESEXP.XLC

   Answer the following:
   a) What ranges did you select to create your chart?
   b) Which year had expenses greater than sales?

III. Open DEPR.XLS and make the following changes:

1. Use a multiple selection to create a pie chart that compares sum of years' depreciation for each year.
2. Add a legend.
3. Add a title *Sum of Years' Depreciation*
4. Use Format Main Chart to change the angle of the first pie slice to 30.
5. Add an arrow that points to the largest slice.
6. Add unattached text that explains your arrow. Add: *Depreciation greatest in year 10*
7. Save your chart as DEPRCHR.XLC.

Answer the following:

a) What command did you use to move your arrow?
b) What command did you use to annotate your arrow?

CHAPTER 5 - CREATING AND USING A DATABASE

Besides building worksheets and creating charts, Microsoft Excel can be used for creating and using a powerful database. As stated in the Getting Started section, a *database* is a collection of data organized in a special way. Its function is to store facts about a set of items, persons, or places. For example, a database can be used to store information about a coin collection (items), a class of students (persons), or the rivers in a state (places).

Once a database is created, it can be used for analysis. This is called a *database application*. An important application is asking questions about data stored in the database. For example, you might ask: "Which coins (in my set of coins) are dated 1909 and are in good condition?" Or, "Which students in my class received a score of 90 or more on the last exam?"

In this chapter you will learn how to create and use a database. When you complete the chapter you will be able to:

* Understand the terms essential to creating a database.

* Create a database.

* Add or modify the database using Data Form.

* Extract records from the database using an extract range.

* Use aggregate functions on extracted data.

* Build and use a one-input and a two-input data table.

5-1 Essential Terms

Figure 5-1 illustrates the difference between a database field, record, and range. A *field* (shown in bold and shaded) is a single fact about an item, a person, or a place, while a *record* is a set of facts about an item, a person, or a place. Since each field must be related to a record, it is sometimes called an attribute of a record. In Figure 5-1, there are 11 fields set aside for each student record. Besides personal information about the student, there are fields for scores on three labs, two exams, and a final exam. There is also a field for the student's total score in the class. A *database range* is the rectangular area of the worksheet that contains the names of all fields and all records defined for the database. The *Data Set Database command* is used to define the range of the database.

	A	B	C	D	E	F	G	H	I	J	K
1	Gradebook for MARSHA FAIRGRADER										
2											
3											
4	CLASS RECORD for Intro To Computing Applications -9/1/90										
5											
6	No	Student number	First Name	Last Name	Lab 1	Lab 2	Lab 3	Exam 1	Exam 2	Final	Total Score
7	1	17211	John	Stark	9	8		85			102
8	2	21414	Mavis	Rushmore	6	7		67			80
9	3	18845	Roger	Liu	9	9		91			109
10	4	20145	Susan	Lanza	6	7		94			107
11	5	22342	Patricia	Lang	8	5		70			83
12	6	22142	Susan	Liu	9	9		83			101

Figure 5-1 A sample database with 11 fields, beginning with NO.; 6 records, beginning with record 1; and the database range A7:K12

5-2 Creating the Database

A database can be created by adding, changing, or deleting fields and records directly---simply open the worksheet and make the changes, or by setting the range of the database and using the *Data Form command*. **Figure 5-2** shows the dialog box that opens when this command is selected. As indicated, all fields and the values assigned to each field for a single record are displayed when Data Form is used. The dialog box shows the number of records in the database and where you are at present (record 1 of 6). With the dialog box open, you can add a value to all boxed-in fields. An open field, such as the value displayed for Total Score, cannot

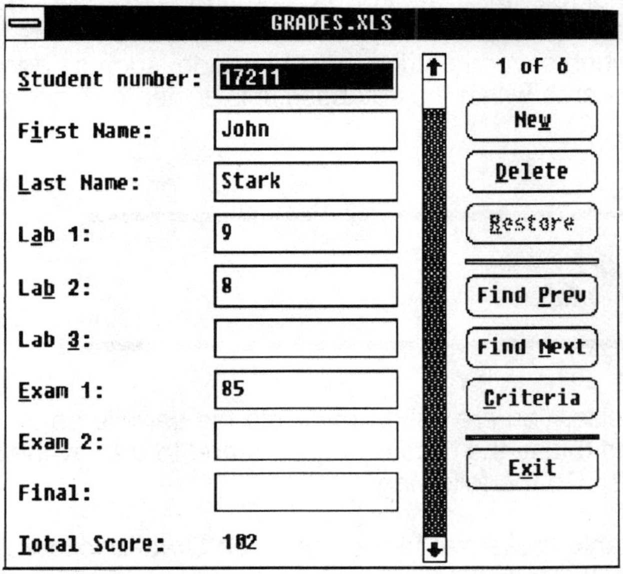

Figure 5-2 The Data Form dialog box

be modified. The seven command buttons on the right-hand side of the form are used as follows:

New permits you to add a new record to the database. If there are no blank records---none were defined within the database range---Microsoft Excel extends the range to include the new record.

Delete drops a record from the database and moves other records up to fill in the space. It does not change the database range.

Restore changes edited fields of a record to their state before the change was made.

Find Prev searches the database in a backwards direction.

Find Next searches the database in a forwards direction.

Criteria searches the database for a defined situation, such as students whose total score is greater than 100.

Exit returns you to the database.

Finally, the dialog box contains a scroll bar. This bar is used to move through a database quickly.

As a general rule, the Data Form command is used when a new record is to be added to the database, or when a single record is to be deleted. In contrast, when several entries must be made, such as adding a new lab score to all records within the database, it is easier to change the database directly.

EXERCISE 5-1
Creating a database

For this exercise, you are asked to create the sample database shown on Figure 5-1 and to use the Data Form command to display the record shown on Figure 5-2. Do the following:

1. With a blank worksheet facing you, type *Gradebook for MARSHA FAIRGRADER* in cell A1.

2. In cell A4 type *CLASS RECORD for Intro To Computing Applications - 9/1/90.*

3. In row 6 type the fields *No, Student number, First Name, Last Name, Lab1, Lab2, Lab3, Exam1, Exam2, Final*, and *Total Score*. After typing a field name, press RIGHT. After typing the last field name, press DOWN, followed by HOME.

4. Add the data shown in the range A7:H12 (see Figure 5-1).

5. In cell K7, type the formula *=SUM(E7:J7)*

6. Copy the formula to cells K8:K12.

7. To align the numbers in the database, use the Forma**t** **A**lignment command (ALT+t and press a) and click on **C**enter and click on OK (ALT+c and press ENTER).

8. Use the Forma**t** **C**olumn Width command to change the columns as follows: No. (width 4), Student number (width 15), First Name and Last Name (width 12), Lab 1, 2, and 3 (width 6), Exam 1, Exam 2, and Final (standard width), Total Score (width 12).

9. The lines under the database headings and the boxes for the database fields and records were drawn using the Forma**t** **B**order command and by selecting either **O**utline (ALT+o) or **B**ottom (ALT+b). You do not have to add these borders to complete this exercise.

10. Once the database is completed, select the range A6:K12. The field names must be included in this range.

11. Select **D**ata and drag to Set Data**b**ase (ALT+d and press b). This sets the database range, with no blank records.

12. Select **D**ata and drag to F**o**rm (ALT+d and press o). John Stark's record should be displayed (see Figure 5-2).

13. Click on **D**elete to remove John Stark's record (ALT+d).

14. Click on Cancel (TAB and ENTER). Otherwise, John Stark's record will be deleted from the database.

15. Experiment with the Find **P**rev and Find **N**ext commands. Experiment with the mouse and the DIRECTION keys. With the mouse, use the scroll bar to review all records in the database. With the keyboard, use UP and DOWN.

16. With John Stark's record facing you, type *7* for Lab **3** and press ENTER (ALT+3, type 7, and press ENTER).

17. Click on **Ex**it.

18. Select **F**ile and drag to Save **A**s (ALT+f and press a).

19. Name this new worksheet *GRADES*

20. Exit to end this exercise.

Questions:

1. What happens when you try to find record 7 in the database? The record previous to record 1?
2. What happens when you type 7 for John Stark and press Enter?
3. What happens to John Stark's record when you press Exit? What does this tell you about making changes to a record in the database?

EXERCISE 5-2
Finding selected records

For this exercise use GRADES.XLS, the database built for the last exercise. **Figure 5-3** shows the completed worksheet. You are asked to fill in all Lab 3 grades.

1. Open GRADES.XLS, if necessary.

2. Type in the Lab 3 grades as shown.

3. Select **D**ata and drag to F**o**rm (ALT+d and press o).

4. Click on **C**riteria (ALT+c).

	A	B	C	D	E	F	G	H	I	J	K
1	Gradebook for MARSHA FAIRGRADER										
2											
3											
4	CLASS RECORD for Intro To Computing Applications -9/1/90										
5											
6	No	Student number	First Name	Last Name	Lab 1	Lab 2	Lab 3	Exam 1	Exam 2	Final	Total Score
7	1	17211	John	Stark	9	8	7	85			109
8	2	21414	Mavis	Rushmore	6	7	1	67			81
9	3	18845	Roger	Liu	9	9	6	91			115
10	4	20145	Susan	Lanza	6	7	9	94			116
11	5	22342	Patricia	Lang	8	5	0	70			83
12	6	22142	Susan	Liu	9	9	6	83			107

Figure 5-3 GRADES2.XLS, the revised database

5. Click in the **T**otal Score box, type *>100*, and press ENTER (ALT+t, >100, and ENTER).

6. Click on Find **N**ext until you reach the end of the database.

7. Click on Find **P**rev until you reach the beginning of the database.

8. Click on **C**riteria (ALT+c).

9. Click in the Lab **3** box, type *>6*, and press ENTER (ALT+3, >6, and ENTER).

10. Click on Find **N**ext until you reach the end of the database.

11. Click on Find **P**rev until you reach the beginning of the database.

12. Click on E**x**it.

13. Select **F**ile and drag to Save **A**s (ALT+f and press a).

14. Name this new worksheet *GRADES2*.

Questions
1. How many students have total scores >100?
2. How many students have total scores >100 and a score >6 on lab 3?
3. What does this exercise tell you about Criteria?

EXERCISE 5-3
A chart based on database values

Besides using the criteria command button to answer specific questions, stored values can be analyzed by using charts. **Figure 5-4** illustrates the chart you are asked to create.

1. Open GRADES2.XLS if necessary.

2. Select the range D6:G12.

3. Select **F**ile and drag to **N**ew (ALT+f and press n).

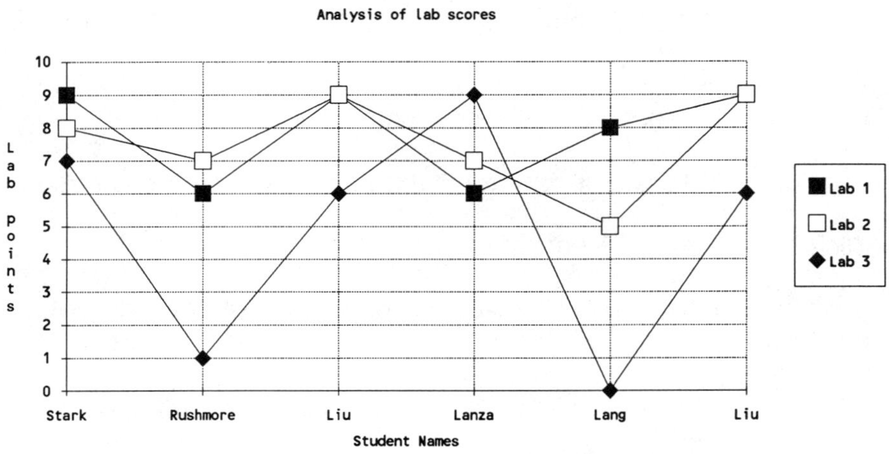

Figure 5-4 A line graph of lab scores

4. Click on **C**hart and click on OK (DOWN and press ENTER).

5. Select **C**hart and drag to Add **L**egend (ALT+c and press l).

6. Select **G**allery and drag to **L**ine (ALT+g and press l).

7. Click on format 4 and click on OK (RIGHT to 4 and press ENTER).

8. Select **C**hart an drag to Attach **T**ext (ALT+c and press t).

9. Click on OK to add Chart Title (press ENTER).

10. Type *Analysis of lab scores* and press ENTER.

11. Repeat steps 8 through 11 to add the **V**alue Axis title *Lab points* and the **C**ategory Axis title *Student Names*.

12. Click on "Lab points" (LEFT to highlight).

13. Select Forma**t** and drag to **T**ext (ALT+f and press t).

14. Click on **V**ertical Text and click on OK (ALT+v and press ENTER).

15. Click on the vertical axis, such as the number 9 (LEFT to highlight).

16. Select Forma**t** and drag to **S**cale (ALT+t and press s).

17. Type *10* for Ma**x**imum (ALT+x).

18. Type *1* for Major unit and click on OK (ALT+a and press ENTER).

19. Print this chart.

20. Save this chart. Call it *LABSCORE.XLC*.

Questions:
1. What does the line chart tell you about the scores for the three labs?
2. How does a chart simplify the analysis of stored database values?

5-3 Finding and Extracting Data from a Database

Once a database has been created, a *criteria range* can defined. This range is used to perform three important database functions: to find records of interest, to copy selected records to another area of the worksheet, and to delete records. Unlike the Data Form Criteria option, which is limited to findings records, the criteria range is more powerful. As shown in this section, this type of range permits the identification *and* extraction of records in a database that satisfy prescribed criteria.

5-3-1 Defining the criteria range

The *criteria range* is a small table placed on a worksheet that contains criteria names and test conditions. **Figure 5-5** shows such a table. The *criteria names*---Last Name, First Name, Final, Total Grade---are field names shown in shaded and in bold. These names must be identical to database names. The *test conditions* must begin with one of the six comparison operators (=,>,<,>=,<=, and <>). In Figure 5-5 these test conditions state: Find those students whose final exam score is less than 150 or those students whose total score is less than 300.

Once the names and test conditions are defined, the criteria range can be set. This range must have a minimum of two rows, one for the criteria names and one for the text condition. However, there can be more than two rows if more than one test condition is indicated.

Criteria Names

	Last Name	First Name	Final	Total Score
Criteria range			<150	
				<300

Figure 5-5 A criteria range

5-3-2 Using the criteria range to find records

Three commands are important in using the criteria range to simply find records: the Data Set Criteria command, the Formula Goto command, and the Data Find command. The *Data Set Criteria command* sets the criteria range. Microsoft Excel responds by calling this range *Criteria*. The *Formula Goto command* is used to go to the database or to the criteria range. This command is especially important for complex worksheets. It allows you to move quickly between the two. The *Data Find command* is used to find data that meet the test conditions, if test conditions are satisfied. For example, it might not be possible to find a student whose final exam score is greater than 150 and whose total score is less than 300.

EXERCISE 5-4
Creating and using the criteria range

For this exercise, complete the GRADE2 database by adding Exam 2 and Final scores to the worksheet. Following this, add a criteria range to the bottom of the worksheet. **Figure 5-6** illustrates the completed worksheet.

1. Open GRADES2.XLS.

2. In columns I and J add the Exam 2 and Final scores to the worksheet.

3. Click on cell D6.

	A	B	C	D	E	F	G	H	I	J	K
1	Gradebook for MARSHA FAIRGRADER										
2											
3											
4	CLASS RECORD for Intro To Computing Applications -9/1/90										
5											
6	No	Student number	First Name	Last Name	Lab 1	Lab 2	Lab 3	Exam 1	Exam 2	Final	Total Score
7	1	17211	John	Stark	9	8	7	85	72	186	367
8	2	21414	Mavis	Rushmore	6	7	1	67	60	156	297
9	3	18845	Roger	Liu	9	9	6	91	89	191	395
10	4	20145	Susan	Lanza	6	7	9	94	88	182	386
11	5	22342	Patricia	Lang	8	5	0	70	62	147	292
12	6	22142	Susan	Liu	9	9	6	83	75	167	349
13											
14											
15											
16		Last Name	Final	Total Score							
17			<150								
18				<300							
19											
20											
21											

Figure 5-6 A criteria range added to the GRADES2.XLS database

4. Select **E**dit and drag to **C**opy (ALT+e and press c).
5. Click on cell B16.
6. Select **E**dit and drag to **P**aste (ALT+e and press p).
7. Select the range J6:K6.
8. Copy and paste this range to cells C16:D16.
9. In cell D17 type *>350* and press ENTER.
10. Select the range B16:D17.
11. Select **D**ata and drag to Set **C**riteria (ALT+d and press c).
12. Select Fo**r**mula and drag to **G**oto (ALT+r and press g).
13. Click on database and click on OK (ALT+g, TAB, and press ENTER).
14. Select **D**ata and drag to **F**ind (ALT+d and press f).
15. Select **E**dit and drag to **R**epeat Find (ALT+e and press r or use arrow keys).
16. Continue to repeat step 15 until Microsoft Excel beeps. To escape from Find, press ESCAPE or drag Data to Exit Find.
17. Select Fo**r**mula and drag to **G**oto (ALT+r and press g).
18. Click on criteria and click on OK (ALT+g, DOWN, UP, and press ENTER).
19. In cell C17 type *<150* and press ENTER.
20. Delete >350 in cell D17.
21. In cell D18 type *<300* and press ENTER.
22. Select the range B16:D18.
23. Select **D**ata and drag to Set **C**riteria (ALT+d and press c).
24. Select Fo**r**mula and drag to **G**oto (ALT+r and press g).

25. Click on database and click on OK (ALT+g, TAB, and press ENTER).

26. Select **D**ata and drag to **F**ind (ALT+d and press f) and find the number of records that meet this condition. Exit Find.

27. Repeat steps 17 to 26 but type _="=L*"_ in cell B17. Define the criteria range as B16:B17. The asterisk after the letter L is called a wild string. It looks for all last names that begin with the letter L.

28. Save this revised worksheet. Call it *GRADES3*

Questions:
1. Why are copy and paste commands advised when building the criteria table?
2. How many records are found on your first search with Data Find? On the second search? On the third search?
3. What question does your first search ask? For example, find those students whose...(complete this question). What question does your second search ask? What question does your third search ask?
4. What happens if you do not delete >350 in cell D17 before you begin your second search? What question would you be asking if you forgot to delete this test condition?

5-3-3 Using the criteria range to extract records

Besides finding records one at a time using the Data Find command, the criteria range can be used to extract a set of records by using the *Data Extract command*. To extract records you must define the database range, a criteria range, and an extract range. Following this you can select the Data Extract command and decide if you want to extract all records or unique records that satisfy test conditions. By turning on the *Unique Records Only box* (see **Figure 5-7**), duplicate records are eliminated from the extracted list.

The *extract range* resembles a database range, with no values added under the field names. It can contain a single field name or all field names found defined for the database. The range should be large enough to include all extracted records. If the range is too small, Microsoft Excel will issue a message telling you that there are more records to fit.

Figure 5-7 The Data Extract dialog box

EXERCISE 5-5
Extracting grade records

For this exercise, use the GRADES3.XLS worksheet. **Figure 5-8** shows the records you are asked to extract. It also shows three different ranges: the database range, the criteria range, and the extract range.

1. Open GRADES3.XLS.

2. Click on column E and increase the Column Width to 12.

3. In cell C15, type *Criteria Range*

4. Revise the range as follows: type *Last Name* in B16, *First Name* in C16, *Final* in D16, and *Total Score* in E16.

5. Delete all values in cells B17:D17.

6. Select the range B16:E17 (see the shaded area on Figure 5-8). By placing no test conditions in the criteria range, *all* records in the database will be selected.

7. Select **D**ata and drag to Set **C**riteria (ALT+d and press c).

8. In cell C21 type *Extract Range.*

	A	B	C	D	E	F	G	H	I	J	K
1	Gradebook for MARSHA FAIRGRADER										
2											
3											
4	CLASS RECORD for Intro To Computing Applications -9/1/90										
5											
6	No	Student number	First Name	Last Name	Lab 1	Lab 2	Lab 3	Exam 1	Exam 2	Final	Total Score
7	1	172'1	John	Stark	9	8	7	85	72	186	367
8	2	214'4	Mavis	Rushmore	6	7	1	67	60	156	297
9	3	18845	Roger	Liu	9	9	6	91	89	191	395
10	4	20145	Susan	Lanza	6	7	9	94	88	182	386
11	5	22342	Patricia	Lang	8	5	0	70	62	147	292
12	6	22142	Susan	Liu	9	9	6	83	75	167	349
13											
14											
15			Criteria Range								
16		Last Name	First Name	Final	Total Score						
17											
18											
19											
20											
21			Extract Range								
22		Last Name	First Name	Final	Total Score						
23		Stark	John	186	367						
24		Rushmore	Mavis	156	297						
25		Liu	Roger	191	395						
26		Lanza	Susan	182	386						
27		Lang	Patricia	147	292						
28		Liu	Susan	167	349						

Figure 5-8 GRADES4.XLS, showing extracted records

9. Select the range B16:E16.
10. Select **E**dit and drag to **C**opy (ALT+e and press c).
11. Click on B22 (DIRECTION keys).
12. In cell B2, type *Final Grade Sheet*
13. Press ENTER.
14. Select the range B22:E27.
15. Select **D**ata and drag to **E**xtract (ALT+d and press e).
16. Click on OK (press ENTER).
17. When the message appears, click on OK again (press ENTER).
18. Select the range B22:E28.
19. Repeat steps 15 and 16.
20. Save this worksheet. Call it *GRADES4*
21. Select **F**ile and drag to **P**rint (ALT+f and press p).
22. Because the change in column width might extend the worksheet to span two pages, click on **F**rom (ALT+f and TAB).
23. Type *1*
24. Click on **T**o (TAB) and type *1* again.
25. Click on OK (press ENTER), to print the first page of the two-page worksheet.

Questions:
1. What message appears when the extract range is too small?
2. What is the value in being able to extract data from a database? Give more than one reason.

5-4 Sorting Data

The *Data Sort command* is used to change the sequence of records stored in the database or placed in an extract range. This command allows you

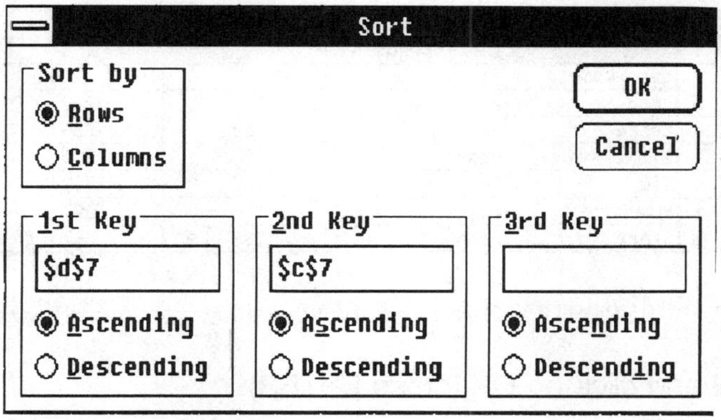

Figure 5-9 The Data Sort dialog box, showing 1st and 2nd sort key locations

to sort by rows or columns, using up to three sort keys. **Figure 5-9** shows the dialog box for this command. You are asked to indicate the direction of the sort and to indicate the value of the first, second, and third sort key. The first sort key must contain a value---the other two keys are optional.

EXERCISE 5-4
Sorting the extracted data by student name

For this exercise use GRADES4.XLS. **Figure 5-10** shows the grade sheet report before records are sorted. The records are copied from GRADES4 to this new worksheet. **Figure 5-11** shows the sorted listing of student grades.

1. With a blank worksheet facing you, select the columns A:D.

2. Select Forma**t** and drag to **C**olumn Width (ALT+t and press c).

	A	B	C	D
1		Grade Sheet		
2	Last Name	First Name	Final	Total Score
3	Stark	John	186	367
4	Rushmore	Mavis	156	297
5	Liu	Roger	191	395
6	Lanza	Susan	182	386
7	Lang	Patricia	147	292
8	Liu	Susan	167	349

Figure 5-10 REPORT1.XLS showing the worksheet before records are sorted

	A	B	C	D
1		Final Grade Sheet		
2	Last Name	First Name	Final	Total Score
3	Lang	Patricia	147	292
4	Lanza	Susan	182	386
5	Liu	Roger	191	395
6	Liu	Susan	167	349
7	Rushmore	Mavis	156	297
8	Stark	John	186	367

Figure 5-11 REPORT2.XLS showing the worksheet after records are sorted

3. Type *12* and click on OK (press ENTER).

4. Click on E1 to remove the range area (press RIGHT).

5. Open GRADES4.XLS.

6. Select **W**indow and drag to **A**rrange All (ALT+w and press a).

7. On GRADES4.XLS, select the range B21:E28.

8. Select **E**dit and drag to **C**opy (ALT+e and press c).

9. Click on cell A1 on the blank worksheet (ALT+w and press the sheet number).

10. Select **E**dit and drag to **P**aste (ALT+e and press p).

11. Important! Press ENTER.

12. In cell B2, type *Grade Sheet*

13. Add shading, as shown, if desired.

14. Select **F**ile and drag to Save **A**s (ALT+f and press a).

15. Call this new worksheet *REPORT1*

16. Click on GRADES4.XLS to activate this worksheet (ALT+w and press the number of GRADES4.XLS).

17. Select **F**ile and drag to **C**lose (ALT+f and press c). Do not save any changes to GRADES4.XLS.

18. With REPORT1.XLS facing you, click on the control icon and drag to Ma**x**imize. (ALT+- and press x).

19. Select the range A2:D8.

20. Select **D**ata and drag to **S**ort (ALT+d and press s).

21. Do not change the 1st key values.

22. Type *$B$2* for the **2**nd key (ALT+2 to type).

23. Click on OK (press ENTER) and note the problem.

24. Select **E**dit to **U**ndo Sort (ALT+e and press u).

25. Select the range A3:D8.

26. Do not change the 1st key values.

27. Type *$B$3* for the **2**nd key (ALT+2 to type).

28. Click on OK (press ENTER).

29. Save this worksheet. Call it *REPORT2*

Questions:
1. What happens when field names are placed in the sort range?
2. What purpose is served by the first sort key? By the second sort key?
3. What happens if the first sort key is $D$3 and the second and third sort keys are blank?

EXERCISE 5-5
Charting the sorted data

For this exercise use REPORT2.XLS. **Figure 5-12** shows the bar chart you are asked to design.

1. Open REPORT2.XLS if necessary.

2. Define the multiple range as A3:A8 and C2:D8.

3. Open a new chart.

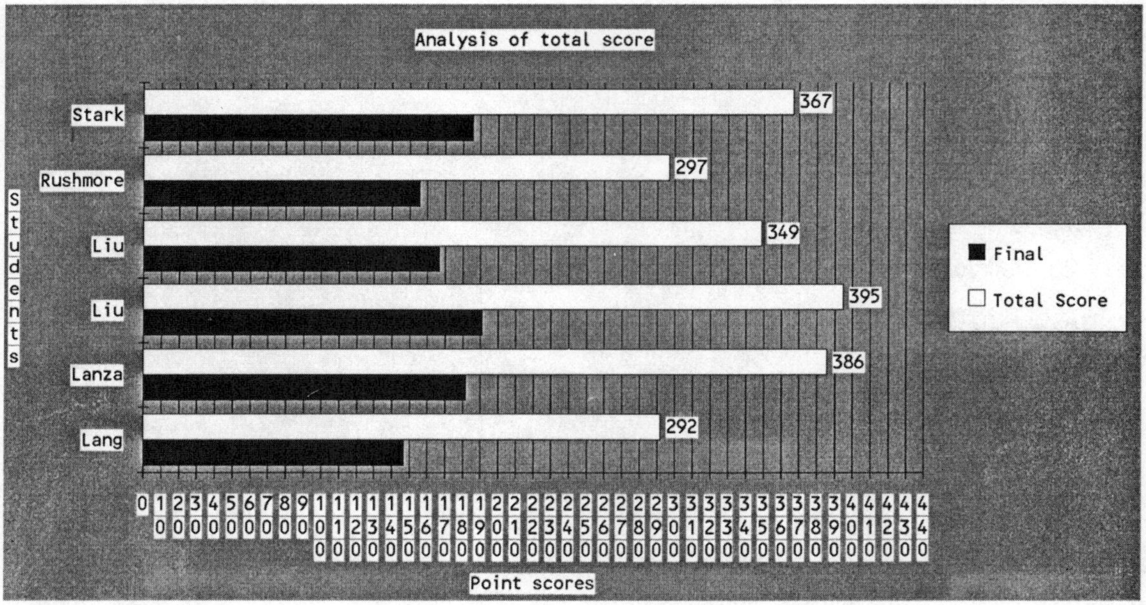

Figure 5-12 Bar chart of final and total scores

4. Select **C**hart and drag to Add **L**egend (ALT+c and press l).

5. Select **G**allary and drag to **B**ar (ALT+g and press b).

6. Click on format 6 and click on OK (RIGHT to 6 and press ENTER).

7. Select the **C**hart Attach **T**ext command to add the Chart **T**itle, *Analysis of total score*; the **V**alue Axis, *Point scores*; and the **C**ategory Axis, *Students*.

8. With Students highlighted (LEFT to highlight), select Forma**t** and drag to **T**ext (ALT+t and press t).

9. Click on **V**ertical Text and click on OK (ALT+v and press ENTER).

10. Click on the horizontal axis (LEFT to highlight).

11. Select Forma**t** and drag to **S**cale (ALT+t and press s).

12. For Ma**x**imum, type *440* (ALT+x, TAB to type).

13. For M**a**jor Unit (ALT+m), type *10* and press ENTER (TAB to type and press ENTER).

14. Select **C**hart and drag to Select **C**hart (ALT+c and press c).

15. Select Forma**t** and drag to **P**atterns (ALT+t and press p).

16. Click on Area **P**attern 2 and click on OK (ALT+p, RIGHT, and press ENTER).

17. Click on one of the Total Score bars on the chart (LEFT to highlight).

18. Select **C**hart and drag to Attach **T**ext (ALT+c and press t).

19. Click on **D**ata Point (ALT+d).

20. For the **S**eries number, type *2* and press TAB.

21. For the **P**oint, type *1* and click on OK (press ENTER).

22. Repeat steps 17 (if necessary) and 18 through 21 to add text to the remaining five data points.

23. Save this chart. Call it *Scores*

24. Print this chart. On many printers, it will take considerable time to print the finished chart.

Questions:
1. What is the first data series?
2. If REPORT1.XLS were used in place of REPORT2.XLS, how would the bar chart differ?

5-5 Using Aggregate Functions

Microsoft Excel provides eleven aggregate functions, designed especially for use with databases. Each function is used to analyze a set of data stored within the database, where the specifics of the analysis are determined by test criteria. A brief description of each function is as follows:

Function	Description
DAVERAGE	Averages values in a field column.
DCOUNT	Counts the cells that contain numbers in a field column.

DCOUNTA	Counts the cells that are not blank in a field column.
DMAX	Returns the largest number in a field column.
DMIN	Returns the smallest number in a field column.
DPRODUCT	Multiplies the values in a field column in the database that satisfy the criteria.
DSTDEV	Estimates the standard deviation of a population, based on a sample, using the values in a field column.
DSTDEVP	Estimates the standard deviation of a population based on the entire population, using the values in a field column.
DSUM	Adds the numbers in a field column.
DVAR	Estimates the variance of a population based on a sample, using a sample, based on the values stored in a field column.
DVARP	Estimates the variance of a population based on the entire population.

Each of these eleven functions contain three arguments: *database (name or range), field name*, and *criteria (name or range)*. For example, to find the average score of a population you would type:

=DAVERAGE(database, "Score", criteria), or
=DAVERAGE(database_range, "Score" ,criteria_range), as in
=DAVERAGE(A6:E55, "Score", A3:D3)

EXERCISE 5-6
Analyzing stored data

For this exercise, use REPORT2.XLS. **Figure 5-13** shows the worksheet with a criteria range added.

1. Open REPORT2.XLS, if necessary and maximize the screen size (if necessary) to make this worksheet easier to work with.

2. In cell B10, type *Criteria range*

	A	B	C	D
1	Final Grade Sheet			
2	Last Name	First Name	Final	Total Score
3	Lang	Patricia	147	292
4	Lanza	Susan	182	386
5	Liu	Roger	191	395
6	Liu	Susan	167	349
7	Rushmore	Mavis	156	297
8	Stark	John	186	367
9				
10	Criteria range			
11	Aggregate function		Final	Total Score
12	Average		171.50	347.67
13	Maximum		191	395
14	Minimum		147	292
15	Standard deviation		16.13	40.31
16	Count		6	6
17	Counta		6	6

Figure 5-13 The analysis of grades

3. In cells A11:A17, type *Aggregate function, Average, Maximum, Minimum, Standard deviation, Count*, and *Counta*.

4. Select the range C2:D2.

5. Select **E**dit and drag to **C**opy (ALT+e and press c).

6. Select cell C11.

7. Select **E**dit and drag to **P**aste (ALT+e and press p) and press ENTER.

8. Select A2:D8.

9. Select **D**ata and drag to Set Data**b**ase (ALT+d and press b).

10. Select C11:D17.

11. Select **D**ata and drag to Set **C**riteria (ALT+d and press c).

12. Click on cell C12.

13. Select Fo**r**mula and drag to Paste Func**t**ion (ALT+r and press t).

14. Click to Paste **A**rguments (ALT+a).

15. Scroll to DAVERAGE() and click on OK (DOWN and press ENTER).

16. Select Fo**r**mula and drag to **P**aste Name (ALT+r and press p).

17. Click on Database and click on OK (DOWN and ENTER).

18. In the formula bar, type after database *"final",C$3:C$8)*. The completed formula should read: =DAVERAGE(database,"final",C$3:C$8).

19. Select C12:C17.

20. Select **E**dit and drag to Fill Do**w**n (ALT+e and press w).

21. In cells C13:C17, edit to store the formulas
    =DMAX(Database,"final",C$3:C$8)
    =DMIN(Database,"final",C$3:C$8)
    =DSTDEVP(Database,"final",C$3:C$8)
    =COUNT(Database,"final",C$3:C$8)
    =COUNTA(Database,"final",C$3:C$8)

22. Select the range C12:D12.

23. Select **E**dit and drag to Fill Rig**h**t (ALT+e and press h).

24. In the formula bar, type after database *"final",D$3:D$8)*.

25. Select D12:D17.

26. Select **E**dit and drag to Fill Do**w**n (ALT+e and press w).

27. In cells D13:D17, edit to store the formulas
    =DMAX(Database,"final",D$3:D$8)
    =DMIN(Database,"final",D$3:D$8)
    =DSTDEVP(Database,"final",D$3:D$8)
    =COUNT(Database,"final",D$3:D$8)
    =COUNTA(Database,"final",D$3:D$8)

28. In cell C8, type *test* and note the change to Count and Counta. Restore by returning 186 to this cell.

29. Save this worksheet. Name it *ANALYSIS*

Questions:

1. Why must the criteria range be C$3:C$8, rather than C3:C8?
2. What is the difference between COUNT and COUNTA?
3. Why can the name "criteria" be pasted to a formula in place of the cell range?

5-6 Building One- and Two-input Tables

A special type of database is a *data table*. This type of table consists of a range of cells that shows the results of a formula. A common use of data tables is the creation of payment tables, where values change as the rate of interest varies, or as the term or the amount of the purchase varies.

A *one-input data table* is used to determine how changes in the value of one variable of a formula affect the overall result. A *two-input data table* is similar. This type of table makes changes to the value of two variables in a formula in order to examine the result.

Figure 5-14 illustrates a one-input table, while **Figure 5-15** illustrates a two-input table. In the first case, the value of the purchase is varied, when the interest rate and the term are held constant. In the second case, the value of the purchase and the interest rate are varied.

Both the Data Table command and the Data Series command are used in creating one- and two-input tables. The *Data Table command* is similar to the Data Set Database and the Data Set Criteria commands. This command is used to define the *data table range*. The range, itself, defines three things: the test condition (or formula), the set of test values, and the location to store test results. In Figure 5-14, the test formula is stored in cell C10 (not shown), the test values are stored in cells B11:B18, and the test results are stored in cells to the right of the test values, namely, C11:C18.

The test formula for the two illustrated data tables is *=ABS(PMT(rate, periods,present value))*, where ABS is the absolute value, PMT is the payment function, RATE is the monthly interest rate, PERIODS is the number of monthly payments, and PRESENT VALUE is the purchase cost.

	A	B	C	D
1	Car Payment Table			
2				
3	Purchase cost (in dollars)			0
4	Term (no of monthly payments)			48
5	Interest rate (yearly rate)			9.50%
6				
7				
8	Data		Monthly	
9	Table		Payments	
10			0	
11		11000	276.35	
12		11500	288.92	
13		12000	301.48	
14		12500	314.04	
15		13000	326.60	
16		13500	339.16	
17		14000	351.72	
18		14500	364.29	

Figure 5-14 A one-input table

	A	B	C	D	E	F	G	H
1	Car Payment Table							
2								
3	Purchase cost (in dollars)			0				
4	Term (no of monthly payments)			48				
5	Interest rate (yearly rate)			0.00%				
6								
7								
8	Data	Monthly						
9	Table	Payments						
10		0	9.00%	9.25%	9.50%	9.75%	10.00%	10.25%
11		11000	273.74	275.04	276.35	277.67	278.99	280.31
12		11500	286.18	287.55	288.92	290.29	291.67	293.05
13		12000	298.62	300.05	301.48	302.91	304.35	305.79
14		12500	311.06	312.55	314.04	315.53	317.03	318.54
15		13000	323.51	325.05	326.60	328.15	329.71	331.28
16		13500	335.95	337.55	339.16	340.78	342.39	344.02
17		14000	348.39	350.05	351.72	353.40	355.08	356.76
18		14500	360.83	362.56	364.29	366.02	367.76	369.50

Figure 5-15 A two-input table

The completed formula is: *=ABS(PMT(D5/12,D4,D3)*. This formula is stored to the right of the test values and above the cell where the first test result is to be stored.

Figure 5-16 illustrates the dialog box for the Data Table command. If the test results are to be placed in a column, as in Figure 5-14, only the Column Input Cell must be indicated. In our example, the entry is d3, the cell that stores the value of the purchase cost---since this is the value to be varied. If the test results are to be placed in a row and a column, as in Figure 5-15, both the Row Input Cell and the Column Input Cell must be indicated.

The two-input table is built in the same way as a one-input table except that two sets of test values must be specified: cells B11:B18 store the purchase cost values; cells C10:H10 store the interest rate values. The test formula is placed in cell B10. Likewise, a row and column cell input must be specified (see Figure 5-16). The results of processing are placed in a two-dimensional table, called an *array*. This differs from a one-input table where results are placed in a one-dimensional table, or a list.

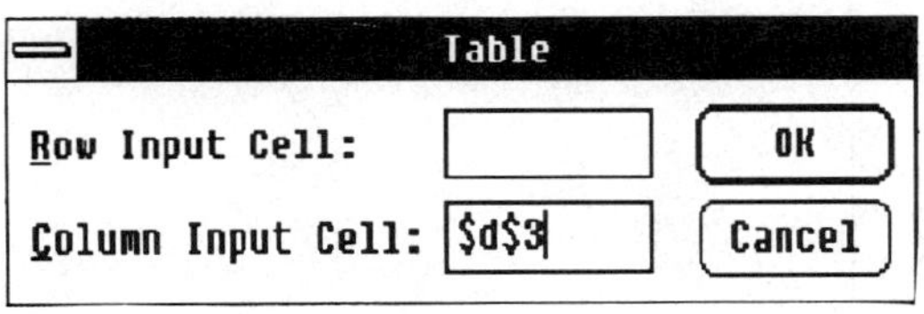

Figure 5-16 The Data Table Dialog box

EXERCISE 5-9
Building a one-input table

For this exercise, you are asked to build the one-input table shown on Figure 5-14.

1. Open a new worksheet.

2. Type the headings shown in cells A1:A9 and C8:C9.

3. In cell D3, type *0* (you will be asked to vary this value later in the exercise).

4. In cell D4, type *48*.

5. In cell D5, type *9.50%*.

6. Type *11000* in cell B11.

7. Define the range B11:B18.

8. Select **D**ata and drag to Se**r**ies (ALT+d and press r).

9. Type *500* for the **S**tep Value and click on OK (type and press ENTER).

10. In cell C10, type *=ABS(PMT(D5/12,D4,D3))*

11. Define the range B10:C18.

12. Select **D**ata and drag to **T**able (ALT+d and press t).

13. In the **C**olumn Input Cell, type *d3* and click on OK (ALT+c to type and press ENTER).

14. Define the range C10:C18.

15. Select Forma**t** and drag to **N**umber (ALT+t and press n).

16. Click on 0.00 and click on OK (DOWN and press ENTER).

17. Save this worksheet. Call it *ONEPUT*

18. In cell D3, type *11500*.

19. Exit at this time, or continue to the next exercise. Do not save these last changes.

Questions:
1. What happens after the Data Table command is selected?
2. What happens when 11500 is typed in cell D3?
3. What is the value of a table such as this one?

EXERCISE 5-10
Building a two-input table

For this exercise build the two-input table shown on Figure 5-15.

1. Open ONEPUT.XLS, if necessary.

2. In cell D5, type *0.00%*

3. Cut and Paste to move monthly payments from cells C8:C9 to cells B8:B9.

4. Select the range C11:C18.

5. Select **E**dit and drag to Cl**e**ar (ALT+e and press e).

6. Cut and Paste to move the PMT formula stored in cell C10 to cell B10.

7. In cell C10, type *9.00%*

8. Define the range C10:H10.

9. Select **D**ata and drag to Se**r**ies (ALT+d and press r).

10. Type *0.0025* for the **S**tep Value and click on OK (type and press ENTER).

11. Define the range B10:H18.

12. Select **D**ata and drag to **T**able (ALT+d and press t).

13. In the **R**ow Input Cell, type *d5* and click on OK.

14. In the **C**olumn Input Cell, type *d3* and click on OK (TAB to type and press ENTER).

15. Define the range C11:H18.

16. Select Forma**t** and drag to **N**umber (ALT+t and press n).

17. Click on 0.00 and click on OK (DOWN and press ENTER).

18. Save this worksheet. Call it *TWOPUT*

19. In cell D3, type *11500*

20. In cell D5, type *9.75%*

21. Exit at this time. Do not save these last changes.

Questions:
1. What happens after the Data Table command is selected this time?
2. What happens after the values of the two variables are entered?
3. What is the value of a table such as this one?

5-7 Summary

This chapter is designed to acquaint you with nine Data commands and how they are used in the building of a database and database applications.

Creating a database can be done in two ways: By defining fields and typing in records, one after another; or by defining fields and using the Data Form to add, delete, or modify a database record. As a general rule, the Data Form is advised whenever a single record is to be processed.

Once the database is complete, the database range is set by the Data Set Database command. Both field names and records in the database must be included in the database range.

Criteria, consisting of test conditions, are used with the Data Find command to locate records in the database. Criteria are placed within a criteria range and are set using the Data Set Criteria command. A second possibility is to use Data Form to specify criteria and find records.

Stored records can be found by using the Find options on the Data Form or by using the Data Find command. With Data Form a sequential search of the database can be performed.

Records can be extracted from a database using the Data Extract command. Extracting data requires the setting of the database range, the criteria range, and the extract range---a range for storing the fields of records that satisfy test conditions.

Records in a database or in an extract range can be sorted using the Data Sort command. This command leads to an ordered listing of fields of records.

Records stored in a database can be analyzed using charts to plot stored values or by employing one of the 11 built in database aggregate functions. A database function always begins with the letter D, as in DAVERAGE.

A special type of database is a data table. A one-input data table provides a list of results to show how values change when one variable in a formula is permitted to vary. A two-input data table provides an array of results. This array shows how values change when two values in a formula are permitted to vary.

KEY TERMS

Aggregate function
Array
Criteria
Criteria range
Data table range
Database
Database application
Database range
Extract range
One-input data table
Two-input data table

COMMAND REFERENCE

Data Delete: Data menu. Deletes active database record.

Data Extract: Data menu. Copies matching records from the database to a specified extract range. All data extracts must include a database table, criteria range and extract range.

Data Find: Data menu. Finds records meeting the specified criteria and locates them in the database. Use ESC to exit Data Find.

Data Form: Data menu. Allows you to edit and search your database for specified criteria through a user-friendly form that contains all the fields in your database.

Data Series: Data menu. Creates numerical series, for example, 1, 2, 3, 4, 5, and 6. You must select the location of series, then specify series type, step and stop values.

Data Set Criteria: Data menu. Sets criteria to query your database. Can search for numerical relations like >100, text like ="=hunt" or wildcards like ="=L*".

Data Set Database: Data menu. Defines the database. The first command step in all database applications.

Data Sort: Data menu. Sorts the database according to defined criteria. Can sort up to three different keys.

Data Table: Data menu. Defines a cell range as a data table. First enter the necessary formulas and variables, then select the cell range and use Data Table to define the table. Table ranges cannot be copied.

ON YOUR OWN

1. In figure 5-1 the entry in cell C6 is a database _______.
   a) record
   b) field
   c) application
   d) column
   e) number

2. The _______ command is used to define the range of a database.
   a) Data Set Criteria
   b) Data Series
   c) Data Set Database
   d) Data Form
   e) Data Find

3. Names in a criteria range must be
   a) entered in bold
   b) entered using the Formula GoTo command
   c) identical to record names in the database
   d) identical to field names in the database
   e) test conditions

4. To extract records using the Data Extract command, you must define which three ranges?
   a) database, criteria, test conditions
   b) criteria, formula names, application range
   c) database, criteria, extract
   d) extract, data find, data set database
   e) cell, worksheet, database

5. In figure 5-6, if the criteria range contained >185 in cell C17 and >350 in cell D18, which students would be extracted?
   a) John Stark, Roger Liu, Susan Lanza
   b) John Stark, Roger Liu, Susan Lanza, Susan Liu
   c) John Stark
   d) John Stark, Roger Liu
   e) Roger Liu

6. The _______ command is used to change the sequence of records stored in a database or extract range.
   a) Data Order
   b) Data Series
   c) Data Arrange
   d) Data Find
   e) Data Sort

7. A data table range defines which of the following three items?
   a) test condition or formula, interest payments, database
   b) test condition or formula, test values, location for results
   c) formula, values, cells
   d) one-input, two-input, sort key
   e) test values, location for results, sort key

8. The formula =Count(Database,"name",H$2:H$9) means
   a) Count the number of cells in the database with the entry "name."
   b) Count the number of entries in the field name, "name" by looking in the cell range H2:H9.
   c) Count the number of entries in the field name, "name" and put the answer in cell range H2:H9.
   d) Count the number of names in the database.
   e) Count the number of names in cell range H2:H9.

9. A two-dimensional table is called a(n)
   a) double input table
   b) data table
   c) application
   d) array
   e) field

10. In the two input table in figure 5-15, the two variables are
   a) input and output
   b) purchase cost and monthly payment
   c) interest rate and purchase cost
   d) term and purchase cost
   e) term and interest rate

MORE PRACTICE

I. Open GRADES4.XLS and make the following changes:
1. Insert two rows between 13 and 14.
2. Add two new student records(remember to give them numbers):

   35462, Kevin Johnson, 8,8,7,79,85,187,369
   22156, Dennis Hogan, 7,7,5,83,81,190,383

3. Clear cells B23:E28.
4. Query the database to extract all students with final scores greater than 180.
5. Print your database using your name as a header.
6. Do not save changes.

Answer the following:
a) Which students were extracted?
b) Did you have to redefine the database? Why or why not?

II. Open TWOPUT.XLS and make the following changes:
1. Delete A8 and A9.
2. Cut and paste the cell range B8:H18 to A8:G18.
3. Enter 5.00% in cell B10, select the cell range B10:I10 and use Data Series to add the new column headings for your revised table.
4. Select A10:I18 and redefine your table using the Data Table command. (Hint: D5 and D3 are your row and column inputs).
5. Format the cell range H11:H18 as 0.00.
6. Save your new table as *TWOPUT2.XLS*

Answer the following:
a) What is the monthly payment for a $12,000 car at 6.00% interest?
b) What row input cell did you enter in the data table command?

III. You have recently inherited $1000.00 from your little known but highly appreciated Aunt Clara. With the rampant changes in computers, you decide there may be some investment opportunities in technology stocks. Create a database using the following information and make the queries noted.

1. Enter and center the following as Field Names (in order left to right):
   Exchange (the stock exchange selling the stock, O for Over the Counter or N for New York)
   Name (company name)
   Symbol (company symbol)
   Div (Dividend paid)

Yield (Yield)
P/E (Price/Earning ratio)
Recent Price (Latest closing price)
Sales Vol (Recent daily sales volume)

2. Enter the following data:
   Stocks:
   O,Samna,SMNA,0,0,0,4.675,542
   O,Oracle Systems,ORCL,0,0,38,24.675,15194
   O,Microsoft,MSFT,0,0,24,77.75,9407
   O,Lotus Development,LOTS,0,0,27,30.675,7426
   O,Ashton-Tate,TATE,0,0,0,11.25,4367
   O,Adobe Systems,ADBE,.14,.8,12,16.75,1166
   N,Compaq,CPQ,0,0,13,100,26337
   N,AT&T,T,1.20,2.8,22,43.675,21081
   N,IBM,IBM,4.84,4.8,11,100.75,17059
   N,Hewlett-Packard,HWP,.42,.8,14,49.75,7613

3. Change column B and G to widths 18 and 12 respectively.
4. Add the title, "Technology Stock Analysis" to cell A1.
5. Sort your database alphabetically.
6. Set up a criteria range and extract range and extract all stocks with prices less than 45.
7. Save your database as *TECHSTOC.XLS*

Answer the following:

a) Were the stocks extracted in alphabetical order?
b) Which of the extracted stocks had the highest sales volume?

CHAPTER 6 - RECORDING AND RUNNING MACROS

With Microsoft Excel it is possible to write a set of instructions to tell or command Microsoft Excel to perform a specific action or set of actions. In this way, it is possible to automate frequently performed actions. Each set of instructions is called a *macro*. There are two kinds of macros, command macros and function macros. *Command macros* consists of a sequence of individual commands joined together. For example, a macro can be designed to compute a square root, to center text in a cell, or to center text in a cell and to place a border around the cell. *Function macros* are like worksheet functions. You can write a function macro to make a specialized calculation, such as transforming miles per gallon to kilometers per liter.

When you complete this chapter you will be able to:

* Record and run a command macro.

* Record and run a function macro.

* Edit a macro.

* Add a dialog box to a macro.

* Create macros to use as shortcut keys.

6-1 Recording and Running a Command Macro

Before you can run a command macro, you must create and name one, or open a macro stored on file. In Microsoft Excel, five macro commands are used with macros (see **Figure 6-1**). Besides these commands, all command macros must be named. Naming a macro can be done in two ways: by using the Formula Define Name command, or by letting Microsoft Excel name the macro for you.

```
Macro
-----------------
Record...
Run...
-----------------
Start Recorder
Set Recorder
Relative Record
```

Figure 6-1 The Macro drop-down menu

There is a long and a shortcut way of creating a macro. The long way requires the use of the Macro Set Recorder, Start Recorder, Stop Recorder, and Formula Define Names commands. The shortcut method uses the Macro Record command. In the next section, we explain the long way of creating a macro. This slower method allows you to determine step-by-step how a Macro is designed. The next section simplifies this process through use of the Macro Record command.

6-1-1 Using the Macro Set Recorder command

Creating a macro is called *recording*. Before a recording can take place, five steps are required for setup. These steps are as follows:

1. Open a worksheet, such as SHEET1.XLS.
2. Open a new or a saved macro sheet.
3. Activate the new macro sheet.
4. Select the cell or the cell range on the macro sheet that you wish to record on.
5. Select the *Macro Set Recorder command*.

Opening a new or a saved macro sheet is done in the same way as opening a worksheet or chart. For a new macro sheet, select File and drag to New. When the dialog box opens, click on the Macro Sheet selection (see **Figure 6-2**). For a saved macro sheet, select File and drag to Open. When the dialog box opens, scroll to the macro you want to open. A macro, unlike a worksheet or chart, ends with a .XLM extension. For example, a macro SQRT is saved as SQRT.XLM.

The selection of the cell or the cell range on the macro sheet means different things. If a single cell is selected, such as A1, and this cell is blank, the macro is recorded beginning in column A1. The next statement is recorded on A2, then A3, and so on, until the entire macro is recorded. When a macro exceeds the number of cells in column A, it begins recording in column B.

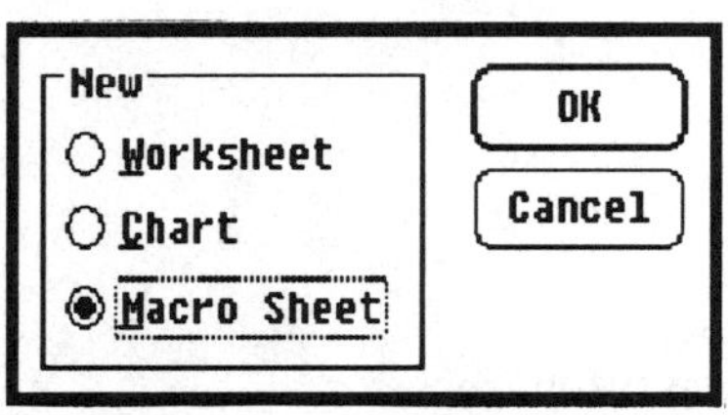

Figure 6-2 The File New dialog box showing a Macro Sheet selection

Once the range is set, the *Macro Set Recorder command* is selected. This command is similar to the Data Set Database and the Data Set Criteria commands. Once selected, Microsoft Excel knows where to start the recording.

6-1-2 Recording a command macro

Recording a macro also requires several steps. These are:

1. Go to the cell on the worksheet (not the macro sheet) where the recording is to begin.

2. Select the *Start Recorder command.*

3. Make the entries you want to record on the worksheet.

4. Select the *Stop Recorder command.*

The *Start Recorder command* "turns on" the recorder, much like an ordinary tape recorder. The status bar at the bottom of the screen will specify recording. The *Macro Stop Recorder command* "turns off" the recorder. This command replaces the Macro Record command on the drop-down menu.

EXERCISE 6-1
Creating a macro

In this exercise you are asked to create a macro that places the formula to compute a square root on a macro sheet. **Figure 6-3** illustrates the macro you are asked to record.

1. If necessary, select **F**ile and drag to **N**ew to open a new worksheet. Otherwise, begin with SHEET1.XLS.

2. Select **F**ile and drag to **N**ew once again (ALT+f and press n).

	A
1	SQRT macro
2	=FORMULA("The square root is")
3	=SELECT("R2C3")
4	=FORMULA("=SQRT(R[-1]C)")
5	=RETURN()

Figure 6-3 Square root macro sheet

3. Click on **M**acro Sheet and click on OK (ALT+m and press ENTER).

4. Click on column A.

5. Select Forma**t** and drag to **C**olumn Width (ALT+t and press c).

6. Type *20* and click on OK (press ENTER).

7. Select **W**indow and drag to **A**rrange All (ALT+w and press a).

8. Type *SQRT macro* in cell A1.

9. Click on A2.

10. Select **M**acro and drag to Se**t** Recorder (ALT+m and press t). This indicates where you want to begin the recording on the macro sheet.

11. Click to activate the new worksheet (ALT+w and press the worksheet number).

12. In cell A1 type, *The number is*

13. In cell C1, type *100*

14. Click on cell A2.

15. Select **M**acro and drag to **S**tart Recorder (ALT+m and press s). From this point on you will record the instructions you enter from the keyboard.

16. In cell A2 type, *The square root is* and press ENTER. This adds the following statement to the macro sheet: =FORMULA("The square root is").

17. Select cell C2. This adds the statement: =SELECT("R2C3") to the macro.

18. Select Fo**r**mula and drag to Pas**t**e Function (ALT+r and press t).

19. Click on Paste **A**rguments (ALT+a).

20. Scroll to SQRT() and click on OK (ALT+f, DOWN to SQRT() and press ENTER).

21. For the argument in the formula bar, type *C1* and press ENTER. Following this step, the statement =FORMULA("=SQRT(R[-1],C)") is added to the macro.

22. Select **M**acro and drag to Stop Rec**o**rder (ALT+m and press c). This stops the recording and adds =RETURN() to the macro sheet.

23. Click on the new macro (ALT+w and press the macro number).

24. Select **F**ile and drag to Save **A**s (ALT+f and press a).

25. Call this new macro *SQRT*

26. Exit or continue on with the next exercise.

Questions:
1. How is text saved on a macro sheet?
2. What is meant by =SELECT("R2C3")?
3. What statement is added to the macro sheet when the Macro Stop Recorder command is given?

6-1-3 Naming a macro

After a macro has been created, it must be named and saved. The *Formula Define Name command* is needed to name the macro. The procedure to use is as follows:

1. Activate the macro you have recorded.

2. Insert a new row at the top of the macro, if a name has to be assigned.

3. Type a name that best describes the recording. In the last exercise, a row was used to name the macro. The name typed was SQRT macro.

4. Select the Formula Define Name command. This command opens the dialog box shown on **Figure 6-4**.

5. Type the name of the macro if the displayed name is not the one you want. Otherwise, continue.

6. Click on Command if you are defining a command macro or Function if you are defining a function macro.

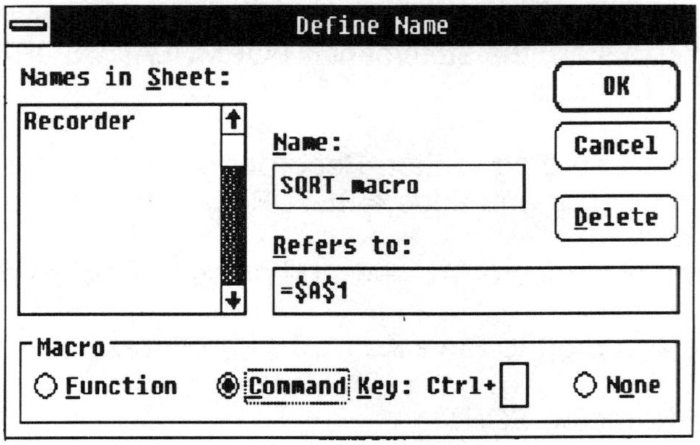

Figure 6-4 The Define Name dialog box

7. For a command macro, you can enter a single-letter shortcut key, such as the letter q.

8. Click on OK to define the new macro.

9. Save the new macro, using the File Save As or File Save command.

EXERCISE 6-2
Naming a macro

For this exercise you are asked to name SQRT.XLM, the macro created for the last exercise. Once named, you are asked to test your work.

1. Open SQRT.XLM, if necessary.

2. Click on A1.

3. Select Formula and drag to **D**efine Name (ALT+r and press d).

4. Keep the name SQRT_macro shown in the text box.

5. Click on **C**ommand (ALT+c).

6. For the shortcut key, type *q* in the **K**ey: Ctrl+ box (TAB to type).

7. Click on OK (press ENTER).

8. Select **F**ile and drag to **S**ave (ALT+f and press s).

9. Select **F**ile and drag to **C**lose (ALT+f and press c).

10. Open macro SQRT.XLM once again.

11. Select Formula and drag to **D**efine Name (ALT+r and press d).

12. Click on OK.

13. Exit at this time, or continue on to the next exercise, where you are asked to run the new macro.

Questions:

1. When you select the Formula Define Name the second time, what names appear in the Names in sheet box?
2. If you want to delete the name and start over with a new name, what procedure would you follow?

6-1-4 Running a macro

After a macro has been recorded and named, it can be run. The *Macro Run command* (or by using the CTRL+shortcut key combination) is used to run a macro. The procedure to follow in running a macro is as follows:

1. Open the macro(s) you wish to use.

2. To free space on the screen, a useful practice is to hide the macros from view.

3. Select the cell or cell range on the worksheet or chart where you intend to apply a macro.

4. Select the Macro Run command and choose the macro to run (or press the CTRL+shortcut key to run the macro).

Figure 6-5 shows the dialog box for the Macro Run command. In this illustration, the only macro available to run is SQRT.XLM, that is named SQRT_macro. The letter q appears at the beginning of this reference. This is the shortcut key.

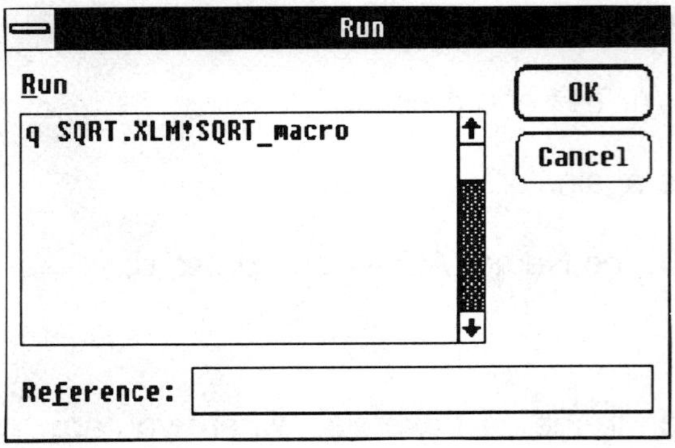

Figure 6-5 The Macro Run dialog box

EXERCISE 6-3
Running the stored macro

For this exercise you are asked to use the macro SQRT.XLM, created and saved by the last two exercises. **Figure 6-6** shows the worksheet you will be asked to build.

1. Open macro SQRT.XLM, if necessary.

2. With the macro sheet active, select **W**indow and drag to **H**ide (ALT+w and press h).

3. With a blank worksheet facing you, type in cell A1 *The number is*

4. In cell C1 type *166*

5. Click on cell A2.

6. Select **M**acro and drag to **R**un (ALT+m and press r).

7. When the dialog box opens, select SQRT_macro and click on OK (ALT+r, RIGHT, and press ENTER).

8. In cell A4 type *The number is*

	A	B	C
1	The number is		166
2	The square root is		12.8840987
3			
4	The number is		188

Figure 6-6 The first test of the macro

9. In cell C4 type *188*

10. Click on cell A5.

11. Repeat steps 6 and 7 and note the problem.

12. Select the range A2:C2.

13. Select **E**dit and drag to Cl**e**ar to clear the information in these cells (ALT+e and press DEL).

14. Click on cell A2.

15. Press CTRL+q.

16. Save this worksheet. Call it *TEST1*

17. Exit or continue on with the next exercise.

Questions:

1. What square root is computed when you run the macro from cell A5? Why does this happen? (Hint: review the macro code or read the next section first.)
2. Why is there an exclamation point in the name SQRT.XLM!SQRT_macro?

6-1-5 Editing a command macro

A macro can be edited just like a worksheet. This means that any macro formula can be added, changed, or deleted using the standard edit commands. Consider each of the formulas on your SQRT_macro sheet.

---

* *=FORMULA ("The square root is")*. This formula is used to place text or a constant in a cell. It could be edited to read *=FORMULA("The square of the number is")*.

* *=SELECT("R2C3")*. This formula is quite specific---it states, select the cell in row 2, column 3, using the row and column format. It can be edited to read, *=SELECT("RC3")*, which means the cell in column 3, but same row.

* *=FORMULA("=SQRT(R[-1]C)")*. This formula inserts the built-in function SQRT and the location of the argument for the function in a cell. It states:

compute the square root of the number stored one row above in the same column, where the row number is set by the previous select formula. This formula can be edited to read *=FORMULA("=SQRT(R[-2]C)")*, which means compute the square root of the number stored two rows above in the same column.

* *=RETURN( )*. This formula means return to the worksheet. All command macros end with this statement. With a command macro, the value of the return argument is set to null.

Working with a R1C1 reference style on a macro sheet and an A1 reference style on a worksheet can be (and often is) confusing. If you want to use only the R1C1 reference style, activate the worksheet and choose the Option Workspace command to open the workspace dialog box (see **Figure 6-7**). Click on R1C1, to changeover from A1 style to the R1C1 style. Observe that this command can be used for other functions as well. For example, it can be used to set a decimal place. If the Fixed Decimal is set to 2, the number type number 4567 will be displayed as 45.67. It can also be used to turn on or off the status bar, the scroll bars, and the formula bar. It can even be used to define a new ALT key combination.

EXERCISE 6-4
Editing the stored macro

For this exercise, use the macro SQRT.XLM and the worksheet TEST1.XLS once again. **Figure 6-8** shows how your revised macro should look when you complete this exercise; **Figure 6-9** shows the revised worksheet.

Figure 6-7 The Options Workspace dialog box

	1
1	SQRT macro2
2	=FORMULA("The square of the number is")
3	=SELECT("RC3")
4	=FORMULA("=SQRT(R[-2]C)")
5	=RETURN()

Figure 6-8 The final edited version

1. Open SQRT.XLM and TEST1.XLS, if necessary.
2. Arrange the screen to see both sheets. If SQRT.XLM is hidden, select Window Unhide.
3. Activate TEST1.XLS.
4. Click on column A (SHIFT+DOWN).
5. Select Forma**t** and drag to **C**olumn Width (ALT+t and press c).
6. Increase the column width to 17.
7. Activate SQRT.XLM.
8. In cell A1, edit to change the name to *SRQT_macro2*
9. In cell A2, edit to change the formula to *=FORMULA("The square of the number is")*
10. In cell A3, edit to change the formula to *=SELECT("RC3")*
11. Activate TEST1.XLS to conduct the first test of the revised macro.
12. Select cell A5.
13. Press the macro's shortcut keys: *CTRL+q*
14. Activate SQRT.XLM.

	1	2	3
1	The number is		166
2	The square root is		12.8840987
3			
4	The number is		188
5	The square of the number is		13.7113092
6			
7	The number is		144
8			
9	The square of the number is		12

Figure 6-9 The second test of the macro

15. In cell A4, edit to change the formula to *=FORMULA("=SQRT(R[-2]C)")*

16. Click on A1.

17. Select Formula and drag to **D**efine Name (ALT+r and press d).

18. Keep the name SQRT_macro2.

19. Click on **C**ommand (ALT+c).

20. Type *q* for the shortcut key (TAB to type). Notice that the shortcut key can be the same for more than one macro.

21. Click on OK (press ENTER).

22. Save the revised macro. Call it *SQRT2*

23. Activate TEST1.XLS to conduct the second test for the revised macro.

24. In cell A7 type *The number is*

25. In cell C7 type *144*

26. Select cell A9.

27. Press the macro's shortcut keys: *CTRL+q*

28. Select **O**ptions and drag to **W**orkspace (ALT+o and press w).

29. Click on R**1**C1 and click on OK (ALT+1 and press ENTER).

30. Click on R9C3 and study the formula.

31. Save the revised test sheet. Call it *TEST2*

32. Select **O**ptions and drag to **W**orkspace (ALT+o and press w).

33. Click on R**1**C1 to turn it off and click on OK (ALT+1 and press ENTER).

34. Exit at this time.

Questions:
1. For this example, why are editing changes important?
2. When would the same shortcut key give you trouble? To test your thinking open SQRT and SQRT2 and experiment with the two on TEST1 and TEST2.

6-2 Using the Macro Record Command

A shortcut way to setup, create, and define the name of a macro is to use the *Macro Record command*. This command (1) opens a macro sheet for you, (2) uses the file name for the name of the macro sheet, (3) allows you to add a shortcut key, and (4) starts the recording---all in one easy step. Because of its simplicity, the Macro Record command is a powerful feature of Microsoft Excel. **Figure 6-10** shows the dialog box for this command. Entering the Name SUM and the Key:CTRL+s tells Microsoft Excel to open a macro sheet named SUM, with a shortcut key of s, and to begin recording. To stop recording, select Macro once again and drag to the Stop Recording command.

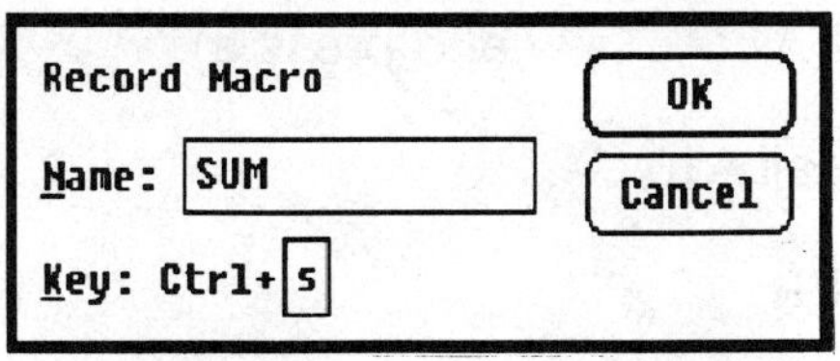

Figure 6-10 The Macro Record dialog box

EXERCISE 6-5
Recording with the Macro Record command

For this exercise, you are asked to build the summation macro shown on **Figure 6-11**. Once this is done, you are asked to test the macro using the numbers on **Figure 6-12**.

	A
1	SUM
2	=ARRANGE.ALL()
3	=SELECT("R10C1")
4	=FORMULA("=SUM(R[-9]C:R[-1]C)")
5	=RETURN()

Figure 6-11 The SUM9.XLM macro

	A
1	100
2	50
3	234
4	13
5	445
6	
7	
8	
9	
10	842

Figure 6-12 The test data for SUM9.XLM

1. Open a blank worksheet.
2. Select **M**acro and drag to Re**c**ord (ALT+m and press c).
3. In the **N**ame box type *SUM* and press TAB.
4. In the **K**ey box, type *s* for the shortcut key.
5. Click on OK (press ENTER). Your recording has started. (Generally, you will not be able to see the macro as it is created.)
6. Select **W**indow and drag to **A**rrange All (ALT+w and press a).
7. With the worksheet active, click on cell A10.
8. Type *=SUM(A1:A9)* and press ENTER.
9. Select **M**acro and drag to Stop Re**c**order (ALT+m and press c). This shuts off the recorder.
10. Activate A1 in the macro sheet.
11. Select Fo**r**mula and drag to **D**efine Name (ALT+r and press d).
12. Click on SUM in the Names in **S**heet box (DOWN).
13. Click on Cancel (TAB and press ENTER).
14. Activate the macro sheet.
15. Change the column width of column A to 15.
16. Click on A1 (UP).
17. Save this macro sheet. Name it *SUM9*

18. Close all files. Do not save changes to SHEET1.XLS.

19. Open SUM9.XLM.

20. Select **F**ile and drag to **N**ew (ALT+f and press n).

21. Click on **W**orksheet and click on OK (UP and press ENTER).

22. In cells A1:A5 only, type the numbers shown on Figure 6-12.

23. Click on cell A10.

24. Press CTRL+s.

25. Save this test worksheet. Name it *TEST3*

26. Exit at this time or continue on with the next exercise.

Questions:
1. Compare the Macro Record command to the Macro Set Recorder and Macro Start Recording commands. What are the advantages and disadvantages of the Macro Record command?
2. What names are in the Names in Sheet box when you select the Formula Define Name command? What does the Macro Record command do that the Macro Start Recorder command does not do?
3. What happens to the display screen when you type CTRL+s?

6-3 Recording and Running a Function Macro

Recording a function macro differs from recording a command macro. With a function macro, recording commands are generally not used. Instead, formulas are typed directly. Another difference is that function macros return a value to the worksheet. The formula =RETURN(*VALUE*) means: Return the computed value to a cell on the worksheet.

6-3-1 Creating a function macro

The procedure to follow in creating a function macro is quite simple.

1. Open a macro sheet.

2. Enter the name of the macro in the first cell.

3. Type the formulas needed for processing the value to be returned.

4. Name the new function using the Formula Define Name command.

5. Test the saved function, using the Formula Paste Function command.

When typing, use lower-case letters, such as return(a3). Microsoft Excel will convert names such as "return" to upper-case. In doing this, it will check your spelling.

6-3-2 Adding comments to a function macro

For both function and command macros, comments can be added to a macro sheet. Comments are added to help you understand how a macro works. To add comments, use the adjacent cell to the right of the typed formula. As a general rule, make comments brief. The goal is to be able to display all formulas and comments on a single display screen. With comments, do not use an equal (=) sign. If you do, Microsoft Excel will attempt to interpret the formula.

EXERCISE 6-6
Building a function macro

For this exercise, you are asked to write the function named SQUARE, shown on **Figure 6-13**. This function is designed to receive the argument "feet" and to return the squared value.

1. Open a new macro sheet.

2. In cell A1, type *Square* to name the function.

3. In cell A2, type *=argument("feet")* to show the formula for accepting a value from the worksheet.

	A	B
1	Square	Name of the macro
2	=ARGUMENT("feet")	Receives the input value
3	=feet*feet	Computes the square of the input
4	=RETURN(A3)	Returns the computed value

Figure 6-13 The SQUARE.XLM function macro

4. In cell A3, type *=feet*feet* to compute the square of feet.

5. In cell A4, type *=return(A3)* to return the computed value to the worksheet.

6. Change the width of column B to 15.

7. Add the comments shown on Figure 6-13.

8. Click on cell A1 and format the title to Bold.

9. With cell A1 active, select Formula and drag to **D**efine Name (ALT+r and press d).

10. Accept Square as the name and click on Function (TAB and LEFT).

11. Click on OK (press ENTER).

12. Select Formula and drag to Paste Function (ALT+r and press t).

13. Scroll to the end of the Paste List box (press END).

14. Click on cancel (TAB and press ENTER).

15. Save this macro sheet. Name is *SQUARE*

Questions:

1. When you select the Formula Define Name command, what name is suggested?
2. What is the name of the last function in the Paste List box?
3. Why is it important to add comments to a macro sheet?

6-3-3 Running a function macro

Running a function macro is just like running any of Microsoft Excel's built-in functions. To run a macro:

1. From the worksheet, choose the Formula Paste Function command.

2. Select the function name.

3. Type the argument and press ENTER.

EXERCISE 6-7
Running a user-defined macro

For this exercise, you are asked to use the SQUARE.XLM macro built for the last exercise and to revise TEST2.XLS. **Figure 6-14** illustrates this revised worksheet.

1. Open SQUARE.XLM, if necessary.
2. Open TEST2.XLS.
3. In cells A3, A6, and A8 type *The square is*
4. Click on cell C3.
5. Select Formula and drag to Paste Function (ALT+r and press t).
6. Scroll to the end of the Function box to SQUARE.XLM (END).
7. Click on OK (press ENTER).
8. In the formula bar, type *C1* (for the argument) and press ENTER.
9. Click on C6.
10. Repeat steps 5 to 7.
11. In the formula bar, type *188* and press ENTER.
12. Click on C8.
13. Repeat steps 5 to 7.

	A	B	C
1	The number is		166
2	The square root is		12.8840987
3	The square is		27556
4	The number is		188
5	The square of the number is		13.7113092
6	The square is		35344
7	The number is		144
8	The square is		20736
9	The square of the number is		12

Figure 6-14 The revised TEST2.XLS worksheet

14. In the formula bar, type *12*12* and press ENTER.

15. Save this test sheet. Call it *TEST4*

16. Print this worksheet. To remove the gridlines, use the **F**ile Page Se**t**up command (ALT+f and press t) and turn off gridlines. After printing, turn gridlines back on.

Questions:
1. What does this exercise tell you about the types of arguments a function macro can accept?
2. What happens if SQUARE.XLM is not opened before you begin this exercise? What does this tell you about function macros?

6-4 Special Macro Functions

Several special functions can be added to macros to make them more interactive. In this section, we consider three types of special functions: dialog box functions, input functions, and alert functions. Each function has a special makeup known as the *syntax* of a function. If you want a better understanding of the complete range of special functions and their syntax, you must use the *Microsoft Excel Reference Guide*, that comes with the full version of the software.

6-4-1 Dialog box functions

Special statements can be written to tell Microsoft Excel to halt the execution of a macro, to drop down a dialog box, and to await the input of values. In some cases no new values need to be entered. Even so, it is necessary to click on OK (press ENTER) to continue.

The syntax for a dialog box function is *=command_name?()*, where the question mark indicates that a dialog box is to be opened. The statement *=INSERT?()* tells Microsoft Excel to halt, to select Edit, to open the Insert dialog box, and to wait for the receipt of further processing instructions.

6-4-2 Input functions

This type of function tells Microsoft Excel to halt and to wait for the receipt of new values from the keyboard. The complete syntax is:

=INPUT(prompt,type,title,default,x-pos,y-pos)

For example, the statement:

=INPUT("Enter font type:reg(1),bold(2),italics(3),bold(4)",1)

tells Microsoft Excel the prompt (or message) to be displayed and the type. The type indicates the nature of the input to be keyed to processing. For example, with the INPUT function, several type choices are available. The table of choices is as follows:

Type	Input
0	Formula
1	Number
2	Text
4	Logical
8	Reference
16	Error
64	Array

Thus, type 1 tells Microsoft Excel to expect a number.

Once the INPUT is received, Microsoft Excel will wait for the type to be keyed to processing. The other four arguments in the syntax---title, default, x-pos, and y-pos---are not to be changed and are left blank in the example above. These values are not changed.

6-4-3 Alert functions

This special function displays one of three dialog boxes: Type 1, a message that asks a question; Type 2, a message that makes a statement; and Type 3, a message that indicates an error. The syntax for this type of function is:

=ALERT(message_text,number)

Thus, *=ALERT("Great Job",2)* opens a dialog box to make this statement.

EXERCISE 6-8
Adding special functions to a macro

This exercise asks you to add several new statements to the macro entitled SUM and saved as SUM9.XLM (see Figure 6-11). **Figure 6-15** shows the revised macro. Once this macro is built, it is to be tested, using the TEST3.XLS worksheet. **Figure 6-16** shows how this worksheet will look when you complete this exercise.

1. Open SUM9.XLM.

2. In cell A1 type *REVISED_SUM*

	A
1	REVISED_SUM
2	=ARRANGE.ALL()
3	=SELECT("R10C1")
4	=FORMULA("=SUM(R[-9]C:R[-1]C)")
5	=SELECT("R1C1:R10C1")
6	=INSERT?()
7	=COLUMN.WIDTH?()
8	=SELECT("R10C1")
9	=FORMULA("The sum is")
10	=INPUT("Enter font type: reg(1), bold(2), italic(3), bold ital(4)",1)
11	=FORMAT.FONT(,,A10)
12	=ALERT("Great job",2)
13	=RETURN()

Figure 6-15 The revised SUM9.XLM macro

3. Cut and paste *=RETURN* to place this formula in cell A13.

4. In cell A5 define the range A1:A10 as *=SELECT("R1C1:R10C1")*

5. In cell A6 type *=INSERT?()* to add a dialog box function to the macro.

6. In cell A7 type *=COLUMN.WIDTH?()* to add a second dialog box function to the macro.

7. In cell A8 type *=SELECT("R10C1")* to specify an individual cell.

8. In cell A9 type *=FORMULA("The sum is")* to add text to the worksheet.

9. In cell A10 type *=INPUT("Enter font type:reg(1),bold(2),italics(3), bold(4)",1)* to add an input function to the macro. This will display a message on the screen and wait for you to enter a number (since type is 1).

10. In cell A11 type *=format.font(,,A10)* to specify where to change the font on the worksheet.

	A	B
1		100
2		50
3		234
4		13
5		445
6		
7		
8		
9		
10	The sum is	842

Figure 6-16 The test of the revised macro

11. In cell A12 type *=ALERT("Great Job",2)* to add a type 2 alert message to the macro.

12. Click on A1.

13. Select Formula and drag to **D**efine Name (ALT+r and press d).

14. Keep the name REVISED_SUM.

15. Click on **C**ommand (ALT+c).

16. Type *s* for the shortcut key (TAB to type).

17. Click on OK (press ENTER).

18. Save this revised macro. Call it *SPECIAL*

19. Open TEST3.XLS.

20. Delete 842 from cell A10.

21. With A10 active, press *CTRL+s*

22. When the Edit Insert dialog box opens, click on OK (press ENTER).

23. When the Column Width dialog box opens, type *15* and click on OK (press ENTER).

24. When the INPUT dialog box opens, type *2* and click on OK (press ENTER).

25. When the ALERT dialog box opens, click on OK (press ENTER).

26. Close all files and exit. Do not save changes to TEST3.XLS.

Questions:

1. What are three advantages in placing dialog box, input, and alert statements in a macro?
2. What happens if you place the formula =BORDER?() in a macro? What happens if you place the formula =INPUT("What is your name", 2) in a macro? What happens if you place the formula =ALERT("Oh, no",3) in a macro?

6-5 Creating Shortcut Keys

An important use of macros is creating shortcut keys. These allow you to customize Microsoft Excel to meet your particular needs. For example, instead of selecting Edit and dragging to Clear (or pressing DEL and ENTER), you might find it easier to press CTRL+d, where d stands for Delete. Or, instead of selecting Edit Undo, it might be more convenient for you to type CTRL+u, where u stands for Undo. The next exercise describes how you can create these shortcut keys.

EXERCISE 6-9
Customized shortcut keys

For this exercise, you are asked to create and test two shortcut macros DELETE.XLM and UNDO.XLM. **Figure 6-17** illustrates the first new macro; **Figure 6-18** illustrates the second new macro. When you have completed both macros, store them in workspace MACROS.XLW.

1. With a blank worksheet facing you, type *135* in cell A5.

2. Drag **M**acro to Record (ALT+m and press c).

3. Type *Delete* in the **N**ame box and press TAB.

4. Type **d** in the **K**ey box and click on OK (press ENTER). This starts your macro recording, even though you will not see the instruction steps.

5. With cell A5 continuing to be active on the worksheet, drag **E**dit to Cl**e**ar (ALT+e and press e).

6. Click on OK to clear the number 135 from A5 (press ENTER).

7. Drag **M**acro to Stop Re**c**order (ALT+m and press c). This stops the recording of the macro.

	A
1	Delete
2	=CLEAR(3)
3	=RETURN()

Figure 6-17 The DELETE.XLM macro

	A
1	Undo
2	=UNDO()
3	=RETURN()

Figure 6-18 The UNDO.XLM macro

8. To determine how the macro looks, select **W**indow and drag to **A**rrange All (ALT+w and press a).

9. Test this macro. Make an entry on the worksheet in a cell other than cell A5. Press CTRL+d to activate the shortcut key. The entry should be deleted.

10. Save the new macro. Call it *DELETE*

11. Type *34* in cell A5.

12. Press *CTRL+d* to delete the entry.

13. Drag **M**acro to Re**c**ord (ALT+m and press c).

14. Type *Undo* in the **N**ame box and press TAB.

15. Type **u** in the **K**ey box and click on OK (press ENTER). This starts your macro recording once again.

16. Select **E**dit and drag to **U**ndo Clear (ALT+e and press u).

17. Select **M**acro and drag to Stop Re**c**order (ALT+m and press c).

18. Test this macro. Make an entry on the worksheet and type *CTRL+d* to delete the entry. Then type *CTRL+u* to undo the deletion.

19. Save the new macro. Call it *UNDO*

20. Close the worksheet. Save DELETE and UNDO in a single workspace. Call it *MACROS*. Since this is a workspace, the .XLW is added to the file.

Questions:

1. What is the advantage of a customized shortcut key?
2. Why should customized shortcut keys be saved using a single workspace?
3. How many customized shortcut keys can be created?

6-6 Summary

This final chapter is designed to introduce you to four of the five Macro commands in building Command and Function macros. Command macros consist of a sequence of individual commands. They are designed to accomplish a processing task, or set of tasks. They are not created to compute a value and return it to the worksheet. Function macros are. These macros are like the built-in functions provided by Microsoft Excel.

Creating a Command macro can be done in two ways: (1) by setting the recording area, using the Macro Set Recorder command and by starting and stopping the recording, using the Start Recorder and Stop Recorder commands, or (2) by using the Macro Record and Macro Stop Recorder commands. The first method provides flexibility in the way macros are recorded and named. Once recording is stopped, the Formula Define Name command is used to name the macro, indicate whether the macro is a command or function macro, and indicate whether the macro is to be assigned a shortcut key. The second method names the macro and the shortcut key, as part of the setup. This method is the one most often recommended. Regardless of which method is used, once a Command macro has been recorded, it is run by using the Macro Run command.

Creating a Function macro is done in the same way as creating a Command macro, with two exceptions. When the macro is named, it must be defined as a Function Macro. In addition, a function macro is done using the Formula Paste Function command.

Macros can be edited like a worksheet. When adding new statements to a macro, each statement beginning with an equal sign (=) will be executed. When adding a statement, the syntax prescribed by Microsoft Excel must be followed.

Comments can be added to a macro. When adding comments, remember not to begin the statement with an equal sign.

Several types of special functions can be added to macros. The three functions considered were Dialog box functions, Input functions, and Alert functions. These functions help to make macros more interactive. They allow the user to enter processing requirements during run time.

Shortcut keys can be built using command macros. These keys allow the user of Microsoft Excel to customize processing commands, such as DELETE, UNDO, or even OPEN and CLOSE files. With Microsoft Excel a set of shortcut keys will save you considerable time in building and changing worksheets, charts, and databases.

KEY TERMS

Alert function
Command macro
Dialog box function
Function macro
Input function
Recording
Shortcut key

COMMAND REFERENCE

Macro Record: Macro menu. Tells Microsoft to begin recording your keystrokes for use in a macro. If you have not already opened a macro sheet, Macro Record will open a new macro sheet and allow you to give it a name and a shortcut key.

Macro Run: Macro menu. Runs open macro files. If more than one macro is open, it will ask which macro you wish to run.

Macro Set Recorder: Macro menu. Tells the macro at which cell to begin recording on the macro sheet. Especially useful for adding recorded key sequences to an existing macro.

Macro Start Recorder: Macro menu. Starts the macro recorder.

Macro Stop Recorder: Macro menu. Stops the macro recorder and adds the function =RETURN() to your macro sheet.

ON YOUR OWN

1. A _______ is a set or string of instructions you create that tells Microsoft Excel to perform a specific action or set of actions.
   a) function
   b) command
   c) directory
   d) chart
   e) macro

2. In figure 6-3, the cell entry in A3 will
   a) select the third row and second column.
   b) change the height of the selected row to 3.
   c) go to the intersection of the third row and the second column.
   d) change the height of the column to 2.
   e) enter the string R2C3 into the active cell.

3. The macro shown in figure 6-3 is an example of a(n) _______ macro.
   a) function
   b) command
   c) format
   d) open
   e) worksheet

4. The statement _______ must be the last cell entry in every macro.
   a) =FORMULA("=SQRT(R[-2]C)")

b) =RETURN("Last cell entry")
c) =SELECT("R1C4")
d) =RETURN()
e) =SELECT()

5. The Formula Define Name **will not** perform which of the following actions?
   a) Open a new macro sheet
   b) Assign a name to your macro
   c) Assign a control key to your macro
   d) Designate a macro as a function or command macro
   e) Delete a previously defined name

6. The _______ command will open a macro sheet, name it, allow you to add a shortcut key and start the recording.
   a) Macro Set Recorder
   b) Macro Record
   c) Macro Start Recorder
   d) Macro Stop Recorder
   e) Macro Run

7. The statement =ALERT("Nice move, Slick!",3) would
   a) Enter "Nice move, Slick" into your worksheet
   b) Give an Alert message, "Nice move, Slick"
   c) Give an Alert question, "Nice move, Slick"
   d) Give an Alert error message, "Nice Move, Slick"
   e) Give an Alert message, "Nice move Slick" in cell 3

8. CTRL+S is an example of a(n) __________ key.
   a) command
   b) macro
   c) function
   d) shortcut
   e) action

9. The _________ command could be used to change the default cell address from A3 to R3C1.
   a) Formula Define Name
   b) Options Workspace
   c) Display Options
   d) Formula Select Special
   e) Formula Reference

10. The statement =INSERT?() will
    a) insert a question mark into the active worksheet.
    b) insert a new row into the active worksheet.

c) stop the macro and prompt the user for further instructions regarding the Edit Insert command.
d) stop the macro and prompt the user for text to insert into the active cell.
e) insert a new row or column automatically.

MORE PRACTICE

I. Record a macro that automatically creates a pie chart of any selected cell range(s).
   1. After recording, insert a new row at the top of your macro and title your macro: **Chart**.
   2. Define the macro name as **Pie**.
   3. Print your macro using your name as a header.
   4. Save your macro as *PIECHART*

   Answer the following:
   a) How did you guarantee that your macro would chart any cell range?
   b) What is the macro statement that opens and selects the Pie chart?

II. Write a function macro that will compute the distance travelled for any given time and speed. Hint: the formula for computing distance is DISTANCE = RATE x TIME.
   1. Title, save and define your macro's name as **Distance**.
   2. Print your macro using your name as a header.
   3. Test your macro using 60mph and 1 1/2 hours as figures.
   4. Save and print your test worksheet as *DIST1*

   Answer the following:
   a) How would you change your macro to compute TIME given DISTANCE and RATE?
   b) How many variables are in your formula?

III. Edit the macro you wrote in I above so that it will ask the user what type of chart would you like to create. Your macro should also give the user a message "You've selected a most attractive chart" at the very end of the macro.
   1. Name and define your macro as *PIE2*
   2. Print you macro using your name as a header.

   Answer the following:
   a) How many lines did you have to add to your macro?
   b) What type of input is required in the macro instruction that questions the user?

COMMAND SHORTCUT KEYS AND SPECIAL CONTROL KEYS

For experienced users of Microsoft Excel, shortcut keys become important. These keys are alternatives for choosing many of the worksheet, chart, and macro sheet commands. The following function key and function-key combinations show you the shortcut-processing features built into Microsoft Excel.

Key	Command or Action
F1	Help (inactive)
SHIFT+F1	Context-sensitive help (inactive)
ALT+F1	File New command (Chart option)
ALT+SHIFT+F1	File New command (Worksheet option)
ALT+CONTROL+F1	File New command (Macro sheet option)
F2	Activate formula bar, in Edit mode
SHIFT+F2	Formula Note command
CONTROL+F2	Window Show Info command
ALT+F2	File Save As command
ALT+SHIFT+F2	File Save command
ALT+CONTROL+F2	File Open command
ALT+CONTROL+SHIFT+F2	File Print command
F3	Formula Paste Name command
SHIFT+F3	Formula Paste Function command
CONTROL+F3	Formula Define Name command
CONTROL+SHIFT+F3	Formula Create Names command
F4	Formula Reference command
CONTROL+F4	Control Close command (active document window
ALT+F4	Control Close command (application window)
F5	Formula Goto command
SHIFT+F5	Formula Find command
CONTROL+F5	Control Restore command (active document window)
ALT+F5	Control Restore command (application window)

F6	Next pane
SHIFT+F6	Previous pane
CONTROL+F6	Next document window
CONTROL+SHIFT+F6	Previous document window
F7	Formula Find command (next cell)
SHIFT+F7	Formula Find command (previous cell)
CONTROL+F7	Control Move command (active document window)
ALT+F7	Control Move command (application window)
F8	Turns Extend on or off
SHIFT+F8	Turns on Add
CONTROL+F8	Control Size command (active document window)
ALT+F8	Control Size command (application window)
F9	Options Calculate Now command
SHIFT+F9	Options Calculate Document command
ALT+F9	Control Minimize command (application window)
F10	Activate menu bar
CONTROL+F10	Control Maximize command (active document window)
ALT+F10	Control Maximize command (application window)
F11	File New command (Chart option)
SHIFT+F11	File New command (Worksheet option)
CONTROL+SHIFT+F11	File New command (Macro sheet option)
F12	File Save As command
SHIFT+F12	File Save command
CONTROL+F12	File Open command
CONTROL+SHIFT+F12	File Print command

Besides shortcut keys based on the twelve function keys, there are twenty-two processing shortcuts based on the control key plus a special character or number. These shortcut combinations are shown next.

Key	Command or Action
CONTROL+~	Format number (general format)
CONTROL+!	Format number (0.00 format)
CONTROL+@	Format number (h:mm AM/PM format)
CONTROL+#	Format number (dd-mm-yy format)
CONTROL+$	Format number ($#,##0.00;($#,##0.00) format)
CONTROL+%	Format number (0% format)
CONTROL+^	Format number (0.00E+00 format)
CONTROL+1	Format Font (Font 1 option)
CONTROL+2	Format Font (Font 2 option)
CONTROL+3	Format Font (Font 3 option)
CONTROL+4	Format Font (Font 4 option)
CONTROL+?	Formula Select Special (notes option)
CONTROL+*	Formula Select Special (current region option)
CONTROL+/	Formula Select Special (current array option)
CONTROL+\	Formula Select Special (row differences option)
CONTROL+:	Formula Select Special (column differences option)
CONTROL+[	Formula Select Special (Precedents: direct only option)
CONTROL+{	Formula Select Special (Precedents: all levels option)
CONTROL+]	Formula Select Special (Dependents: direct only option)
CONTROL+}	Formula Select Special (Dependents: all levels option)

CONTROL+ =	Calculate now
CONTROL+ '	Options display (toggles between formulas and values)

INDEX

D

E

T

U

V

W